JOURNAL FOR THE STUDY OF THE OLD TESTAMENT
SUPPLEMENT SERIES

408

The Priests in the Prophets

The Portrayal of Priests, Prophets and Other Religious Specialists in the Latter Prophets

Edited by

Lester L. Grabbe and Alice Ogden Bellis

T & T CLARK INTERNATIONAL
A Continuum imprint
LONDON • NEW YORK

Copyright © 2004 T&T Clark International
A Continuum imprint

Published by T&T Clark International

The Tower Building   15 East 26th Street
11 York Road   Suite 1703
London SE1 7NX   New York, NY 10010

www.tandtclark.com

British Library Cataloguing-in-Publication Data
A catalogue record for this book is available from the British Library.

ISBN 0-567-08166-4

Typeset by Tradespools, Frome, Somerset
Printed on acid-free paper in Great Britain by Antony Rowe Ltd, Chippenham,
Wilts.

CONTENTS

Contents

CONTRIBUTORS

Alice Ogden Bellis is Professor of Old Testament Language and Literature at Howard University School of Divinity, Washington, DC.

Ehud Ben Zvi is Professor in the Department of History and Classics at the University of Alberta.

Bryan Bibb is Assistant Professor of Religion at Furman University in Greenville, South Carolina.

Daniel E. Fleming is Associate Professor in the Skirball Department of Hebrew and Judaic Studies at New York University.

Julie Galambush is Associate Professor of Religion at The College of William and Mary in Williamsburg, Virginia.

Lester L. Grabbe is Professor of Hebrew Bible and Early Judaism at the University of Hull.

James R. Linville is Assistant Professor of Religious Studies at the University of Lethbridge in Alberta.

Richard D. Nelson is W. J. A. Power Professor of Biblical Hebrew and Old Testament Interpretation, Perkins School of Theology, Southern Methodist University, Dallas, Texas.

Margaret S. Odell is Associate Professor of Religion at St Olaf College in Northfield, Minnesota.

Corrine Patton is Associate Professor of Theology at the University of St Thomas, St Paul, Minnesota.

Joachim Schaper is Privatdozent (Lecturer) in the Evangelisch-theolo-
gische Fakultät of the Eberhard-Karls-Universität in Tübingen.

Ziony Zevit is Distinguished Professor of Bible and Northwest Semitic
Languages and Literatures at the University of Judaism in Los Angeles.

ABBREVIATIONS

AB	Anchor Bible
AJSL	*American Journal of Semitic Languages*
AnBib	Analecta Biblica
AOAT	Alter Orient und Altes Testament
ARM	Archives royales de Mari
ARMT	Archives royales de Mari, transcrite et traduite
BBB	Bonner biblische Beiträge
BHS	*Biblia Hebraica Stuttgartensis*
Bib	*Biblica*
BibInt	*Biblical Interpretation*
BKAT	Biblischer Kommentar, Altes Testament
BR	*Biblical Review*
BTB	*Biblical Theology Bulletin*
BZ	*Biblische Zeitschrift*
BZAW	Beihefte zur *Zeitschrift für die altestamentliche Wissenschaft*
CAD	*The Chicago Assyrian Dictionary of the Oriental Institute of the University of Chicago*
CBQ	*Catholic Biblical Quarterly*
CR: BS	*Currents in Research: Biblical Studies*
CRRAI	Compte- rendu de la rencontre assyriologique internationale
ETL	*Ephemerides Theologicae Lovanienses*
FAT	Forschungen zum Alten Testament
GKC	*Gesenius' Hebrew Grammar* (ed. E. Kautzsch, transl. A. E. Cowley, 1910 2nd ed.)
GLAJJ	M. Stern, *Greek and Latin Authors on Jews and Judaism* (1974–84)
GTA	Göttinger theologischer Arbeiten
HAT	Handbuch zum Alten Testament
HB	Hebrew Bible
HdO	Handbuch der Orientalisk
HSM	Harvard Semitic Monographs
HSS	Harvard Semitic Studies
ICC	International Critical Commentary
Int	*Interpretation*

JAOS	*Journal of the American Oriental Society*
JBL	*Journal of Biblical Literature*
JNSL	*Journal of Northwest Semitic Languages*
JQR	*Jewish Quarterly Review*
JSOT	*Journal for the Study of the Old Testament*
JSOTSup	Supplements to *Journal for the Study of the Old Testament*
JSP	*Journal for the Study of the Pseudepigrapha*
JSPSup	Journal for the Study of the Pseudepigrapha–Supplementary Series
JSS	*Journal of Semitic Studies*
KAI	H. Donner and W. Röllig, *Kanaanäische und aramäische Inschriften* (1966–69)
LSTS	Library of Second Temple Studies
MARI	*Mari: Annales de recherches interdisciplinaires*
MT	Masoretic text
NAC	New American Commentary
NCB	New Century Bible Commentary
NICOT	New International Commentary on the Old Testament
NRSV	New Revised Standard Version
OBO	Orbis biblicus et orientalis
Or	*Orientalia*
OTE	*Old Testament Essays*
OTG	Old Testament Guides
OTL	Old Testament Library
OtSt	*Oudtestamentische Studiën*
RA	*Revue d'assyriologie et d'archéologie orientale*
RB	*Revue biblique*
RGG	*Religion in Geschichte und Gegenwart*
RlA	E. Ebeling, et al. (eds.), *Reallexikon der Assyriologie*2 (1928-).
SAA	State Archives of Assyria
SBLDS	Society of Biblical Literature Dissertation Series
SBLMS	Society of Biblical Literature Monograph Series
SBLSBS	Society of Biblical Literature Sources for Biblical Study
SBLSP	Society of Biblical Literature Seminar Papers
SBLSymS	Society of Biblical Literature Symposium Studies
SBT	Studies in Biblical Theology
Sem	*Semitica*
SFSHJ	South Florida Studies in the History of Judaism
SJLA	Studies in Judaism in Late Antiquity
SSN	Studia semitica neerlandica
TSAJ	Texte und Studien zum antiken Judentum
TynBul	*Tyndale Bulletin*
USQR	*Union Seminary Quarterly Review*

VT	*Vetus Testamentum*
VTSup	Supplements to *Vetus Testamentum*
WBC	Word Bible Commentary
WMANT	Wissenschaftliche Monographien zum Alten und Neuen Testament
ZAW	*Zeitschrift für die attestamentliche Wissenschaft*
ZDPV	*Zeitschrift des Deutschen Palästina-Vereins*

Lester L. Grabbe

The present volume is the publication of the papers read at the SBL meeting in Toronto, 17–20 November 2002, on the theme of the priests in the Latter Prophets. It is one of a series of volumes that has arisen out of the work of the Prophetic Texts and their Ancient Contexts Group, a Society of Biblical Literature unit founded and chaired by Ehud Ben Zvi.[2] The papers were all related to the general theme but took a variety of approaches. The theme of the priests in the Latter prophets represents a focus, not a rigid confinement, since it was not always desirable or even possible to stick precisely to the texts in the Latter Prophets. A number of themes arise out of these essays and will be discussed here, following a summary of each of the papers.

Summaries of Papers

Ehud Ben Zvi ('Observations on Prophetic Characters, Prophetic Texts, Priests of Old, Persian Period Priests and Literati') begins with two fundamental observations on the relation between the mental image of the prophet and that of the priest: (1) an absence: there is no essential opposition between priests and prophets (only a contingent opposition between particular priests and prophets in some texts); and (2) a presence: the slippage of attributes associated with priests, prophets, and literati. The prophets had to stand against a corrupt elite, including some priests. Post-exilic readers would have identified with the prophetic critique of the monarchy, but would not have learned of any categorical opposition between priests and prophets. It is likely that the temple filled a central role in supporting the literati who composed and read the prophetic books in Persian Judah. Most of the critique was of long-dead priests of the monarchic period. The literati accepted the main ideological claims of the temple. Although not all the literati were priests or Levites, there was a major overlap of the two categories. The social circumstances of Yehud priests and literati were reflected in the authoritative discourses, and the

---

1. I wish to thank the contributors for their comments, corrections, and suggestions on the contents of this introductory paper to the volume. I also wish to thank the University of Hull and the British Academy who provided funding for me to attend the 2002 Annual Meeting of the Society of Biblical Literature.
2. Ben Zvi/Floyd 2000; Grabbe/Haak 2001; Sweeney/Ben Zvi 2003; Grabbe/Haak 2003.

attributes associated with one image became assigned to the other. Moses was a pivotal figure who allowed the association of *torah* and *davar*. Normative literature was expected to be coherent with the ideology of the elite who controlled the temple. The prophetic message was known mainly through the prophetic books. The times were a fertile ground for developing the mental category of godly communicators in the Jerusalem discourses, which included prophets of old, priests of Yehud and Yehud literati.

Bryan D. Bibb ('The Prophetic Critique of Ritual in Old Testament Theology') begins with a quote from L. Koehler that the Israelite cult was not instituted by God, but was taken from 'the heathens'. Although most OT theologies show more sympathy toward the cult, they still tend to follow what is seen as the 'prophetic critique' of the cult. The basic thesis of the article is that OT theologies have taken a Christian worldview, inspired by the prophetic critique, to reconstruct a misleading – even libelous – presentation of Israel's cultic life. This alleged critique is based on a few paradigmatic texts (Amos 5.21–25; Hos. 6.6; Isa. 1.11–14; Mic. 6.6–8; Jer. 6.20, 14.12). To the writers of OT theologies the message has seemed to be self-evident, and they have been content with the superficial. If they had gone below the surface, however, they would have seen that the prophetic critique is part of a larger prophetic rhetoric to convict of sin, explain God's plans, and sometimes to hold out the hope of salvation. Prophets went to great lengths to get their message across. It is within this rhetorical freedom that one must interpret the prophetic critique of ritual. Could the prophets have imagined a world without the cult and ritual? The prophetic critique performed a rhetorical function in four ways: (1) the rejection of the cult tied to the denunciation of idolatry; (2) the use of cultic imagery to describe God's judgmental acts; (3) the central role played by priests and other religious leaders in the prophetic denunciations (Ezek. 22); (4) implicit in the criticism, the vision of a true, positive cultic reality. The second part of the paper looks at three OT theologies: those of W. Eichrodt, T. Vriezen, and W. Brueggemann. Eichrodt's *Theology* is remarkable in not only mirroring the prophetic critique of priests, but also identifying with it, extending it into the Christian theological world and using it as a hermeneutical key to organize his OT theology. Although claiming admiration for the high ideals expressed in the Israelite cult, Eichrodt's interest is ultimately a Christian one; however, the Christian reflection is a second stage: he sees the initial stage as a neutral description from the OT text. But his theology is logocentric, with the true value of the cult centered in words and ideas. Vriezen's theology is even more explicitly Christian than Eichrodt's. He structures his book around questions asked by Christians, seeing a sharp contrast between the prophetic demand for spiritual and moral adherence to the covenant and the cultic rituals. Both the priests and prophets are necessary, but also conflict. The 'secret of the

OT' is that the OT itself springs from the prophets. Although Brueggemann is in the same theological tradition as Eichrodt and Vriezen, he makes a deliberate decision to repudiate their basic point of view. He justifies the cult by arguing for its sacramental quality as the mediator of Yahweh's real presence; that is, he identifies it with the eucharist. The prophets take the cultic life of Israel seriously, but use rhetorical strategies to warn of the danger of the cult becoming manipulative and self-satisfied so that it no longer communicates the word.

Daniel E. Fleming ('Prophets and Temple Personnel in the Mari Archives') does not strictly write on the priests in the Latter Prophets, but his discussion in the context of Mari brings out some important aspects of the relationship between priests and prophets that are very much relevant for the biblical situation. The terminology at Mari resists the priest/ prophet dichotomy. No single group of temple personnel can be called 'priests' as opposed to the others. Real power and status lay with diviners who were employed by the palace and might rise in rank to have direct contact with the king. There is also no single word for 'prophet' at Mari. The two principal titles are *āpilum* (often translated as 'answerer', though there is no direct evidence) and *muḫḫûm*. There are also some other terms, but the most interesting is *nābû*, which is clearly cognate with Hebrew *nābî'*. This occurs in a letter from an official visiting Ashmad who assembled the *nābû* among the tent-dwellers and took an omen (though the precise mode is uncertain). It has long been observed that many episodes of prophecy at Mari took place in temples. The temples in Syria had a different place in society (being smaller and less influential) than in southern Mesopotamia even though the same terminology was used in the texts. The king and the palace were the center of power and wealth. The temples were less influential, but played an important social role. It is not clear which of the figures lived in temple lodgings or had their full income from temple resources. What we do not know for sure is whether the prophetic figures were a part of the temple staff. Although the *bārûm* diviners were the main authorities, there is no evidence of rivalry between them and the prophetic figures. After all, all prophecies required confirmation by divination. The priests and prophets were further removed from the center of power. Mesopotamian priests did not include finding out the divine will in their portfolio, which means that the prophets were the only specialists in divine communication available to the temples. They offered a coordinated alternative to divination in another social location. Temple deities could deliver their messages only through the *āpilum*, the *muḫḫûm*, and other temple personnel. In Zimri-Lim's kingdom Mari was the capital of the Binu Sam'al tribe. Pastoralists and townspeople existed on an equal footing. Few if any Mari institutions had their power base in an urban elite. A multiplicity of cultures co-mingled at Mari. It is not clear that prophecy was only on one side of the Akkadian/Amorrite divide, though it might be more characteristic of Syria. Interestingly, though, not one of the prophetic episodes is reported by a leader of the pastoralists, and only the one text on the *nābû* associates prophecy with pastoralism. The paper concludes with a long appendix on the etymology of *nābû* and *nāvî'*.

Julie Galambush ('The Northern Voyage of Psammeticus II and its Implications for Ezekiel 44.7–9') sets out to find an explanation for the 'foreigners' in the temple, presumed by this passage. It is a major puzzle because Ezekiel's general practice is to comment on contemporary events, yet scholarly explanations of this passage have generally looked to find the answer in Israel's past. Some recent suggestions are promising but ultimately do not answer all the questions. A notable aspect of the passage is that these foreigners 'broke the covenant', an apparently strange statement since foreigners had no covenantal relationship with YHWH. There is an exception, though: Zedekiah's vassal treaty with Nebuchadnezzar was sealed with an oath in the name of YHWH. It was Zedekiah who broke the covenant, not Nebuchadnezzar, but Ezekiel seems to blame the Egyptians because they facilitated Judah's sins. Quite a few prophecies against Egypt are found in the book. The foreigners are said to be 'uncircumcised', but the Egyptians were circumcised. This can be explained by the fact that the Egyptians were not considered properly circumcised and therefore remained uncircumcised as far as Ezekiel was concerned. The question is whether there were Egyptians in the temple? A context might be found in Pharaoh Psammetichus' tour of Palestine in 592 BCE. The text describing this tour indicates that a delegation, including cult personnel, was left behind for a period of time after Psammetichus returned to Egypt. Although our knowledge ceases at this point, it is not unreasonable to suppose that the Egyptian delegation (as part of its duties on the state visit) carried out some liturgical functions in association with the temple, and that this event is what provoked Ezekiel's denunciation.

Lester Grabbe ('A Priest Is without Honor in his Own Prophet: Priests and Other Religious Specialists in the Latter Prophets') surveys the individual texts in the Latter Prophets about priests and some other religious specialists. The main points and themes which emerge become the basis for asking broader questions about the priestly *gestalt* and the situation of priests in society and also extends the investigation into other texts. Some of the main conclusions are the following: First, the criticisms of the cult do not reject it *per se* but usually relate to specific points. The critique is often based on the later religious criteria of the final editors rather than those likely to have exercised the religious leaders of the earlier period (e.g. the accusation that the cult in question has to do with Baal or that the Bethel cult was regarded as illegitimate). Secondly, the ostensibly separate roles of priest, prophet, diviner, and the like were often entangled in real life (e.g. the same individual might have more than one role).

Thirdly, we have a glimpse of the priesthood's development over several centuries, the main one being a dimorphic priesthood, with the Levites acting as lower clergy and only 'Aaronic' priests being allowed to preside at the altar. Fourthly, the priestly role included engagement with 'mantic wisdom', including divinatory skills. Fifthly, priests functioned as scribes and teachers. This included having custody of the Torah and its interpretation, a duty that increased in importance as the Second Temple period progressed. They were the educated class and pursued intellectual activities other than theology. Finally, beginning with the Persian period the high priest had an important leadership role with regard to the Jewish community. Thus, although the Latter Prophets do not by any means give a full picture, they are an important source and contribute to an understanding of the priesthood in its interaction with the community, the leadership, and other religious specialists.

James R. Linville ('The Day of Yahweh and the Mourning of the Priests in Joel') asks how the book of Joel imagines its own role and the status of the priesthood in its symbol constructions and 'word-world'. Scholars have often minimized the place of the temple, ritual, and priesthood in the book. Actually, the book allows for the priesthood to be taken for granted in viewing ritualization as having the capacity to overcome great social distresses. Priests have an importance in this word-world out of proportion to the actual amount of text devoted to them: they are essential players in the divine/natural/human economy of the cosmos. There are different interpretations of the locusts in Joel 1 and 2, but whatever real catastrophe might have been experienced by Joel, he is representing a literary world. There is also debate over what the people had done to suffer their fate, but Joel is concerned not so much with guilt and innocence as with the cosmic themes of chaos and restoration. God, nature, and human life are linked; crises are presented as the result of divine action. We are confronted with an ambivalent Yahweh acting as the 'profane Other' who subverts the sacred order. The resolution is initiated through 'ritualization' (i.e. redefining the situation by imposing its own conceptual order) by a call to public lamentation and fasting. The cessation of sacrifice marked a break in tradition, but the priests still took the lead in the one ritual act remaining open to the people: mourning and fasting. The hunger they are suffering becomes the positive ritual act of fasting. Yahweh is no longer the 'profane Other' who sends the famine but the savior, the 'numinous Other'. Priests are the only authority figures in Joel 1–2 (except for the occasional reference to elders). They cease to be mentioned after 2.17, but allusions to priestly functions and temple imagery are found in the rest of the book. The re-integration of 2.18–4.1 requires accepting the divine hierarchy of God, priests, and populace. The defeated nations become the sacrifice which is a prelude to the re-creation of the primal paradise. The rituals that address the rupture in the social order reaffirm the social hierarchies. Thus, the lack of explicit reference to priests in the oracles of salvation does not suggest a program to replace them. The priestly leadership is in fact validated by prophecy. The message of the book revolves around a conception of temple and its liturgies as a microcosm of the cosmos and society. The book affirms that the temple is necessary to the stability of the cosmos and the relationship with the creator.

Richard D. Nelson ('Priestly Purity and Prophetic Lunacy: Hosea 1.2–3 and 9.7') begins by exploring the social roles of prophets. He emphasizes that they are characterized by stereotypical behavior. One of the most important of these is ecstatic behavior, but there are others. Indeed, a characteristic of a prophet is peculiar behavior in general, whether diet, speech, or actions outside or even contrary to social norms (these characteristics are surveyed in some detail in the paper). They could be judged as the acts of a madman, especially by their opponents, but priests also had their own stereotypical behavior. Of particular interest here is the strange action of Hosea described in the prophetic sign act report in Hos. 1.2–9 in which Hosea takes a 'promiscuous woman'. A number of factors mark off Hos. 1 from 2–3. Chapter 1 on its own has no analogy of Yahweh's relationship with Israel, but marrying the woman is a self-contained prophetic act to be seen as having separate significance from the symbolic signs of the children. This metaphor of marrying a promiscuous woman undermines the analogy of divine election followed by infidelity. It is the language of promiscuity, not adultery; the children are Hosea's, not someone else's. The sign of 1.2–9 is composed of four prophetic acts, explained by the use of four 'for' (כִּי) clauses. Gomer is the first-stage sign followed by three second-stage signs. So why the wedding which seems unnecessary? Gomer's contribution to the story is motherhood: she and her children stand for the land, but the marriage stands for nothing in the story. The answer is that this is an example of prophetic 'mad' behavior (cf. 9.7). By taking her, Hosea performed a prophetic act designed to undermine the priestly claims of purity and to mimic the nation's apostasy. He seems to be imitating the sins of the priests and people, both undercutting the priestly claims to purity and criticizing the people's promiscuous behavior. Acting as a peripheral prophet, Hosea's criticism of the Yahwistic cult and priesthood is part of a wider assault on the religious apostasy of the nation. He uses the language of ritual purity to condemn the priests for immoral intercourse. His action is an example of the 'outrageous' prophetic action which led to his being labeled a fool and lunatic.

Margaret S. Odell ('What Was the Image of Jealousy in Ezekiel 8?') looks at a rather intriguing statement that has long exercised students of Ezekiel. It has been conventional to see Ezek. 8 as a collage of idolatries of the House of Israel. This study takes the view that the 'image of jealousy' cannot be interpreted in isolation from the chapter or the book as a whole.

The conventional view that this is an idol, perhaps of Asherah, that provokes YHWH's jealousy ignores the language (*semel* is not used of idols, and 'image of jealousy' does not mean 'image that provokes to jealousy'), the context (the image is not worshipped), and the theology (Asherah worship is not condemned in the book). *Semel* is used in Phoenician and Punic for anthropomorphic statues. 'Jealousy' here is the hithpael participle of *qnh* 'create' and suggests an image to invoke divine blessings. Ezekiel 8.5–6 is closely related to Ezek. 43.7–10 where the word *pgr* may refer to 'monuments' that were intended as a substitute for sacrifices. Evidence for this can be found in the Phoenician context where votive statues were dedicated to temples as thanks for weathering a great crisis (e.g. illness). Ezekiel 20.30–32 indicates that these monuments had become the focal point of the Judean cult. Israel is condemned not because it sacrificed children to idols, but because it was making offerings in conjunction with cult statues, substituting these monuments for proper sacrifice. The men worshipping in 8.16–17 are worshipping YHWH, in association with the symbol-rich sun imagery, as an expression of confidence of the deity's faithfulness to Israel. But YHWH sees this as an evasion of his demand for real devotion involving the hearts and minds. He would not be satisfied with the tokens of devotion, the votive images.

Corrine Patton ('Layers of Meaning: Priesthood in Jeremiah MT') explores the reading of the text's final form as the product of a dialogue between the layers of redaction. She notes that ritual matters in Jeremiah are usually ignored or thought to be late additions, but there is a unified social definition of the nature and function of the priesthood in the final form of the text, despite conflicting ideologies in the various layers. Condemnation of the priests is characteristic of the oracles in 1–25, often coupled with condemnation of prophets as a part of the religious leadership responsible for the fall of Jerusalem. Priestly opposition to Jeremiah comes to the fore in chs. 26–33. In this and later layers of the book, the authors use characterization as a way to communicate ideology. Although the text characterizes priests mainly through negative qualities, Jeremiah is both identified as a priest in the superscription to the book and functions as a cultic functionary in a temple environment in many passages. The rhetorical effect is that he comes across not as an outsider opponent of ritual, but as an insider critic of a cult gone bad. As the book progresses, a greater distance between Jeremiah, the temple cult, and even the priests is found. In chs. 34–45 he is no longer a cultic functionary but rather a voice outside the temple. As Jeremiah is literally placed outside of the temple, scribes and written oracles become more important. The written word seems to have replaced both priests and prophets as the effective vehicle for divine mediation. However, the dialogue between the various layers in the text in the final form of the book reveals that, even though later redactors have tried to steer the book in certain ways, a fundamental question remains: why did neither priest, prophet, nor written scroll save the city? Was it a failure of human vehicles of mediation or a problem with God?

Joachim Schaper ('The Priests in the Book of Malachi and their Opponents') aims to identify the priests criticized in Malachi and also their opponents (by which is meant the author[s]/redactor[s] of the book who criticize the priests). Several indications put the book in the period between 460 to 398 BCE: references to God as being active against Edom (1.4–5), the mention of a 'governor' (1.8), the problem of mixed marriages which had not yet been addressed (2.11–12), and the poor economic circumstances presupposed in the book. The passage 1.6–2.9 is the central one. This seems to be referring to the altar priests, not the lower cult personnel (since the priests are the ones who 'draw near' to the altar). Four basic positions have been taken on the priests and Levites in the book: (1) the book is prior to P and the 'priests' and 'Levites' are used synonymously; (2) although the language is heavily reliant on D, the actual description of tithes is more like P, suggesting a transition from D legislation to P; (3) the author was aware of P legislation, but still saw no differentiation in the priesthood; (4) the priests and Levites were in deep tension, and the book does not support the P legislation (the view of P. D. Hanson). The author(s)/redactor(s) of the book do not make a distinction between priests and Levites, not because of an ignorance of P and Ezekiel but *despite* them. Malachi gives no hint that Levites were second-rank cult personnel, yet we know from other Persian-period sources that they were already so at this time. Malachi goes further than D, H, and P in equating blemished animals for offerings as 'impurity'. The book also turns the priestly blessing on its head in ironic mockery of the priesthood. Nevertheless, the priests are also praised, which means that the book is not criticizing priestly *office*, but rather the priestly *incumbents* to the office. This shows that the author(s) of the book were not Levites but priests – dissident priests who are denouncing the Zadokite priests in charge of the temple. Evidence of a rift in the Jerusalem priesthood is also found in Neh. 13.4–14.

Ziony Zevit ('The Prophet versus Priest Antagonism Hypothesis: Its History and Origin') argues against the common scholarly position that there was an institutional antagonism between priests and prophets. This is a false dichotomy – on historical, textual, and phenomenological grounds. (The same applies to the one long alleged between pre-classical and classical prophets.) Although there is some justification for distinguishing between the different types of prophets, these are technical rather than essential and owe more to the different types of literature from which we learn about them. The classical prophets did not necessarily have ethical or moral concerns: the total number of verses on the subject is only about 11 percent and is missing entirely from a number of prophetic books. The prophets give no practical remedies; nothing suggests any attempt to replace the Israelite ethos or the ruling elite with a new order (except perhaps Ezek. 40–48). Prophets function as public scolds, but their overriding interest is cultic behavior. The priest/prophet antagonism hypothesis has a long history with roots in Christian theological interests and the development of the psychology of religion as a discipline. Yet a number of recent studies have begun to give a more positive perspective and do justice to the priests. When one surveys the relevant biblical passages on priests, a number of points emerge. For example, priests were not always considered necessary except for manipulation of the blood at the 'sin-offering'. Neither Elijah nor the prophets of Baal are identified as priests, despite making offerings. Josiah did not interfere with the Jerusalem priesthood even though he did away with certain cult practices. The priests are seldom referred to in the Latter Prophets (only 78 times, mostly in Jeremiah and Ezekiel). For Amos and Hosea there is no antagonism toward the cult performed properly and no animus when conducting the priestly functions. Jeremiah did not single out the priests for particular criticism. In fact, only Malachi accuses the priests of malfeasance while in office (the issue seems mainly the definition of acceptable animals). The Latter Prophets show many criticisms of cult practices of the people, but the priests are not singled out. When prophets did not like the cult or aspects of it, they did not attack the officients who were essentially technicians. There is no principled objection to the cult or those overseeing it. On the contrary, the Prophets contain many positive passages toward the temple and cult. So what is the origin of the antagonism hypothesis? It lacks a basis in biblical texts and is unsubstantitated by the poorly articulated psychological arguments advanced to support it. It originated at a particular stage of biblical scholarship: although it fits the prejudices of the Enlightenment image of religion (informed by Reformation and post-Reformation theology), its roots appear to be much earlier, probably in the priestly condemnation of Jesus and some of the disciples in the Gospels and Acts. This was picked up in later religious polemics but reached its culmination in Wellhausen and the religious developments of the late-nineteenth century from which it was bequeathed to us as a modern scholarly tradition.

Antagonism between Priests and Prophets?

It was a nineteenth-century view that saw priests and prophets not only as two different professions but as having two different and conflicting world views. A strong theme that cuts through many of the contributions to this volume is to question – indeed, to object to – this old dichotomy. A number of the contributors address the problem explicitly, while others do so more implicitly. The centrality of the cult to worship in ancient Israel is now widely recognized in scholarship, even if some of the old attitudes have not entirely disappeared. Yet the question of the precise relationship between priests and prophets – and of the prophetic attitude toward the cult – is still debated, and the idea of a 'prophetic critique' of the priesthood is still very much alive. Two writers (Zevit, Grabbe) survey the passages throughout the Latter Prophets; others treat the subject in relation to broad topics (Ben Zvi, Bibb, Patton); while yet others focus on specific passages (Galambush, Linville, Nelson, Odell, Schaper).

Z. Zevit argues that the supposed antagonism between priest and prophet is an invention of modern scholarship. How this critique is part of a modern scholarly position is also emphasized by B. Bibb who looks at the priest/prophet dichotomy as it is characterized in two classic theologies of the twentieth century (though a more recent OT theology from the late 1990s resists the older view). Agreeing generally with Zevit's analysis does not mean, however, that a definite prophetic critique of priests in certain passages has been overlooked. The question is the significance of this critique and how it is to be interpreted in the broader context of the Latter Prophets' message(s). No one refuses to believe that priests are attacked at length in some prophetic passages, but they are hardly the only ones coming under strong criticism (cf. Grabbe). As Zevit notes, the prophetic critique was only part of the prophets' role as public scolds. Significantly, none of the prophets was evidently suggesting a replacement of the present order with a new one. Similarly, J. R. Linville argues that the book of Joel shows no plans to replace the cult with anything else, but rather validates the priestly leadership by prophecy. In Joel's 'word-world' the priests have a disproportionate importance. In fact, in spite of their critique the prophets cannot imagine a world without priests and the cult (Bibb). Their criticisms of the priests have to be interpreted in the context of the overall prophetic rhetoric. R. D. Nelson accepts that Hosea does indeed condemn the priests, ironically making use of priestly purity language, but this is only part of a general condemnation of apostasy that extends to all the people. E. Ben Zvi points out that there is a contingent opposition in the sense that the prophets indicted corrupt individuals, including priests. If the literature was the product primarily of the Persian period, the priests being criticized would have long since been dead in many cases, while the literati who produced the literature accepted the general ideology of the temple establishment. One can go further and say that the temple is necessary for the very stability of the cosmos (Linville).

The way in which the prophetic critique is much more complex than often appreciated is well illustrated by the study of M. S. Odell. She investigates the striking imagery of Ezek. 8 in which leaders of the community are pictured as worshiping in the temple in what is usually interpreted as grotesque pagan rites. Odell gives this a new interpretation, particularly in regard to two aspects of it: the image of jealousy is a monument dedicated to YHWH, and the worship is an expression of confidence in YHWH's faithfulness. There is no question that Ezekiel is giving a negative portrait of the individuals involved; however, it is not about Asherah worship or child sacrifice, but about the substitution of votive offerings for proper sacrifice. C. Patton's study of Jeremiah reaches a number of conclusions, including a deconstruction in which the book ultimately admits its own failure. But, like Ben Zvi and others, she also argues that Jeremiah comes across as a critic from the inside, not the outside, who condemns individual priests, but not the priesthood as a whole. The one genuine prophetic attack on the priesthood as such that Zevit allows is Mal. 1.6–14. Yet J. Schaper's study of the priesthood in Malachi suggests that what is being criticized is the practice of the priestly incumbents and not the office itself. There is a criticism in Ezek. 44.7–9, but this actually refers to foreign (Egyptian) priests, according to J. Galambush.

In sum, if the present volume does nothing else, it should serve as a witness to a sea change in attitudes about the relationship between priests and the temple cult, on the one hand, and prophets on the other.

Priests and Society

The place of priests in society is not always appreciated by a modern audience. The sacrificial cult was central to Israelite and Judean society. As Zevit points out, some biblical passages take the position that priests were not always necessary for sacrifice. These are texts, of course, and one can still ask to what extent they reflect historical reality. Many scholars would take the view that sacrifices without priests were possible in some historical periods, but not in others. By the Persian period, when many prophetic books may have been edited, there does appear to be only one place of sacrifice: the Jerusalem temple.[3] This may also have been true in the late pre-exilic period, though the question of when Jerusalem became the sole place of sacrifice is debated.

At some point, however, the Jerusalem temple became the center of worship for Jews, at least for those in Palestine, and also the spiritual center for those in the Diaspora. At that time the priests were the only ones allowed to officiate at the altar, which meant that the priestly office was vital. Prophets may have been willing to criticize priests in some form or other, but there is little indication that they wanted to change society to a non-temple, non-priestly one (Zevit). As Linville points out, the temple was regarded as essential by at least some of the prophets. For example,

---

3. This is a large subject, but see the discussion in Grabbe (2004, ch. 10).

the message of the book of Joel centers on the temple and its liturgies as a microsm of the cosmos and society. The temple and priesthood were an integral part of Israelite and Judean society.

What further roles priests had is to some extent a matter of speculation. That some temple personnel acted as scribes can be demonstrated.[4] Ben Zvi emphasizes the close relationship that the literati (which would include not only scribes but other educated and upper-class individuals with the leisure and ability to write) would have had with the temple establishment, at least in the Persian period if not earlier. The interaction would have been mutual, with the priests communicating with and influencing the literati, and the literati in turn having an influence – perhaps more subtle – on the priests. (In this scenario we must not lose sight of the fact that the literati overlapped with the priesthood and temple personnel.) Although much has been made of stereotypical behavior on the part of prophets, we should keep in mind that priests also had their own stereotypical behavior intimately associated with their roles. This is especially evident in priestly language (though their activities in the cult would also have been according to a stylized routine in most cases). Priestly blessings and proclamations have been widely studied, but one suspects that even ordinary conversation might have had certain characteristics (even as one notices characteristic 'clerical' modes of speaking among some clergy today).

The sociology of the priesthood also includes inner-priestly relations. Schaper has recently published a monograph study of how he thinks the priesthood developed between the time of Josiah and the end of the Persian period.[5] In Malachi he has identified an inter-priestly controversy. Although he argues that the author of Malachi knew of and accepted the division between the altar priests and Levites, he deliberately made no reference to it. The reason was that the book was produced by dissident priests who were writing against the actual servers at the altar as perpetuating unlawful practices.

Schaper's argument ties in closely with Galambush's interpretation of Ezek. 44.7–9. The latter suggests that Egyptian priests may have actually engaged in cultic activity in the Jerusalem temple: if so, we should expect that the incident would have evoked considerable criticism in some circles: priestly, prophetic, prominent lay leaders. We have only the passage in Ezekiel which is not long or detailed enough to suggest the whole range of response to the incident, but a conservative reaction from a variety of social groups would have been likely. Ezekiel's views can be widened by looking at what he thought of the worship described in Ezek. 8. Odell's

---

4.   Grabbe 1995: 169–71; Schams 1998.

5.   Schaper 2000. For a discussion and critique of this and some other recent studies, see Grabbe (2004, ch. 10).

interpretation that this is a fully Yahwistic temple routine suggests a good deal of official tolerance toward a variety of cultic activity during the early-sixth century, yet Ezekiel's disapproval is expressed in strong language and imagery. He cannot have been alone in this. The religious conflict would have divided priest from priest, priest from prophet, and lay worshiper from temple. In Schaper's view this conflict continued on into the Persian period.

Cult Prophets

The question of cult prophets was not explored in a major way in these papers (though several addressed the issue to some extent; see below), yet this is an issue that must be taken into account for a full picture of the priesthood. Just as scholars of the past were often dismissive of the priests, they were also frequently hostile toward cult prophets. The prophet call, prophetic freedom to speak, and prophetic submission to the will of God were seen to be incompatible with a cultic office. Cultic prophets had all the disadvantages of priests and none of the advantages of prophets, according to the prevailing theological ethos. Of course, this presupposed that none of the 'classical' prophets was a cultic prophet. S. Mowinckel's seminal study on cultic prophecy (Mowinckel 1922) did not identify any of the classical prophets as cultic, but subsequent studies have not been so reluctant (e.g. Jeremias 1970).

Yet perhaps the question needs to be looked at in a wider context: the association between some prophets and the temple. For example, the book of Jeremiah is potentially central to the question. According to both the superscription of the book (1.1) and also the familial relations described in the book itself (Long 1982), he was from a priestly family based in Anathoth. What one cannot help noticing in particular, however, is how much time Jeremiah spends in and around the temple – how much it is used as a forum for his messages and a platform for his activities, especially in chs. 1–33. This is one of the points made by Patton, though she notes that in chs. 34–45 he becomes more a voice outside the temple. Ezekiel is also a priest, even if he appears to fulfill no explicit priestly functions; however, he gives a quite explicit description of activities in the temple in ch. 8 (Odell). A recent study of Zechariah argues that he was priest of the temple, as well as a prophet (Pola 2003: 45).

Fleming's study raises the issue in the context of Mari. He points out that the relationship of the 'prophetic' individuals to the temple where they often deliver their messages is actually often unknown. Whether they were officials in the temple or derived part or all of their living from the temple cannot be answered from the data available. These might be cult prophets in some sense, but we do not know for certain. What we do know is that the messages are often delivered in a temple context, just as are those of some of the Israelite prophets according to the text.

Priests and Other Religious Specialists

Only to a lesser extent do the essays in this volume explore the place of other religious specialists besides priests and prophets.[6] A survey of the texts relating to priests (Grabbe), however, finds references not only to prophets but also to divination. The biblical text is clearly negative toward many sorts of divination (e.g. Mic. 3.5–8), but not to all. The priestly divinatory mechanism of the Urim and Thummim is not mentioned in the Latter Prophets, though the ephod is (Hos. 3.4; cf. Jer. 23.33–40), but these were considered divinely approved forms of divination. The language sometimes used in reference to prophets is the language of divination. For example, several passages in Jeremiah speak disparagingly of divination (14.14, 27.9–10, 29.8–9), but one reference is different. In Jer. 21.1–2 the king sends two individuals (one of them Zephaniah the priest) to inquire (דרש) of YHWH. 'To inquire' is the language of divination. We also find it in a number of passages in Ezekiel where the elders come to 'inquire' of YHWH through him (14.1–4, 20.1–3).

The situation at Mari provides an interesting parallel about the interaction of different religious specialists (Fleming). The diviners (*bārûm*) held the most prestigious position. Although they were employed by the palace, theirs can be classified as a religious office. There was no conflict between them and the temple priests who tended to have a less significant role in Mari than in southern Babylonia. The same applied to the prophetic figures who seem to have often functioned in the temple, even if their exact formal relationship with the temple is not usually clear to us. Since the priests did not include finding out the divine will in their portfolio, the prophets were useful to them in filling this role. On the other hand, all prophecies had to be confirmed by divination. Each specialist fulfilled his (and occasionally her) function, apparently without any serious conflict.

Ben Zvi highlights the 'slippage' of attributes between priests, prophets, and literati.[7] Although not every member of the literati was a priest or Levite, the majority probably were. The literati also identified with the central tenets of Jerusalem temple ideology. The image of priest and prophet – whether presented as a positive model or critiqued from a negative point of view – would have been assimilated to some extent to the

---

6. For a study devoted to the range of religious specialists in ancient Israelite society, including the king, see Grabbe (1995).

7. See also the discussion and arguments in Grabbe 1995: 217–21.

image that the literati had of themselves, especially those figures pictured as living toward the end of the monarchy. In addition, we have the fact that several prophets are said or implied also to be priests. Malachi construes the priest as the messenger of YHWH, a role elsewhere taken by the prophet. Moses is characterized as a prophet (Deut. 18.15–22), but Aaron is said to act as Moses's own prophet (Exod. 4.16, 7.1). Finally, we hear the voices of both priest and prophet through the literati – through the books composed and edited to present a particular message and ideology by the small elite literate circle responsible for writing and book production.

The point is made that the priests and prophets consitute different social groups (Patton). This is by and large true. Most priests were not prophets and most prophets were not priests. Temple personnel were generally set apart from lay Israelites and Judeans, holding their office by heredity alone. Prophets, on the other hand, could come from any social group (including the temple personnel) and served because of a call experience from God.[8]

We cannot conclude a great deal about the interrelationships between religious specialists on the brief bit of information found in this particular study. What we can say is that the priests, prophets, and others each had their own sphere and need not be in competition. We should also be aware that the judgment of the biblical editors about various priests, prophets, diviners and the like represents only one viewpoint. Many people evidently found divination useful and it apparently had an important place in society. The scribal element (literati) was essential to shaping and transmitting the image and tradition of the different religious specialists. Although we still see a variety of viewpoints even in the final text of the Bible, there was clearly a certain amount of assimilation to particular images and ideology that the writers wanted to pass on. This conforms to the views of the temple establishment.

Conclusions

The essays in the present volume cover a range of issues relating to priests and also to some other religious specialists in ancient Israelite and Judean

---

8.   Judging from sociological studies of prophecy in other cultures, such call experiences are normal. Some have wanted to deny that so-called 'false prophets' had a call, drawing on Jer. 23.21–22 as evidence. This is use of blatant religious prejudice as data. It is part of the polemic within prophetic conflict to deny that one's opponent has any genuine qualifications to act as a prophet, but this does not mean that such accusations are true. Using biblical passages in such a neo-fundamentalist way, as if it constituted observed sociological data, is a caricature of scholarship and does not make it evidence. See further the discussion and bibliography in Grabbe (1995: 113–15; see also especially Buss 1982).

society. We can summarize some of the main issues raised or addressed in the following points:

1. There was no natural or inevitable opposition between priests and prophets. The role of prophet entailed being a public 'scold' (Zevit's word), which included attacking any group from the monarchy to those at the bottom of society for doing what the prophet thought was wrong – or all of the above. Thus, priests might well be targeted by some prophets, but it was usually an attack on specific priests for their individual failings rather than on the priesthood or temple cult as such. The idea of a deep conflict between the priestly and prophetic is basically a modern scholarly invention.

2. The temple and its priesthood were seen as an essential part of ancient Israelite and Judean society. This seems to be the assumption of most prophets who generally appear to take the temple and cult for granted. There is little evidence of wanting to remove them or to create a cultless society.

3. This acceptance of the temple's place in society does not mean that relations were all happy and harmonious. There is evidence of inner-priestly strife at certain times. This appears to be the case in the late monarchy at a time when the Levites evidently wished to have full priestly status. Schaper argues that this conflict continued into the Persian period. Priests were also apparently ready to criticize each other, as in the case of Malachi who seems to be giving an inner-priestly critique (Schaper; Grabbe 1995: 49).

4. Although we do not have evidence of cult prophets in the classical sense, as postulated by Mowinckel and others, we do have examples of prophets strongly associated with temples and carrying out their activities often or mainly in the temple (e.g. Isaiah, Jeremiah, perhaps Zechariah). This is paralleled by the Mari prophets who seem to do their work in temples even though their precise relationship with the temple is generally not certain. According to the biblical text a number of prophets were also priests (Jeremiah, Ezekiel, perhaps Zechariah). It has also been argued that Habakkuk and also even Jeremiah and Amos were cult prophets (though this question was not examined at length in the essays here).

5. A certain overlap of functions (Ben Zvi calls it 'slippage') can be seen between some religious specialists. This is not inevitable, but varies according to the society in question. For example, at Mari the diviners were separate from the temples, whereas prophets were often associated with temples. In ancient Israel divination was among the duties of the priesthood, at least in the early days, though its use seems to have declined later. The scribal class (literati) was apparently made up largely, but not entirely, of

priests and Levites. Finally, as already noted, some prophets are stated to be priests.

For a full story of the priests, one needs to go beyond the Latter Prophets. Nevertheless, a study of how the priests have been represented in this corpus of literature has given particular insights not only on priests but also on prophets, the relationships between priests and prophets, and interactions with some other religious specialists. These insights have fully justified the meeting in which the papers were originally read and the present volume in which they are published.

BIBLIOGRAPHY

Ben Zvi, Ehud, and Michael H. Floyd (eds.)
2000   *Writings and Speech in Israelite and Ancient Near Eastern Prophecy* (SBLSymS; Atlanta: Society of Biblical Literature).

Buss, M. J.
1982   'An Anthropological Perspective upon Prophetic Call Narratives', *Semeia* 21: 9–30.

Grabbe, Lester L.
1995   *Priests, Prophets, Diviners, Sages: A Socio-historical Study of Religious Specialists in Ancient Israel* (Valley Forge, PA: Trinity Press).
2002–3   Review of J. Schaper, *Priester und Leviten im achämenidischen Juda*, *JQR* 93: 609–11.
2004   *A History of the Jews and Judaism in the Second Temple Period*, vol. I: *Yehud: A History of the Persian Province of Judah* (LSTS 47; London/New York: T & T Clark).

Grabbe, Lester L., and Robert D. Haak (eds.)
2001   *'Every City Shall Be Forsaken': Urbanism and Prophecy in Ancient Israel and the Near East* (JSOTSup, 330; Sheffield Academic Press).
2003   *Knowing the End from the Beginning: The Prophetic, the Apocalyptic, and their Relationships* (JSPSup 46; London/New York: T & T Clark).

Jeremias, Jörg
1970   *Kultprophetie und Gerichtsverkündigung in der späten Königszeit Israels* (WMANT, 35; Neukirchen: Neukirchener Verlag).

Long, Burke O.
1982   'Social Dimensions of Prophetic Conflict', in Robert C. Culley and Thomas W. Overholt (eds.), *Anthropological Perspectives on Old Testament Prophecy* (*Semeia*: 21; Chico, CA: Society of Biblical Literature), 31–53.

Mowinckel, Sigmund
1922   *Psalmenstudien. III. Kultprophetie und prophetische Psalmen* (Skrifter utgit av Videnskapsselskapets i Kristiania II: Hist.-Filos. Klasse 1922, No. 1; Oslo: Dybwad).

Pola, Thomas
    2003   *Das Priestertum bei Sacharja: Historische und traditionsgeschichtliche Untersuchung zur frühnachexilischen Herrschererwartung* (FAT, 35; Tübingen: Mohr Siebeck).
Schams, Christine
    1998   *Jewish Scribes in the Second-Temple Period* (JSOTSup, 291; Sheffield Academic Press).
Schaper, Joachim
    2000   *Priester und Leviten im achämenidischen Juda: Studien zur Kult- und Sozialgeschichte Israels in persischer Zeit* (FAT, 31; Tübingen: Mohr Siebeck).
Sweeney, Marvin A., and Ehud Ben Zvi (eds.)
    2003   *The Changing Face of Form Criticism for the Twenty-first Century* (Grand Rapids, MI: Eerdmans).

OBSERVATIONS ON PROPHETIC CHARACTERS, PROPHETIC TEXTS,
PRIESTS OF OLD, PERSIAN PERIOD PRIESTS AND LITERATI

Ehud Ben Zvi

1. *Introduction*

There is probably no historian of ancient Israel, or biblical scholar for that
matter, who has not heard of constructions of 'the prophet' as a historical
and institutional character opposed to 'the priest' in ancient Israel. These
constructions have a long history and have been central to biblical studies
strongly informed by theological concerns in some Protestant and
(classical) Reform Judaism circles. They have also been associated with
the construction of the biblical prophets of old as ancient leaders for social
justice – and forerunners, to some extent, of those who advocated these
positions – in more than one version of contemporary biblical or biblically-
informed theologies. The study of this and similar ideological constructions is taken up in other contributions to this volume and in any case
belongs to the realm of the sociology of knowledge rather than to that of
the historical study of ancient Israel. This writer is particularly interested in
the latter, and so is his contribution.

In the following pages I will make a number of observations that deal
directly with the most likely relation between the mental image of 'the
prophet' and 'the priest' as discursive categories within the social
discourse/s of the postmonarchic period, or to be more precise, within
that of the literati of Yehud who were not only responsible for most of the
biblical literature in its present form, but also who constituted their
primary (re)readership.[1]

This contribution consists of two main sets of observations. The first one
deals with that which may be called observations of absence, whereas the
second, of presence. The absence referred to here is that of ideological
constructions of mental images of opposition between 'the priest' and 'the
prophets' that are *not* contingent on particular sets of prophets and priests,

---

1. The books that eventually were included in the HB were not read only once. Most
readers were actually rereaders. For the sake of simplicity I will be using, for the most part,
the terms readers and readership, but it is worth stressing that they point at rereaders and
rereaderships. Occasionally, however, to emphasize the point I will refer to (re)readers and the
like.

their circumstances, individual characters, and the like.[2] In other words, these are observations about the absence of categorical opposition between these two categories within the discourse of the mentioned postmonarchic communities. The second set deals with observations about the presence of slippage of attributes usually associated with mental images of the prophets of old, priests, and the literati who identified with these characters. The resulting partial overlaps or instances of partial intertwining of images and attributes are not due to any substantial constraint of the characterization of priests or prophets.[3] This being the case, the mentioned tendencies towards partial convergence within the discourse of postmonarchic Yehud demand particular attention. This contribution would relate these discursive and ideological trends and their relation to the social realia of the period.

2. Categorical Oppositions in the Constructed Monarchic Past?

The constructions of the past communicated by the prophetic books and the so-called deuteronomic history, and later, and to some extent, Chronicles, reflected and shaped the images of the past within the world of these literati.[4] Since the monarchic past is the ideological and temporal realm that, according to some, was populated with categorical oppositions between priests and prophets, this is the era that bears most of the attention for the present purposes. If so, how did they construe the relation between prophets and priests in the crucial monarchic period?

The intended and primary readers of the prophetic books certainly learned that there were many prophetic characters whose world was set in the monarchic period that strongly opposed unfaithful priests (e.g. Jer. 18.18, 23.11; Ezek. 7.26, 22.26; Hos. 5.1; Mic. 3.11; Zeph. 3.4). But they also certainly learned that these prophetic characters stood alongside with YHWH against anyone else who was unfaithful to YHWH. They opposed other prophets (e.g., Isa. 28.7; Jer. 8.1–2, 18.18; Ezek. 13.1–16, 22.25, 28; Mic. 3.5–6; Zeph. 3.4), political and judicial leaders (e.g. Isa. 5.23; Jer.8.1–2;

---

2. In plain words, oppositions that are not related to, for instance, a conflict between a good, pious prophet or prophets and a group of sinful priests, or an evildoer priest. Biblical texts assume that there were priests and prophets who were sinful and were supposed to be confronted by pious people. All of these confrontations are situationally bound, that is, contingent. On these matters see below.

3. After all prophets do not have to be, or share any particular attributes of priests and *vice versa*,

4. Chronicles was not, and probably was never meant to be, a 'classical' text that could have enjoyed the same, or a higher degree of authority than the books included in the so-called deuteronomic history. These matters, however, stand beyond the scope of this contribution and, in any case, deserve a separate study.

Ezek. 22.6–12, 27; Mic. 3.1–4, 9–11; Zeph. 3.3), sages (e.g. Isa. 5.21; Jer. 8.8–9, 18.18), characters carrying attributes associated with any of the above (e.g. Ezek. 11.1–13), and certainly strongly denounced Jerusalem (e.g. Isa. 1; Ezek. 22.1–5, 23; Amos 2.4–5; Mic. 3.9–12; Zeph. 1.4–6) and Israel, Judah, northern Israel or 'the people (e.g. Isa. 1, Jer. 7.28–33; Amos 2.4–5, 6–16; Hos. 1.2–2.3, 11.1–7; Mic. 1.2–9; Zeph. 2.1–3). These literati could not have learned from these texts about any essential, non-contingent opposition between 'the prophets' and 'the priests' any more than they could have learned about any essential, non-contingent opposition between 'the prophets' and 'Israel', or 'Jerusalem', 'the political leadership of the monarchic period', 'the sages', or even, and to show to the absurdity of the claim, 'the prophets'.

It is worth stressing that the fall of the monarchic polities, and particularly that of Judah loomed large on the postmonarchic communities within which the prophetic books were written or reached their present form, and certainly loomed large on the literati for whom they were written. Reflections on these issues that were informed by the assumption of YHWH's justice led by ideological necessity to stern condemnations of monarchic Judah (and its forerunner, monarchic Israel) for sins so great that justified YHWH's destruction of Jerusalem and its polity.[5] Since the faithful prophets of old were conceived, among others, as those who were a small minority and warned the people of the impending and fully justified destruction, as those who called the people to turn away from their wrong ways and return to YHWH and YHWH's ways but were unsuccessful,[6] then the prophets had to stand, by necessity, against the corrupt elite and the people of their times, and therefore, against priests, prophets, sages, political leaders, and 'Israel', 'Judah' or 'Jerusalem'. But more important for the present endeavor is the observation that the postmonarchic readers, who are not prophets nor live in the monarchic period, were also supposed to identify with the prophetic characters of their books and their messages. From the viewpoint of the readers of these books the position against 'iniquities' taken by these characters is that which any pious Israelite should have taken when confronted with circumstances described in the books; in fact, it is the position that the readers themselves would like to imagine they would have taken if they had to confront the terrible conditions that characterize these books. These books do construct a non-

---

5. The potential list of types of sins available for these constructions in Israel and in the ancient Near East included what today we may call cultic, social, ethical, political sins. However, all of them are included in, or function as, an expression of an ideologically construed rejection of, or disrespect towards the deity

6. I discussed these matters in E. Ben Zvi, '"The Prophets" – Generic Prophets and their Role in the Construction of the Image of the "Prophets of Old" within the Postmonarchic Readerships of the Book of King', *ZAW* (forthcoming).

contingent, categorical opposition but it consists of those who follow
YHWH and YHWH's ways and those who reject them, be them priests,
prophets, leaders, or 'all Israel/Judah'. In this sense, the ideological
dichotomy that these books describe[7] is not substantially different from
that conveyed by texts in Proverbs and Psalms (e.g. Ps. 1; Prov. 1) which
were also shaped within a similar social and ideological matrix.[8] In all
cases, the texts fulfill an educational purpose as they serve to socialize their
readers into the basic ideological principles held by their communities.

It bears note that in books in which prophets *per se* do not take the
center of the stage – as they do in the prophetic books – the ubiquitous,
although at times implied, essential opposition between those who are
pious and those who are sinful and above all their respective ways led to
the creation of 'functional prophets', that is, characters who are not
prophets, but who serve roles similar to those often associated with the
prophets. For instance, they explain the reason for events – in the real
world to the readers, call people to return to YHWH, warn them from the
consequences of turning away from YHWH and the like.[9] In other words,
from the viewpoint of the readership of these authoritative texts they
served educational purposes.

As one turns to works that existed within the repertoire of Jerusalemite-
centered communities in the Achaemenid period communities and
communicated to their primary readers images of the monarchic or
premonarchic periods besides the prophetic books, it becomes evident that
even a cursory overview of the collection of books we called the
deuteronomic (hi)story, and in particular the books of Samuel and Kings,
show that postmonarchic literati could not have learned from these texts of
any non-contingent, categorical opposition between priests and prophets.

The same holds true for their reading of the pentateuchal books. The
latter construe Moses, to some extent at least, as a prophet (see Deut.
18.15–18, 34.10), and certainly Aaron as the archetypical (and proto-
typical) priest. The postmonarchic readers certainly could not have
construed the relationship between Moses and Aaron as one characterized
by a categorical, non-contingent opposition. In fact, the relation between
Moses and Aaron, provides an exemplary case of a complementary

---

7.   See, for instance Mic. 3 in which the prophetic character is contrasted with anyone else
and notice the emphatic 'as for me' in 3.8
8.   That of Achaemenid Yehud and its basic tenets.
9.   See, for instance, the characterization of Joshua (and cf. with that of Moses). For
'functional' prophets in Judges, cf. the recent paper by Christoph Levin, 'Prophecy in the
Book of Judges', presented at the 2002 meeting of the Society of Biblical Literature that took
place in Toronto, 23–26 November, 2002; for 'functional' prophets in Chronicles, see Y. Amit,
'תפקיד הנבואה והנביאים במשנתו של ספר דברי הימים' *Beit Miqra* 28 (1982/3), pp. 113–33.

relation between priest and 'prophet' in the past.[10] In addition, if the readership of Genesis was supposed to construe to some extent Abraham as a prophet (see Gen. 20.7), then again they cannot learn about any categorical opposition between priestly and prophetic roles.[11]

As one turns to books explicitly set in the Persian period, then one may find again a case of a prophetic diatribe against priests who failed to perform their duties (Mal. 2.1–3), but even this book is certainly not anti-priestly. On the contrary, it reaffirms the importance of proper priests and the centrality of the temple. The books of Haggai and Zechariah communicated to their readership that the presence of a properly run temple is crucial in the divine economy and has worldwide implications. It also bears notice that texts conveying the central role for the Jerusalemite temple in the divine design for the world are not confined to these books, but are part and parcel of the (eventually, biblical) corpus of prophetic literature and voiced by many prophetic characters (see, for instance, Isa. 2.2–4, ch. 60; Mic. 4.1–5; Hag. 2.6–9). It goes without saying that the existence of such a central temple requires by necessity the presence of (faithful) priests.

This being so, it is worth stressing that one of the most ubiquitous ideological topos in prophetic literature and (Hebrew) biblical literature in general is that of the centrality of Jerusalem/Zion.[12] But the centrality of Jerusalem/Zion in these contexts rests fully on its association with the (ideologically) sole legitimate temple for the one and only existing deity in the universe. In other words, Jerusalem is important and unique because of the temple, rather than vice versa. As mentioned above, the ideological presence of a temple implies that of the priests.

---

10.   On Moses and Aaron see also below.

11.   See not only the Melchizedek story in Gen. 14, but also the role of Abraham as a person performing sacrifices, including the 'non-sacrifice' of Isaac at Mt Moriah, which in second Temple period is identified with the site of the Jerusalemite temple.

12.   There is no need here to expand on these matters, since I discussed them and some of their implications to some length in 'Inclusion in and Exclusion from Israel as Conveyed by the Use of the Term "Israel" in Postmonarchic Biblical Texts'. S. W. Holloway and L. K. Handy (eds.), *The Pitcher Is Broken. Memorial Essays for Gosta W. Ahlstrom* (JSOTSup, 190; Sheffield: JSOT Press, 1995), pp. 95–149.

To be sure, there are texts that construe a time in which Israel had no temple, but these periods are always considered transient. They relate to either the period of the wandering in the desert and the ideologically comparable period between the destruction of the 586 BCE and the rebuilding of the temple in Darius' days. The postmonarchic/Yehudite literati responsible for most of the biblical books in their present form certainly thought that the wanderings were meant to lead to the land and eventually to the establishment of the temple in Jerusalem, and were fully aware that there was a temporary period during which there would be no temple in Jerusalem.

These considerations lead to a clear conclusion: Within the Jerusalemite centered, postmonarchic discourse/s that reflected and shaped the ideology of the literati responsible for most of the biblical books in their present form, there was no room for the construction of authoritative characters (prophetic or otherwise) that would have stood in a non-contingent situation of opposition to priests, and indirectly, to the temple *per se*.[13] In other words, this is not a simple case of absence of evidence,[14] but of an absence that is due to ideological systemic constraints within the postmonarchic discourse/s.[15]

None of these considerations *per se* necessarily requires the development of trends conveying a sense of partial convergence between the ideological image of 'the priest' and 'the prophet',[16] beyond the construction of both faithful prophets and priests as included in the category of those who follow YHWH and YHWH's ways. But there is evidence suggesting that such trends did develop within the mentioned discourses.

3. *Social Realia in Postmonarchic Israel and Trends towards Slippage of Attributes between and Partial Intertwining of Images of 'The Prophet' and 'The Priest'*

There is a widespread agreement – though certainly not unanimity – that the prophetic books, and most of, if not all the biblical books, in their present form were composed by literati in the post-monarchic period, and for the most part within the Persian period Yehud. The production of these books necessitated and implied the fulfillment of several conditions. For one it required the existence of bearers of high literacy able to compose these books and to serve as their primary readership. Their presence in turn implies that processes leading to, and social 'institutions' for the (continuing) education and socialization of these literati were in place during Yehud and were effective, at least to some degree. To be sure, the existence of these processes and social institutions requires the allocation of the economic and social resources necessary for

---

13. Significantly, it is within the same ideological matrix that the Pentateuch was composed in its present form, and notice the strong presence of priestly traditions there.

14. One must be cautious about simple cases of absence of evidence, for the latter is not really evidence for absence in these instances.

15. On social relia concerns, see next section.

16. Full convergence is, of course, an impossible proposition. Prophetic and priestly roles could not be absolutely equated in Israel or any ancient Near Eastern society.

the creation and maintenance of a layer (or layers) of literati and their activities.[17] This allocation of resources in turn requires and implies the development of a social need, or claimed to be social need, not only for the literati's activities but also their products, that is, books, readings among the literati, readings to others, and from an ideological or theological perspective, the shaping and communication of that which is claimed to be YHWH's word and teaching as a written text meant to be read, reread, meditated upon, and read to others in various settings and on a range of occasions. This social need is, of course, constructed primarily within the discourse of a certain, elite group (or groups) in the population and it reflects its ideological (or theological) tenets. In any case, the existence of such a social need has to be agreed upon by those groups and institutions in Yehud that were in a position of controlling the allocation of resources necessary to maintain the highly literate elite, its activities and its products.

Since I have discussed these matters elsewhere to some length,[18] it would suffice for the particular purpose of this contribution to emphasize that most likely the Jerusalemite temple fulfilled a central, systemic role in the manifold processes that granted social, economic and ideological sustainability to the cadres of bearers of high literacy that were necessary for the composition and continuous reading and rereading of the prophetic books in Yehudite Jerusalem.[19] Or, in other words, the Jerusalemite Temple of the Yehud period was most likely an important link in the processes leading to the production and 'consumption' of the prophetic books, at the very least in their present form.

The literati themselves, who are in some way also the product of these processes, seemed to have identified fully with the central tenets of the second temple Jerusalemite ideology (e.g., the centrality and unique role of Jerusalem/Zion/temple vis à vis any other city or temple – even if Yhawistic) or at the very least shaped in such a manner the authoritative voices in their writings, including, of course, the prophetic books (see above). This is not surprising at all, given the considerations about the role of the Jerusalemite

17. These activities include writing these type of books for a restricted highly literate Hebrew readership, reading, rereading, meditating on these books, as well as editing, copying, archiving, retrieving them, and reading them or portions of them to others unable to read them by themselves – that is, the immense majority of the population.

18. See my 'Introduction: Writings, Speeches, and the Prophetic Books – Setting an Agenda', E. Ben Zvi and M. H. Floyd (eds.), *Writings and Speech in Israelite and Ancient Near Eastern Prophecy* (Symposium, 10; Atlanta: Society of Biblical Literature, 2000), pp. 1–29; and earlier, 'The Urban Center of Jerusalem and the Development of the Literature of the Hebrew Bible', W. G. Aufrecht, N. A. Mirau and S. W. Gauley (eds.), *Aspects of Urbanism in Antiquity* (JSOTSup, 244; Sheffield: Sheffield Academic Press, 1997), pp. 194–209. See also my commentaries on Micah, Obadiah and Hosea (forthcoming).

19. Or Jerusalemite Yehud.

temple mentioned above and matters of social cohesion and self-identifica-
tion within a very small elite in a small province that advances claims about
its high status and uniqueness in the divine economy.

To be sure, the ideological and social centrality of the temple and,
indirectly, its priests,[20] may lead to particular, time or event-bound
critiques of the latter's perceived misbehavior and of the earth-shattering
consequences that it might lead to in the divine economy.

In other words, it is precisely the fact that the authorship and readership's
discourse is fully permeated by the ideological assumption of the crucial role
of the temple and its priests that provides the background to hyperbolic
critiques of the latter by the prophetic characters that populated the world of
the prophetic books that were composed and (re)read by the literati of
Yehud, as opposed to any claim about an essential, non-contingent
opposition between 'the priests' on the one hand and constructions of
prophets of old, prophetic characters in the prophetic books, and above all,
those who give voice to them, that is the literati themselves.

In other words, it is because the prophetic characters shaped in the
prophetic books, and those who shaped and embodied them in readings
and rereadings thought highly of the office of the priest that the presence of
the so-called 'anti-priest' texts made sense.

It is worth noting, and hardly surprising given the considerations
advanced above, that the harangue of the prophetic characters, and the
composers of the prophetic books in their present form is aimed in the
immense majority of the cases at the long-dead priests of the monarchic
period, rather than at Jerusalemite priests contemporary with the writers
of the books.[21]

It bears notice that not only (a) the Yehudite literati that formed the
authorship and (re)readership of these prophetic books were socialized and
educated to accept the main ideological claims advanced by the social,
religious and ideological center of their days, that is, the Jerusalemite temple,
and (b) their activities and their products were related to the temple in more
than one way, but also (c) they themselves were very unlikely to have run
their lives separate from that of many of the Jerusalemite priests. The entire
population of Jerusalem was small at that time, and the total number of

20. As mentioned above, if the temple is so central, so are its priests. It is extremely
unlikely that anyone in ancient Yehud (or the ancient Near East for that matter) developed an
image of an actual, earthly and 'running' temple devoid of its main human personnel, that is,
devoid priests.

21. The one case in which priests of the second temple are condemned is in Malachi, which
is a text that lionizes the office and roles of the priest, and therefore advances claims about the
actual misconduct of place and time-bound group of them. Moreover, the primary
(re)readership of the book was likely asked to understand the reports in the book as in
their past or as pointing to an ideal future (see Mal. ch. 3).

bearers of high literacy in Persian Yehud or Jerusalem was most likely very small.[22] In such a society it is unlikely that simultaneous and compartmentalized elites of minimal numbers could have existed. It is most likely that the literati closely interacted with the contemporary priests. Moreover, although not every literati was a priest (or Levite), priests of standing could have, and most likely were a substantial contingent among the literati. In other words, there was a partial social overlap between priests and the literati who shaped the images of the prophets of old through their writings and who embodied them, as it were, through their writing and editing texts in which there are numerous reports written in the first person and in which the speaker is a prophet of old, and through their reading of these texts to others who are not literati. Certainly some of priests fulfilled both roles in the Yehudite society.

These considerations regarding the actual social circumstances of Yehud of priests and literati are reflected in various ways in the main authoritative discourse/s of Yehud, and particularly in mental images associated with the prophets of old as they were reflected in, and shaped by books that eventually became 'biblical', including, of course, the prophetic books. In some cases, the text explicitly or implicitly connotes a sense of partial overlap and intertwining of mental images of prophets and priests. For instance, attributes associated with one image are being assigned to the other, or central characters are described as being both prophets and priests, or prophets are described as salient supporters of priests (and temple) and their status in society. A few examples will suffice.

To be begin with, as the prophetic characters of the prophetic books begin to be set in the last days of the monarchic period or the postmonarchic era (i.e. in a time that is closer to that of the literati themselves than, for instance, eighth century monarchic Judah), an undeniable trend is easily recognizable. There are four prophetic books that are explicitly set in these periods by means of their superscription. Even the most cursory analysis, shows that Jeremiah is characterized as a priest, and so is Ezekiel. Moreover, the images of both Haggai and Zechariah are associated with temple building, the centrality of the temple, and even with that of the High Priest. If one were to add Malachi to the list, despite the fact that its superscription does not set it in any particular period, then the crucial role of the temple in the divine economy is certainly communicated by the book.[23]

Even more important for the present purposes is the fact that the book of Malachi explicitly refers to, and asks its readership to construe the priest

---

22. One may also consult the recent population figures in O. Lipschits, 'Demographic Changes in Judah between the Seventh and the Fifth Centuries B.C.E.', in O. Lipschits and J. Blenkinsopp (eds.), *Judah and the Judeans in the Neo-Babylonian Period* (Winona Lake, IN: Eisenbrauns, 2003), pp. 323–76. Lipschits' figures and conclusions about Jerusalem and Yehud during the Persian period are fully consistent with the positions advanced here.

23. On the relation between this concept and its critique of priests see above.

as the messenger of YHWH (מלאך ה' צבאות, see Mal. 2.7).[24] Significantly,
the name of the prophetic character associated with the book is מלאכי, 'my
[YHWH's] messenger.'[25] Moreover, prophets are not only construed as
messengers of YHWH in general (cf. the formula, 'thus says, YHWH...')
elsewhere, or prophetic roles associated to particular מלאך ה' (e.g. Zech.
3.6), but at times prophets are explicitly referred to as מלאך ה' (see Isa.
44.26; Hag. 1.13; 2 Chron. 36.16; cf. Isa. 42.19).[26]

Needless to say, there was a central figure of the past agreed upon
among the literati of Yehud that was construed as both a prophet and a
priest, Samuel.[27] In addition, there were other prophets who were
construed as officiating *ad hoc* priestly roles. In fact, within the world of
the story in 1 Kgs 18, sacrifices are associated with prophetic activities;
priests are nowhere in sight.

Most interesting is the characterization of Aaron, the archetypal priest as

24. See also Qoh. 5.5. The referent of המלאך there is most likely 'the priest'. See, for instance,
R. N. Whybray, *Ecclesiastes* (NCB; Sheffield: JSOT Press, 1989), p. 96; J. L. Crenshaw,
Ecclesiastes (OTL; Philadelphia: Westminster Press, 1987), p. 117; but see also M. V. Fox, *A
Time to Tear Down and A Time to Build Up. A Rereading of Ecclesiastes* (Grand Rapids,
Michigan: Eerdmans, 1999), p. 232. The shift from 'messenger' to 'God' in the LXX (and
Peshitta) is interesting by itself and seems to be a mirror image of the change in the opposite
direction that often appears in the Targumic tradition (e.g. Targ. Onq., Pseudo-Jonathan and
Neofiti Gen 32.31; Targ. Judg. 13.22). On this matter see R. Syrén, 'The Targum as a Bible
Reread, or How Does God Communicate with Humans', *JAB* 2 (2000), pp. 247–64.

25. Within the context of the entire ch. 3, the intended readers seemed asked to identify
the messenger in Mal. 3.1 with Elijah, that is, to associate prophetic attributes to that
messenger. Moreover, if the text in 3.1 was written so as to let the readers ponder whether the
messenger is Malachi or to create a (false) expectation that the messenger is Malachi (cf. B.
Glazier-McDonald, *Malachi: The Divine Messenger* [SBLDS, 98; Atlanta: Scholars Press,
1987], pp. 133–35), it does convey some sense of closeness between the character of Malachi
and the messenger. As such it reflects and reinforces a sense of convergence between prophetic
and (divine) messenger attributes or their bearers, or both.

26. Tendencies to associate divine messengers with prophets or functional prophets
appear also in midrashic literature. See Lev. R. 1.1 that states that prophets were called (at
times) messengers (מלאך), but notice that the decisive argument there comes from Hag. 1.13.
These tendencies seemed to have influenced Targumic traditions. See, for instance, *Targ. Judg.*
2.1. It is worth mentioning that according to Lev. R. 1.1, מלאך ה' (i.e. the messenger of YHWH)
in Judg. 2.1 is to be identified with Phinehas, the priest.
On prophets as messengers see also N. G. Cohen, 'From Nabi to Mal'ak to "Ancient
Figure"', *JSS* 36 (1985), pp. 12–24. For discussion of 'prophets and angels/messengers' from a
different angle, see E. W. Conrad, 'The End of Prophecy and the Appearance of Angels/
Messengers in the Book of the Twelve', *JSOT* 73 (1997), pp. 65–79.

27. He is also construed as the 'leader' of the people. On the characterization of Samuel
and some of its implications see A. G. Auld, 'From King to Prophet in Samuel and Kings', J.
C. de Moor (ed.), *The Elusive Prophet: The Prophet as a Historical Person, Literary Character
and Anonymous Artist* (OtSt; XLV, Leiden: E. J. Brill, 2001), pp. 31–44

Moses' prophet (see Exod. 7.1),[28] that is, he was symbolically construed as the person who embodied the voice of the archetype of all prophets, Moses. This is particularly significant, since in the social world of the Persian period, the authorship and (re)readership of the prophetic books embodied, as it were, the voice of the prophets of old through, among others, their writing, editing, reading and reading to others of these books (see above).

Moreover, the characterization of Moses as a prophet (see Deut. 18.15 and 18, 34.10; Hos. 11.14) is consistent with a sense of partial mental overlapping between the categories of תורה (divine instruction/torah) and דבר ה' (YHWH's word) that allowed the association, or even identification of the two concepts in places such as Isa. 1.10, 2.3; Jer. 6.19; Mic. 4.2; Zech. 7.12. Significantly, the text in 2 Kgs 17.13 explicitly states that החורה (the divine instruction/torah) was sent to Israel through YHWH's servants, the prophets. Thus, prophets of old and, by implication, the literati who inscribed, shaped and voiced them became associated explicitly or implicitly not only with דבר ה' (YHWH's word) but also with תורה (divine instruction/torah).[29] Although the term תורה itself has multiple possible referents in the discourses of the period, even if it is understood in a most general and comprehensive sense, it still includes instructions about how the proper cult of YHWH should take place, and accordingly about the roles that priests should fulfill.[30] To use a biblical metaphor, they become like Moses instructing Aaron the priest. Closer to the likely reality of the period, all the previous examples indicate a sense of discursive and imaginative intertwining within which they may be considered necessary partners in the world of the ideological/theological elite of Yehud, priests and literati, even if the latter remain self-effacing and their presence is felt through the authoritative voices of the past they claim to articulate.[31]

---

28.   My thanks are due to Chris Franke who suggested to me the issue and urged me to follow it during a conversation she, Bob Haak and myself enjoyed over dinner, within the frame of the annual business meeting of the Prophetic Texts and their Ancient Contexts Group.

29.   It is worth noting that given the minimal number of literati in Persian Jerusalem, it is most likely that the same bearers of high literacy composed, read, meditated upon, and read to others books in a variety of genre. There was no sapiential group of literati separate from those who dealt with prophetic literature, nor can the latter be imagined as separate from those who dealt with pentateuchal literature, and therefore shaped תורה (divine instruction/ torah) at least in a pentateuchal sense of the term.

30.   It goes without saying that if תורה (divine instruction/torah) is understood in a very restricted sense, it is directly associated with priests, although this is not the main denoted meaning in this case, there is a strong possibility that the shared use of the term connoted or reflected some sense of mental interconnectedness of concepts among the literati of the period.

31.   I wrote elsewhere on the self-effacing character of the literati of Yehud, and the claim for authority that accompanies such self-characterization, see E. Ben Zvi, 'What is New in Yehud? Some Considerations', Rainer Albertz and Bob Becking (eds.), *Yahwism after the Exile* (STAR, 5; Assen: Royal Van Gorcum, 2003).

The mentioned tendency towards some degree of discursive intertwining was to be expected. If certain books were to hold some normative position within the repertoire of the community, and if for that very reason their production and 'consumption' was supported by the Jerusalemite center, then something of importance was at stake in the production of these books and their meanings for the center itself. This being the case, it is reasonable to assume that the prevalent positions of the authorities of the community – and they themselves exercised some systemic control, whether direct or indirect, on the production and development of the authoritative meanings through the reading, rereading and reading to others of these books. It goes without saying that the Jerusalemite elite of Yehud included many priests. In fact, priests most likely held some of the most important positions of leadership in Yehud,[32] and at least some control over the temple, that is the ideological, cultic, social, and probably economic and political center of Yehud. Under these circumstances normative texts were expected to be, at least, coherent with the positions agreed upon among the elite. In addition, the 'godly' communicators whose voice came, as it were, through these books – and through their authors and readers – despite all their differences, were supposed to share a similar, general viewpoint among themselves and with the contemporary elite of the Jerusalemite center.[33] These circumstances created a fertile ground for the development of a kind of mental category of godly-communicators within the discourses of the Jerusalemite center. This category was populated by the figures of the prophets of old, the associated prophetic characters in the prophetic books, Yehudite pious priests, and Yehudite writers and primary readers and interpreters of prophetic literature, in cases where the last two were not the same person. The existence of such a mental category facilitated the slippage of attributes usually associated with one subgroup to another subgroup, and the occasional development of personages who bear multiple attributes and in whom more than one subgroup is represented. The social realia of many priests who were also literati contributed to these developments.

---

32.   See the characterization of Joshua in the book of Zechariah. See also the description of the Judaic polity in Hecateus, and esp. 'For this reason the Jews never have a king, and authority over the people is regularly vested in whichever priest is regarded as superior to his colleagues in wisdom and virtue. They call this man the high priest, and believe that he acts as a messenger to them of God's commandments.' On Hecateus' testimony see *GLAJJ* 1, pp. 20–35, and for the English quotation, p. 28. See also D. Mendels, 'Hecateus of Abdera and a Jewish "patrios politeia" of the Persian Period (Diodorus Siculus XL, 3)', *ZAW* 95 (1983), pp. 96–110.

33.   Had the latter not been the case, the elite would have construed itself as carrying non-godly messages. This was, of course, not an option in Jerusalemite Yehud.

THE PROPHETIC CRITIQUE OF RITUAL IN
OLD TESTAMENT THEOLOGY

Bryan D. Bibb

1. *Introduction*

In a famous, indeed infamous, moment in his *Theology of the Old Testament* from the first half of the last century, Ludwig Köhler says that

> There is no suggestion anywhere in the Old Testament that sacrifice or any other part of the cult was instituted by God. It is begun and continued and accomplished by man; it is works, not grace; an act of self-help, not a piece of God's salvation. Indeed, the cult is a bit of ethnic life. Israel took it from the heathens.[1]

The idea expressed in this paragraph is obviously not shared by many scholars of the Hebrew Bible today, whether they be Jewish or Christian. This dismissive attitude toward the cultic life of the ancient Israelites (and the cultic life of modern Jews and Roman Catholics by implication) has been deconstructed on two fronts, both historically and theologically. Historians of ancient Israelite religion have come to recognize the dynamic relationship between the idealistic form of religious thought and practice found in the Hebrew Bible and the varied, often syncretistic practices of the multi-faceted Israelite community. Whether Canaanite and Assyrian religious practices encroached on earlier, pure forms of Yahwism, or whether Yahwism was from its inception iconic and nature-oriented, scholars generally agree that Israel did indeed have an authentic sacrificial practice that was not merely a cheap copy of 'heathen' nature religion. On the theological side, biblical interpreters have declawed the old dilemma of whether Israelite theology sipped from the chalice of ancient Near Eastern mythology, or their theology was expressly 'against' their environment. There was certainly a bit of both, and whatever the case, few feel the burden of these questions in light of modern dogmatic commitments.

The fact remains, however, that despite present scholars' attempts to be sympathetic toward Israelite religious practice, the prophetic text still lingers; and it contains a thoroughgoing critique of Israel's cultic practices, rejecting not only the iconic, syncretistic corruption of 'pure' Yahwism,

---

1. Ludwig Köhler, *Theology of the Old Testament* (trans. A. S. Todd; London: Lutterworth, 1957), p. 181.

but also legitimate, totally orthodox festivals, offerings, and prayers. Even though it seems hard to believe that the prophets advocated a religious world without the cult, one could certainly get that impression from the prophets themselves. In fact, scholars, historians, and especially theologians have sometimes come exactly to that conclusion. This paper will address the rhetorical aspect of the prophetic critique of ritual, and argue that 'Old Testament Theologians', operating within a pervasive Christian world-view have been inspired by this fiery rhetoric and have used it to construct a misleading and possibly libelous presentation of Israel's cultic life. Our examples will be drawn from three writers of Old Testament Theologies in the twentieth century, Walther Eichrodt, Theodorus Vriezen, and Walter Brueggemann. Eichrodt and Vriezen represent two different ways of falling victim to the temptation to denigrate cultic practice under the influence of the prophets. Interestingly, both of these theologians are consciously aware of the problem, yet find themselves unable to resist the allure of the prophetic word. Brueggemann will serve as an interesting counter-example. Coming from the same broad theological tradition, Brueggemann's approach raises similar issues and questions, but goes to great lengths to avoid the pitfalls of earlier Christian theologies of the Hebrew Bible. One can hear the strain of theological tradition pulling on his thinking as he strives to free himself from prejudices of the past.

2. Prophetic Critique

First, we need to consider briefly what exactly comprises the prophetic critique of ritual. There are several classic texts that address the inadequacy of ancient Israel's cultic system, and the task is to discern both what their arguments are and why they make them.

The texts most often cited in this discussion are those in which the prophets oppose the cultic and ritual practices of their audience. On one hand, these texts can simply be read as an indictment of *praxis*, an analysis of why these particular ritual acts and specific cultic environments are illegitimate. In their appeal to a higher principle (usually described as one's 'personal' relationship with God, or the 'moral' or 'ethical' dimension of religion), the prophets can be seen as casting doubt on the whole cultic enterprise. These texts appear throughout the eighth and seventh century prophets, but we will focus on a few crucial passages. Amos 5.21–23 is the paradigmatic text, in which God says 'I hate, I despise your festivals, and I take no delight in your solemn assemblies. Even though you offer me your burnt offerings and grain offerings, I will not accept them; and the offerings of well-being of your fatted animals I will not look upon.' Hosea seconds that thought, reporting God's words: 'For I desire steadfast love and not sacrifice, the knowledge of God rather than burnt offerings' (Hos.

6.6). Isaiah declares in the first chapter, '"What to me is the multitude of your sacrifices?" says the LORD; "I have had enough of burnt offerings of rams and the fat of fed beasts; I do not delight in the blood of bulls, or of lambs, or of goats."' (v. 11). He continues by pleading with the Israelites to 'trample my courts no more; bringing offerings is futile; incense is an abomination to me' (vv. 12–13). God has been 'burdened' and 'wearied' by the festivals and sacrifices (v. 14). Micah 6.6–8 asks rhetorically 'With what shall I come before the LORD, and bow myself before God on high? Shall I come before him with burnt offerings, with calves a year old? Will the LORD be pleased with thousands of rams, with ten thousands of rivers of oil? Shall I give my firstborn for my transgression, the fruit of my body for the sin of my soul?' It turns out that God doesn't ask for such things, but only for justice, kindness, and humility. Jeremiah is perhaps the most stringent of all, a bit surprising since he came from a priestly family and may have been a priest himself. God asks derisively through the prophet, 'Of what use to me is frankincense that comes from Sheba, or sweet cane from a distant land? Your burnt offerings are not acceptable, nor are your sacrifices pleasing to me' (6.20). The people seem to be trying hard to get God's attention, but it is to no avail, 'Although they fast, I do not hear their cry, and although they offer burnt offering and grain offering, I do not accept them; but by the sword, by famine, and by pestilence I consume them' (14.12).

The prophetic denunciation of cultic forms of religious expression is almost always voiced by God directly. Thus, it is not just the prophets' observations that ritual practices are not living up to God's standards, but God's own rejection of those practices. This divine 'no' is carried even further by a handful of texts suggesting that sacrificial practices were not part of God's original mandate to Israel! In Isa. 10.12 God asks, 'When you come to appear before me, who asked this from your hand?' Not God, evidently. Amos 5.25 suggests that the ritual practices are not integral to Israel's experience of God, since their wilderness wanderings did not include a cult. God asks, 'Did you bring to me sacrifices and offerings the forty years in the wilderness, O house of Israel?' The implied answer is no, though we suspect that Moses and Aaron would be surprised to hear this, not to mention Nadab and Abihu. Amos' understanding of Israel's earliest religious life is echoed in Jeremiah's Temple Sermon. God provides the history lesson, saying 'For in the day that I brought your ancestors out of the land of Egypt, I did not speak to them or command them concerning burnt offerings and sacrifices. But this command I gave them, "Obey my voice, and I will be your God, and you shall be my people; and walk only in the way that I command you, so that it may be well with you".'

3. *Rhetorical Strategies*

Writers of Old Testament Theologies have found in these texts a very clear message, and indeed the message seems obvious: the rituals found in the ancient Israelite cult were not only corrupt and ineffective, but were also completely abhorrent to God and indeed not even part of God's earliest and deepest requirements for the covenantal relationship. For theologians writing within a tradition that has made exactly that argument about the Old Testament rituals, this prophetic critique is quite alluring.

When the theological argument is so natural, so obviously correct and true, so compelling, there is little reason to take one's analysis much deeper than the surface of the text. If, however, one is not comfortable with the denigration of the cult, the devaluation of bodily, institutional forms of religious expression, the subtle (or not-so-subtle) Protestant Christian supercessionism, then it is imperative to take a deeper look at these passages. When we do, it becomes clear that the strong words of the prophets (indeed the words of God) against cultic practices are part of a larger prophetic rhetorical strategy. For rhetorical impact, the prophets often utter words that should not be said and say things that they cannot mean. Jeremiah is clear at least that he does not want to say the things that he does, and would stop prophesying if he could (ch. 20). By transferring the prophetic voice from themselves to the deity, the prophets tap into a rhetorical stream of great flexibility and power. Their intention is to convict the audience of their sinful activities, to express God's dim view of the situation, and to explain what God plans to do about it. Most of the prophets also hold out a hope for salvation, though rarely in the form that the audience would have wanted to hear most: rescue from the coming punishment. As scholars have increasingly pointed out, the prophets go to remarkable lengths to express their message, utilizing every rhetorical tool at their disposal. From bizarre dramatic acts to offensively sexist and brutal language, the prophets make their enigmatic, mysterious message as clear and as powerful as they can.

It is within this rhetorical freedom that we should interpret the prophetic critique of ritual. Although Amos, Isaiah and Jeremiah denounce the cult of Israel and question its original authority, they surely are not calling for the elimination of ritual practice, are they? How could they envision a world without cult and ritual? Modern interpreters, who can envision such a world, indeed who live in such a world, are the ones who read into this prophetic critique of ritual a preference for a non-ritualistic religion. In actuality, this critique is simply one more aspect of the great prophetic rhetorical device, reversal. As they do with the Passover, the Day of Yahweh, and God's 'family ties' to Israel, the prophets take something valued, assured, and settled, flip it over and use it as a club, as a way to shake up the audience and communicate their point. The rhetorical purpose of the prophetic critique of ritual appears in at least four different ways, and through these it becomes clear that the prophets are trying to convey an important message in an effective way. They are not making a theological argument for the elimination of ritual practices from Israel's religion, but their language points to this possibility as a way of shocking their audience into appropriate response.

First, the rejection of the normative Israelite cult is tied to the prophetic denunciation of idolatry, iconism and syncretism. All of the prophets under investigation have dramatic, powerful passages in which they demonstrate that little human-made statues have no life, cannot save, and are ineffectual in every way. Anyone familiar with the theological traditions that infuse the prophetic speech would not be surprised at these words of judgment. The application of this critique to Israel's own traditions, even as defined in normative Torah, leads to shock and dismay. The subtle technique of reversal, seen powerfully throughout Amos and Jeremiah, serves to convict the people of their shallow religious expression.

A second rhetorically connected theme in the prophets is the use of cultic imagery to describe God's judgmental actions. At least twice in Isaiah's oracles, God performs a cultic action directly, imagining the recipient of God's punishment as a sacrificial offering. In 30.27–33, God appears in divine theophanic glory and celebrates a sacrificial festival. The prophet says, 'See, the name of the LORD comes from far away, burning with his anger, and in thick rising smoke; his lips are full of indignation, and his tongue is like a devouring fire (v. 27). The arrival of God causes the people to rejoice and sing as in a festival, celebrating each stroke of the punishment meted out against the Assyrian king.

> You shall have a song as in the night when a holy festival is kept; and gladness of heart, as when one sets out to the sound of the flute to go to the mountain of the LORD, to the Rock of Israel ... The Assyrian will be terror-stricken at the voice of the LORD, when he strikes with his rod. And every stroke of the staff of punishment that the LORD lays upon him will be to the sound of timbrels and lyres; battling with brandished arm he will fight with him. For his burning place has long been prepared; truly it is made ready for the king, its pyre made deep and wide, with fire and wood in abundance; the breath of the LORD, like a stream of sulfur, kindles it.

This theme is picked up again in ch. 34, in which the prophet praises the LORD's sword, in this case not an instrument of war, but a holy cultic implement. God's sword 'is sated with blood, it is gorged with fat, with the blood of lambs and goats, with the fat of the kidneys of rams. For the LORD has a sacrifice in Bozrah, a great slaughter in the land of Edom.'

The idea expressed here is clear; the prophets are using a quite visceral image, the slaughter of a beast on the altar as a symbol for God's destruction of the enemy. This image has the advantage of illustrating colorfully the downfall of the bad guys while also expressing the reasons behind the destruction. Since those who transgress God's law have disregarded and perverted the righteous commandments, so God will put those commandments into practice as the people are sacrificed. The point of this rhetoric is not to condone human sacrifice, though that is actually what the prophet depicts in this dark passage. The image of God as a direct perpetrator of homicide is troubling, to say the least. Within Isaiah's rhetorical framework, however, it 'works'. It would have grabbed the attention of the ancient audience as well as it grabs our own. We would not necessarily desire to make these passages central to our biblical theology, but they certainly bring some vitality to the conversation.

Ezekiel makes this point even clearer in his intriguing description of the 'bad laws' in ch. 20. God, exasperated after repeated failures of Israel to keep the covenant, says, 'Moreover I gave them statutes that were not good and ordinances by which they could not live. I defiled them through their very gifts, in their offering up all their firstborn, in order that I might horrify them, so that they might know that I am the LORD' (vv. 25–26). Did Ezekiel really mean that God had commanded the people to commit child sacrifice? We certainly do not find record of that in the Bible, unless you count the Abraham and Isaac narrative, and there has been no historical proof that such things were practiced in ancient Israel. The prophet makes an accusation that is beyond the pale of reason and possibility, that God would actually command child sacrifice, in order to make his larger point in a vivid, memorable fashion.

A third aspect of the rhetorical function of the prophetic critique of ritual is the central role that the priests and other religious leaders play in the prophetic denouncements. In many passages that speak against the cult, the real target of the invective is the priesthood. Ezekiel 22 includes harsh words against the priests, officials, and prophets. God says that Israel's 'priests have done violence to my teaching and have profaned my holy things; they have made no distinction between the holy and the common, neither have they taught the difference between the unclean and the clean, and they have disregarded my sabbaths, so that I am profaned among them'. It is significant that Ezekiel's harshest words against the cultic life of Israel come in his vision of the Jerusalem temple's secret abominations. Priests and prophets are both responsible for shepherding the people of Israel, teaching the Torah of God and making known God's requirements. If they follow or promote wicked practices, they are especially accountable for the wickedness that ensues. Ezekiel and Jeremiah each include strong indictments of the priesthood. This does not mean that they envisioned a world without such cultic functionaries. Ezekiel has a special role for the priesthood in his vision of the restored temple. Jeremiah's vision of the new covenant (in which the knowledge of

God will no longer need to be taught because it will be written on everyone's heart) derives in a large way from his dim view of the way that the priestly leadership had failed in its duties. His hopeful vision is a moment of radical desperation, suggesting that perhaps it would be better for everyone if the 'middle man' were bypassed. Jeremiah's words here are not meant to be taken literally on their face. Just like Isaiah's spears and pruning hooks, the idea is symbolic, but it is evocative enough to help the people understand the kind of intimate relationship that Jeremiah had in mind.

Finally, the rhetorical dimension of this prophetic critique of ritual reveals that implicit in the criticism is a vision of true, positive cultic reality. In Isaiah's exalted Mount Zion, the nations stream to the LORD's house to receive instruction. This universalist vision is picked up in Third Isaiah in a more explicitly cultic setting. These non-Israelites who discover the truth in Zion participate in the cultic renewal of Israel. God says in ch.56,

> And the foreigners who join themselves to the LORD, to minister to him, to love the name of the LORD, and to be his servants, all who keep the sabbath, and do not profane it, and hold fast my covenant – these I will bring to my holy mountain, and make them joyful in my house of prayer; their burnt offerings and their sacrifices will be accepted on my altar; for my house shall be called a house of prayer for all peoples (vv.6–7).

Indeed, in the post-exilic period the idea of restored relationships, justice, and righteousness increasingly find expression through cultic symbolism, even transgressing the narrow boundaries of Israel to encompass the broader world community. The semi-apocalyptic visionary of Zechariah imagines a world in which all find God's presence through the Israelite cult. Zechariah 8.20–22 says, 'Peoples shall yet come, the inhabitants of many cities; the inhabitants of one city shall go to another, saying, "Come, let us go to entreat the favor of the LORD, and to seek the LORD of hosts; I myself am going".'[2] Rather than seeing the cult as a temptation to personal glory or as a tool for the manipulation of the deity, the prophets increasingly view it as a vibrant means of God's communication and relationship with humanity. This later idea should not be construed as a shallow, pale imitation of the authentic word from pre-exilic prophets, but rather as the fuller part of the prophetic vision for God's genuine plan for the ritual life of Israel. Seen in this way, the view of Third Isaiah and

---

2. It is perhaps not coincidental that the same theological vision that was so quick to dismiss the role of ritual practices and to judge post-exilic Judaism to be the empty religious husk of a previously vibrant faith is also quick to castigate the apocalyptic literature as spiritualistic mumbo-jumbo, a pale imitation of authentic prophetic world.

Zechariah may be fairly close to what Amos and Jeremiah might have said had they not been involved in a death struggle for the soul of the people. We all know that when fighting tooth and nail, people often say things that could not be said in more rational moments, things that they do not really mean, but have the desired impact.

4. *Critique of Ritual in Old Testament Theology*

Walther Eichrodt's Theology of the Old Testament, through its focus on the covenantal relationship between God and Israel, tends to privilege the 'personal quality of the divine-human relationship'.[3] The prophets speak out against anything that 'de-personalizes' this relationship, and according to Eichrodt,

> this is just what happens when the fear of God is misprized in the relations between God and man, and God himself is sought only in the cultus. God becomes an impersonal source of magical power, which can be manipulated with no feeling of reverence whatsoever simply by means of a meticulous routine; such an attitude declines to recognize the claims of his divine LORD.[4]

The cultus faced a dual temptation, either to devolve into empty, formal performance or to become 'intoxicated' with the divine communion experienced in the cult and thus begin to find 'satisfaction' in the ritual rather than in the subject addressed by the ritual.[5] Eichrodt says that the prophetic response could only be the rejection of such a religious institution, favoring instead an attitude of humble obedience to the moral demands of God.

It is difficult to differentiate in Eichrodt's writings between the prophetic denouncement of cult and the author's own feelings about it. He says that any attempt to escape judgment through the presence of God in the cult is 'objectionable in itself. It is far too cheap a way of enabling man to stand before the God at whose appearing the universe must flee away, and man himself be crushed in the consciousness of his inexpiable guilt.' He describes in glowing terms the 'dynamic power' of the new prophetic word, that 'sweeps away all that is stagnant, and unleashes a forward movement, which can no longer be restrained, and which, once in full career, pauses for nothing'.[6] Notice the present tense in that statement. He continues his own invective by extending the cultic matter to the priests themselves.

---

3. Walther Eichrodt, *Theology of the Old Testament* I (trans. J. A. Baker; Philadelphia: Westminster, 1967), p. 365.
4. Eichrodt, I, p. 366.
5. Eichrodt, I, p. 366.
6. Eichrodt, I, p. 368.

While acknowledging that priests do have some positive role to play in worship, the priesthood is an obstacle to religious development because it tends to segregate into a caste that serves as more of a 'hindrance' than a mediator of divine presence.[7] The priesthood, thus divorced from its intended function through an inexorable 'lust for power' eventually loses its 'religious content'. The work that it does, namely the preservation of the tradition, is itself a problem as it stands in the way of any new religious growth by holding onto 'forms long superseded'. Like the prophets, Eichrodt lumps the normative cultic traditions of Israel in with syncretistic, popular religious expressions, rejecting one along with the other. He says that when the cult underwent the changes described above, it 'became a playground for all the demonic forces of a Nature religion, in which the frontier between God and man was displaced, and the sovereignty of God jeopardized'.[8] Also like Jeremiah, he claims that the only possible remedy for this situation was the dissolution of the old covenant and the creation of a new one. The prophets themselves were not able to envision the path to this revolutionary new covenant, other than 'faithful waiting'.[9] Eichrodt fills in the theological ending that the prophets could not yet clearly see. He says,

> It was only when the mediator of a new covenant, sent by God, had called to himself by an eternally effectual sacrifice the new covenant people, and had given them a new way of life in the 'law of perfectness', that the divine ordinance of the old covenant could be laid aside as 'old and waxing aged'.[10]

For Eichrodt, it is in Christ that the truths found in the ideals of the cult find their fulfillment.

What is remarkable about these comments by Eichrodt is how closely they mirror the statements that prophets themselves make against the cult. He goes beyond simply reporting this prophetic critique to identifying with it, to extending it into the Christian theological world, and to utilizing it as a hermeneutical key for organizing his Old Testament theology. Eichrodt has been completely convinced by the prophets' rhetoric, internalizing their accusations with impressive faithfulness. Because the prophetic critique of cult resonates so piercingly with later Christian supercessionist views, Eichrodt has no need to invoke the critical distance necessary to recognize the rhetorical liberties taken by the prophets.

There is one caveat, however. Whereas theologians of earlier generations did not even realize what was happening in their theological identification

---

7. Eichrodt, I, p. 405.
8. Eichrodt, I, p. 424.
9. Eichrodt, I, p. 433.
10. Eichrodt, I, p. 433. Quoting Heb. 8.13.

with the prophets, Eichrodt is aware of the problem but chooses to
continue the Pauline appropriation of the prophetic message. He admits
that it is a 'disastrous misunderstanding' to judge the cult in general in light
of the particular, perverse forms seen during the time of the prophets.[11] He
does not want to participate in a 'one-sided glorification of prophetism' or
reduce the cult to a pale foreshadowing of truths that are only fully
comprehended later. Rather, he says that the cult is in 'tension' with
prophecy. The interplay between these two, he says, is elevated to its
highest level in Christianity, where the tension between the revealed God
and the hidden God is exemplified in Christ. So, even though Eichrodt
does express some admiration for the high ideals expressed in Israel's cult
(and this is a far cry from others we could name), what he likes about the
cult is its theology of God's sovereignty, not anything related to its actual
praxis. In classic Christian mode, Eichrodt's logocentrism rips the cult
from the messy, physical world of cultic practice and into the rarefied air of
ideas and principles.

A second theological work ends up in this same place, but through a
quite different path. The *Old Testament Theology* of Theodorus Vriezen,
published in its second edition in 1970, is much more explicitly Christian
than Eichrodt's theology.[12] Eichrodt is openly Christian, as seen in the
passages mentioned above, but he sees Christian reflection on the theology
of the Old Testament as a secondary step. His description of the theology
that is contained in the Hebrew Bible is intended to be a neutral
representation. Vriezen, on the other hand, structures the book around
questions asked by Christians about the Old Testament, including for
example an early chapter on whether and in what sense the Old Testament
functions as the Word of God. Very early in his book, he presents a stark
contrast between the prophetic demand for spiritual and moral adherence
to the Covenant and the merely instrumental cultic rituals. Having also
written a *Religion of Ancient Israel*,[13] Vriezen is interested in accounting for
the religious history underlying these theological themes. As a result he
develops a quite odd historical justification for the prophetic contention
that the Israelites had not practiced sacrifice originally. He suggests that
the proliferation of cultic practices happened under influence of Canaanite
religion and the cultic needs of the national religion.[14] Vriezen is tentative
about this suggestion, and backs away from it in other places, but it is
remarkable that he would be compelled to make this argument at all,
seemingly only as a justification of Amos' and Jeremiah's apparently off-

11. Eichrodt, I, p. 435.
12. Theodorus Vriezen, *An Outline of Old Testament Theology* (Oxford: Blackwell, 1970,
2nd edn).
13. Theodorus Vriezen, *The Religion of Ancient Israel* (Philadelphia: Westminster, 1967).
14. Vriezen 1970, p. 37.

handed comments. As for the role of the cult after the Exile, Vriezen makes
the usual comments about the cultic danger of 'ritualism'. He says that this
ritualism was balanced by the development of certain cultic features such
as creedal statements and hymns.[15] This is parallel to Eichrodt's
logocentrism, where the true value of the cult is found in words and
ideas, rather than the actual ritual practices. In any case, he says, the
development of a normative Torah was a negative event because it froze
and eventually silenced the prophetic word, leading to what he calls
traditionalism and observantism, basically meaning the domination of
tradition, ritual and law.[16]

In his chapter on the Old Testament as the word of God, Vriezen
uncovers what he calls 'the secret of the Old Testament', that 'the Old
Testament springs from prophecy'.[17] It is not clear what is so secret about
this, at least among Christian interpreters, unless he is using the term
'secret' to mean a pleasing creamy center that one discovers inside a crusty
shell. This 'secret', he says, is 'elusive and not to be made manageable,
neither in the law nor in institutions nor in forms that have become
historical like the creed or the covenant or any other theological concept.
For all of these forms are merely "answers" to the word of God received
by Israel. From the very beginning it came to Israel through the words of
the prophets.'[18] In Vriezen's approach, the Old Testament can only be the
word of God if it consciously corrects itself, which means that the
prophetic oracles and historical narratives save us from the narrow
ritualism of the cultic impulses in the Torah. The 'inherent danger' of the
priesthood is that it domesticates religion into something 'immutable',
absolutizing the sanctuary as the permanent symbol of God's presence.[19]
He says that 'the prophets could not but protest against this view'. Just as
the prophet and the priest are both necessary and complementary, they are
also in conflict, and in this conflict the priest must always give way to the
prophet, or else it 'destroys the living strengths of its own religion'.[20]
Pervasive in Vriezen's categorization of the priest/prophet relationship is
the prophets' own rhetoric against the cult. The balance between priest and
prophet is in fact more one-sided than it appears.

An interesting contrast to these two Theologies is the view of ritual in
the *Theology of the Old Testament* by Walter Brueggemann. In his section
on the cult as 'mediator' Brueggemann argues for the sacramental quality

15. Vriezen 1970, p. 38.
16. Vriezen 1970, p. 47.
17. Vriezen 1970, p. 101.
18. Vriezen 1970, p. 102.
19. Vriezen 1970, p. 239.
20. Vriezen 1970, p. 239.

of the cult as the mediator of Yahweh's 'real presence'.[21] He is very careful to guard against Christian supercessionism. In a section where he cites the Koehler quote that began this paper, Brueggemann says that 'this general Christian attitude toward the Old Testament is intensified by classical Protestantism, which has had a profound aversion to cult, regarding cultic activity as primitive, magical, and manipulative, thus valuing from the Old Testament only the prophetic-ethical traditions'.[22] Brueggemann springs from the same general theological tradition, of course, and the reader can sense that his comments about the cult are a measured, intentional repudiation of the ideas found in works such as those by Eichrodt and Vriezen. In a masterly rhetorical move, he identifies the Israelite cult with the single ritual tradition with which Protestant Christians have natural sympathy, the Eucharist. He says that Old Testament ritual texts are 'words of institution' through which God's presence is 'made graciously accessible and available to Israel'.[23] Whereas Eichrodt compared the Israelite cult to empty, formalistic religion (reminiscent of the Protestant view of Roman Catholicism), Brueggemann uses the Protestants' own sacramental theology to inspire a bit more sympathy. Priests are not mediators but 'supervisors' who oversee the order, symmetry, coherence and dignity of the ritual procedures. A young graduate of Columbia Theological Seminary could do much worse than these priests as their role models for worship leadership.

Brueggemann addresses Christian stereotypes of the Israelite cult step by step. He insists that 'worship that is visual, active, dramatic, and all-comprehending was a thing of joy for Israel, not a burden'.[24] He contrasts the 'low church' tendencies of the Deuteronomist (sermonic and separatist) with the 'high church' tendencies of the Priestly writer (visual and culturally connected).[25] Whereas Eichrodt and Vriezen adopt the ancient prophetic rhetoric against the cult, Brueggemann wages a rhetorical battle of his own. Like the prophets themselves, he uses a strategy of reversal to convince his audience, taking what is known and accepted and using it in an unexpected manner. If the audience is drawn in by the power of terms like 'words of institution', then they are more likely to follow his lead in appreciating the power of those words and of those ritual texts. Interestingly, Brueggemann concludes his discussion with an analysis of the prophetic critique of cult. This is not accidental or a merely formal point of organization. Like the tradition out of which he writes, the

---

21. Walter Brueggemann, *Theology of the Old Testament: Testimony, Dispute, Advocacy* (Minneapolis: Fortress, 1997), p. 650.
22. Brueggemann, p. 651.
23. Brueggemann, p. 665.
24. Brueggemann, p. 669.
25. Brueggemann, p. 673.

prophetic critique of cult is the final obstacle to an appreciation and affirmation of Israel's ritual practices. Because Brueggemann is aware of the rhetorical dimension of the biblical testimony, he is not automatically captured by the power of the prophets' critique. He acknowledges the dangers of the cult becoming 'manipulative and self-satisfying' (echoing precisely the language of Eichrodt here!), but ultimately situates the prophetic critique as part of the core testimony, saying that Israel's worship must be engaged at all times with the subject of the witness, the LORD of Israel. Implicit in this testimony is the conviction that Israel's worship life does in fact engage and mediate the presence of God.

The prophets take the cultic life of Israel seriously, realizing its potential and power. They use a wide variety of rhetorical strategies to dislodge, even if for a moment, the deep-rooted theological biases that blind their audiences to the word being communicated. The same rhetorical fire that leads them to compare God to a ravenous beast, to a consuming fire, to maggots in rotting meat, and to an abusive husband and father, gives rise to the language of cultic repudiation. It is intended to shock and dismay, not to lobby for a world without cultic practice. Christian theological discussion and appropriation of these texts must pay attention to the rhetorical dynamic, possibly even mirroring their strategies in order to shake up the ingrained theological commitments of modern audiences.

PROPHETS AND TEMPLE PERSONNEL IN THE MARI ARCHIVES

Daniel E. Fleming

Some time during the eighteenth or seventeenth century BCE, a man named Nur-Sin wrote a letter to his master, king Zimri-Lim of Mari, with the one purpose of passing on a message to the king from someone called an *āpilum*. The contents of the letter come straight to the point:[1]

> Abiya, the *āpilum* of Addu Lord of Aleppo, came to me and spoke to me as follows.
> 'Thus (says) Addu:
> 'I gave all the land to Yahdun-Lim, and because of my weapons, he had no rival. He abandoned me, however, and so I gave to Samsi-Addu the land that I had given to him...'

After a break in the cuneiform tablet, we still find Addu to be speaking.

> 'I restored you to the throne [of your father's house]. I gave to you the weapons with which I battled the Sea. I anointed you with the oil of my invincibility(?), so that no one could stand before you.
> Hear this one word of mine: 'When anyone with a case at law appeals to you, saying, "I have been done wrong", stand and give him justice. Ans[wer him strai]ghtaway. This is what I a[sk] of you.'

Addu closes by exhorting king Zimri-Lim to go on campaign only with a favorable oracle from himself, and Nur-Sin draws the letter to a quick close once he has finished the long quote.

Addu Lord of Aleppo is the storm god, the head of the pantheon at Aleppo, the capital of the most powerful kingdom in Syria. The god claims to have power to bestow the Euphrates-based land of Mari, far to the east,

---

1. *FM* VII, 83.5–9, 1'–11', first published as A.1968 in Jean-Marie Durand, 'Le mythologème du combat entre le Dieu de l'orage et la Mer en Mésopotamie,' *MARI* 7 (1993), pp. 41–61. See also the treatments of this text by Nicholas Wyatt, 'Arms and the King: The Earliest Allusions to the Chaoskampf Motif and their Implications for the Interpretation of the Ugaritic and Biblical Traditions,' in M. Dietrich and I. Kottsieper (eds.), *'Und Mose schrieb dieses Lied auf': Studien zum Alten Testament und zum Alten Orient*, (AOAT, 250; Münster: Ugarit-Verlag, 1998), pp. 833–88; Abraham Malamat, 'Deity Revokes Kingship: Towards Intellectual Reasoning in Mari and the Bible', in Jiří Prosecký (ed.), *Intellectual Life of the Ancient Near East* (CRRAI, 43; Prague: Oriental Institute, 1998), pp. 231–36 (= *Mari and the Bible* [Leiden: Brill, 1998], pp. 157–62).

on whomever he favors.[2] Zimri-Lim, the current king of Mari, is said to owe his throne to the god of his western neighbor.

The letter is written in Babylonian-style Akkadian, the Semitic language of eastern Mesopotamia, and none of the terminology is cognate with Biblical Hebrew, but the account immediately brings to mind the prophecy found in the Bible. A man speaks directly to the king in the voice of a god, beginning 'thus (says) Addu'. The god claims to guide the history of Zimri-Lim's kingdom, past, present and future. Kings arise and are deposed by the god's hand, according to their fidelity to him. The god himself has anointed Zimri-Lim, just as Yahweh is said to have anointed Saul (1 Sam. 10.1 and 15.17), David (2 Sam. 12.7; Ps. 89.21), and Jehu (2 Kgs 9.3, 6, 12). Having staked a personal claim on Zimri-Lim by recounting the past, the god makes only one demand, that the king guarantee justice to all who have a good case.

The letter of Nur-Sin is only one of several dozen from the archives of Mari that describe messages from gods that are cast as direct speech, whether delivered in dreams, by a letter from a god, or most often, as a speech repeated out loud by a human intermediary.[3] Mari's archives were created centuries before even the earliest biblical texts, and the very distance in time underscores the need to recognize the antiquity of the phenomenon, and its place in the world beyond Israel.[4] The Bible's books and stories of prophets are unusual and fascinating, but any definition of what is unique to them must be drawn cautiously against the evidence for ancient Near Eastern prophecy outside of the Bible. By far the largest body of such evidence comes from Mari.[5]

---

2. This kind of claim of authority reaching beyond the immediate geographical and political domain is not unique for major deities, especially heads of regional pantheons. See the discussion of Dominique Charpin, 'Prophètes et rois dans le Proche-Orient amorrite: nouvelles données, nouvelles perspectives', *Florilegium marianum* (*FM*) VI (2002), pp. 7–38, especially 28–31.

3. Jack Sasson prefers to gather all of these phenomena under the single heading of 'divine messages', rather than to force a sharp distinction between 'prophecy' and 'dreams' or other related categories ('The Posting of Letters with Divine Messages', *FM* II [1994], pp. 299–316).

4. For a general treatment of Mari, including extensive translations and comment, see the three volumes of Jean-Marie Durand, *Documents épistolaires du palais de Mari, Tomes I, II, III* (Littératures Anciennes du Proche Orient [LAPO], 16, 17, 18; Paris: du Cerf, 1997, 1998, 2000). In English, see also my *Democracy's Ancient Ancestors: Mari and Early Collective Governance* (Cambridge: Cambridge University Press, 2004).

5. For a look at the wider evidence for ancient Near Eastern prophecy, see Martti Nissinen (ed.), *Prophecy in its Ancient Near Eastern Context: Mesopotamian, Biblical, and Arabian Perspectives* (Atlanta: Scholars Press, 2000); Karel Van der Toorn, 'L'oracle de victoire comme expression prophétique au Proche-Orient ancien,' *RB* 94 (1987), pp. 63–97.

In the Bible, perhaps the two most prominent religious personnel are the *kōhēn* and the *nābî'*, generally translated as 'priest' and 'prophet'. Previous generations of scholars often considered priests and prophets to represent two sharply different and opposed voices in Israelite religion, though more recent work has emphasized the continuities between them. Insofar as we are concerned with basic identities and foundational categories, Mari can offer a useful baseline against which to contrast as well as to compare the Bible's prophets and priests. Even the primary terminology from Mari resists classification by the priest-prophet dichotomy, and this itself cautions us to beware universalizing any *kōhēn/nābî'* division as a general duality by which all ancient religious personnel can best be understood.

The larger Mesopotamian temples were served by a variety of sacred personnel, among whom no single rank or group could be identified as 'the priests', against the rest. Scholars tend to speak instead of 'temple personnel', with a wide variety of titles and responsibilities. The prophets of the Mari evidence were at home in temples, considered temples to be an ideal vantage from which to speak for a god, and worked in cooperation with a variety of temple and palace personnel. These prophets were not of the highest social rank, but they were integrated into the core institutions of the Mari kingdom as loyal servants.[6] In the network of personnel who might become involved in Mari prophecy, the real political power and social status were not to be found with the 'priests' who served the temples, but with the diviners who worked directly for the king. If anything, the prophets provided only one key way for the temples to communicate the needs and demands of their gods to the king, when the primary vehicle for divine communication was controlled by diviners who operated without any personal interest in the temple cults.[7]

1. *Mari*

Before returning to the evidence for prophecy, it may be useful to review some basic information about the site of Mari and its finds. The site of ancient Mari or Tell Hariri is on the Euphrates River, just inside Syria's border with Iraq. It has been excavated on and off since 1933, but the most spectacular finds turned up in the first few years, with the discovery of a

6. Esther Hamori presented a paper at the 2001 annual meeting of the American Oriental Society that argued this perspective at length.

7. The basic evidence for the role of divination in the Mari archives was gathered by Durand in the first long section of *Archives Épistolaires de Mari* [*AEM*] I.1 (texts published as Archives Royales de Mari [ARM] XXVI, 1988). On the primacy of the haruspex or *bārûm*-diviner in the communication between gods and kings, see Jack Sasson, 'About "Mari and the Bible"', *RA* 92 (1998), pp. 116–18.

royal palace for the latest levels of the tell.[8] It was already known that a Euphrates-based kingdom centered at Mari had been conquered by king Hammurabi of Babylon. Hammurabi did not have to take Mari by force, but he burned down the palace in order to remove any possibility of reestablishing an administrative capital there, and Mari never regained its political role. Before destroying the palace, Hammurabi had its archives tabulated, perhaps for wholesale removal, but he appears to have decided to take only the most important documents, leaving the rest to be buried in the rubble.[9] This choice preserved roughly 20,000 cuneiform tablets for posterity, the latest of which would date to something like 1761 BCE, by the so-called 'middle chronology'.[10]

I have avoided calling Mari a 'city', because the actual occupation of this site is obscure, in spite of all the excavations. Very few private residences have been found for any period, with almost nothing proven for the early second millennium. In every phase, the site was dominated by its palaces, its temples, and a massive encircling mound.

Mari appears to have been established around 2800 BCE and through the second half of the third millennium it was a hub of political power in eastern Syria. All sorts of new construction took place at the end of the third millennium, contemporary with the last great Sumerian kingdom of Ur, but it is not certain that these buildings were in active use through the first two centuries of the second millennium. A final phase was inaugurated by an Amorite king named Yahdun-Lim, who reoccupied the prestigious site in order to make it the eastern capital of a Euphrates valley kingdom that he hoped to extend northward. Yahdun-Lim did not live long enough to bring this about and after his death a rival named Samsi-Addu (Akkadianized as Shamshi-Adad) quickly moved to annex the entire domain to an even larger kingdom based in the Tigris and Habur Rivers valleys. Samsi-Addu set up his younger son Yasmah-Addu on the throne of Mari, under his own ultimate oversight. This first 'Mesopotamian' kingdom between the two great rivers was held together adroitly by the aging Samsi-Addu, but with his passing the tribal kin of Yahdun-Lim were

8. For general descriptions of the archaeological finds from Mari, see J.-M. Aynard and Agnès Spycket, 'Mari.B.Archäologisch', *RlA* 7 (1987–1990), pp. 390–418; Jean-Claude Margueron, 'Mari, reflet du monde syro-mésopotamien au IIIe millénaire', *Akkadica* 98 (1996), pp. 11–30; 'Mari au IIe millénaire', in *Cinquante-deux réflexions sur le Proche-Orient ancien, offertes en hommage à Léon de Meyer* (Leuven: Peeters, 1994), pp. 313–20.

9. Dominique Charpin, 'La fin des archives dans le palais de Mari', *RA* 89 (1995), pp. 29–40.

10. On the chronology of the Mari kings, see Nele Ziegler and Dominique Charpin, 'Mari (rois)', in Francis Joannès (ed.), *Dictionnaire de la Civilisation Mésopotamienne* (Paris: Robert Laffont, 2001), pp. 496–501. Charpin has written a full history of Zimri-Lim's reign, to appear in *Florilegium marianum* V as 'Mari et le Proche-Orient à l'époque amorrite: essai d'histoire politique. La règne de Zimrî-Lîm (1775–1761)'.

able to take back their Mari capital. Zimri-Lim took the throne of Mari, as the son of Yahdun-Lim, and held it for over 13 years.

Almost all of the Mari tablets came from the royal palace and the overwhelming majority of those from the reign of Zimri-Lim, the last king. A significant number of texts do, however, date to the time of Yasmah-Addu and his father Samsi-Addu, when Mari was ruled as one component of a larger kingdom based elsewhere. The largest number of tablets from both periods is administrative, reflecting the daily affairs of many different offices and institutions. What makes the archives unique, however, is the correspondence, something over 3000 letters collected by the Mari kings.[11] The mere number is rare, but it is the range of participants and preoccupations that is unprecedented. Zimri-Lim in particular fostered a culture of information control, and his officials collected an enormous range of correspondence in the palace archives. Given the random aspect of the finds, it is difficult to know how many Mesopotamian rulers were so assiduous in soliciting and hoarding mail. Zimri-Lim, at least, kept letters from all of his royal officials, whether assigned to Mari, to the district, or to diplomatic posts; he kept letters from his wives and family, from vassals and other political contacts and even secret letters intercepted from his enemies.[12] The king seems to have encouraged his subjects not to hold back and the correspondence shows a lively, usually self-serving, sometimes comical stream of verbiage. Because the letters come from such a variety of settings, their detail illuminates many aspects of life during this period.

Prophecy is not a special interest of the archive, but only one such aspect. Mari prophecy has been known for over 50 years, but there have been key phases of publication that have inspired waves of commentary.[13] After the first trickle of references through the 1950s, the women's correspondence from Mari was published in 1967 as Archives Royales de Mari (ARM) X.[14] Leadership of the Mari publication team passed from Georges Dossin to Jean-Marie Durand in the early 1980s and Durand produced a definitive edition of the letters with references to prophecy and dreams, in 1988, as ARM XXVI/1 (= *AEM* I/1). During the 20 years of

11. There is no published count of the letters found in the Mari archives and, in any case, counting clay tablets is always an inexact procedure, when most of them are found in fragments. Bertrand Lafont has helped me arrive at a rough figure, based on his count of 2550 separate published letters. There are certainly more to be published, mostly from pieces, but probably enough to put the final number at more than 3000.
12. Some idea of the variety can be derived from perusing Durand's three volumes in the LAPO series.
13. A. Lods and G. Dossin, 'Une tablette inédite de Mari, intéressante pour l'histoire ancienne du prophétisme sémitique', in *Studies in Old Testament Prophecy Presented to Prof. Th. H. Robinson* (Edinburgh, 1950), pp. 103–10.
14. The copy appeared alone long before the final publication of transliterations and translations as ARMT X in 1978.

work by the new group, tremendous progress has been made toward reconstructing the historical framework for the archives, with important implications for both the sequence of events and for the interpretation of Mari society. It is now possible to date many of the letters by the events described, even to the level of months or weeks in Zimri-Lim's reign, though letters did not include standard reference to the calendar and formal year names. We also know that Yahdun-Lim and Zimri-Lim were rulers of the Binu Sim'al tribal confederacy, and that we cannot define an opposition between the urban elite culture of the Mari royal administration and the supposed rural or peripheral world of tribally organized populations.[15]

The letters that mention prophecy come from several types of sources. Jack Sasson divides these into letters sent from Mari itself, especially when the king is on campaign, and those sent from elsewhere.[16] In fact, most of the full-time residents of the palace complex at Mari were women and religious life at Mari gave special place to the cultic interests of women. These increasingly revolved around a number of goddesses. Most of the letters sent from Mari concerning prophecy were sent by three women who played leading roles in administering the women's domain, perhaps in successive phases: Addu-duri, Inibshina and Shibtu. Many of the divine messages mentioned in these letters come from goddesses. The remaining letters sent from other locations are sent by men, and their prophecies tend to come from male deities. Sasson discusses the implications of this pattern with marvellous insight.

Almost all of the letters that mention prophecy come from the reign of Zimri-Lim.[17] In Durand's compilation of most of the Mari prophecy, he presents 4 letters to or from gods (XXVI 191–194), 27 texts with what he calls prophecy (195–223), and 17 letters describing dreams (224–240). There are other occasional references to prophets, including the *āpilum*s in ARM XXVI 371 and 414, in *Florilegium marianum* (*FM*) VII 38 and 39 (= A.1968 and A.1121+), and now in *FM* VI 1. A *muḫḫûm* is mentioned in ARM XXVI 243, which Durand had not included in his collection of

---

15. The breakthrough identification of the tribal identity of the Mari kings was made by Dominique Charpin and Jean-Marie Durand, '"Fils de Sim'al": les origines tribales des rois de Mari', *RA* 80 (1986), pp. 141–81. I discuss the implications for the politics of the Mari kingdom at length in my *Democracy's Ancient Ancestors*.

16. Sasson 'Divine Messages', *FM* II (1994).

17. Until recently, it seemed that no letters from the reign of Yasmah-Addu and his father mentioned prophets or prophecy, but Charpin has now published one clear example as *FM* VI 1, which suggests that ARM XXVI 223 may come from the same setting (now *FM* VI 2). Charpin points out that Mari's ritual texts for Eshtar already mentioned male and female *muḫḫûm* and *muḫḫûtum* prophets, and Durand showed that these come from the reign of Yasmah-Addu as well (see *FM* III 2 and 3; in Durand and Michaël Guichard, 'Les rituels de Mari', *FM* III [1997], pp. 9–18).

prophecy, and in ARM XXVII 32.[18] Although king Zimri-Lim showed a real interest in receiving news of divine messages through prophets and dreams, he did not generally accept direct contact from prophets. Prophetic messages were commonly passed to the king by various officials, though a letter to Zimri-Lim from the *āpilum* of the sun god Shamash, written with unabashed authority in the voice of the god (ARM XXVI 194), shows that this was no rule.[19] Charpin cites the still unpublished 'Epic of Zimri-Lim', which has Zimri-Lim march out with confidence at the sight of his *āpilum*-sign of victory: 'Prince of the land – he beheld his prophet-sign. The king – his heart swelled mightily. Addu strides on his left, warlike Erra on his right.'[20]

2. *Mari Prophets*

Even the Bible does not exhibit terminology that permits a simple separation of 'prophet' from 'priest' by the Hebrew itself, under no more than these two titles. Temple and cult responsibilities are attributed to both the *kōhēn* and the *lēwī* (e.g. Judg. 17.5, 7, 10). Bearers of divine messages may be called 'men of god' or 'seers' (*rō'eh*) as well as the ubiquitous *nābî'*. Discernment of divine intention by divination and communication on God's behalf in oral form are both the responsibility of Levites (Deut. 33.8–11) and *kōhênîm* 'priests' (1 Sam. 23.6–12). Priestly and prophetic functions can be distinguished easily enough, but actual practice allows a considerable role for prophecy and related phenomena in cultic settings and by cultic personnel.

In the Mari evidence, people who speak for a god likewise carry a variety of titles, though their use is considerably more balanced, and no single word can be translated as 'prophet'. In some cases the messenger has no title and the entire category of dream messages is never linked to any one professional category, though various classes are represented. Dreams are not generally attributed to people who are identified by any of the titles linked to prophecy, or conversely, prophets are not said to receive their messages as dreams.[21]

18.　On ARM XXVI 243, see Charpin, *FM* VI, p. 7 n. 4 and p. 33 n. 211.

19.　Charpin discusses at some length the evidence for prophecy delivered in face-to-face interviews with the king (*FM* VI, pp. 16–22), in disagreement with Sasson (*FM* II, pp. 301, 306 n. 24).

20.　Lines ii 139–142; [139]*i-mu-ur-ma it-ta-šu a-pí-la-am e-teₙ-él ma-ti-i*[*m*] [140]LUGAL *li-ib-ba-šu da-na-na-am uṣ-ba-am* [141]*i-la-ak Ad-du-um i-na šu-me-li-šu* [142]*Èr-ra da-pí-nu-um-ma i-na im-ni-šu*). This section was published by Durand in *AEM* I.1, p. 393, and is cited by Charpin (*FM* VI, p. 16 n. 82).

21.　Karel Van der Toorn distinguishes four types of revelation: (auditory) dreams, visions, inspiration, and the interpretation of signs ('Old Babylonian Prophecy between the Oral and

Two principal titles are assigned to men and women who speak on behalf of a god, either by seeking an audience with a high-ranking member of the royal court, by speaking out in the temple precincts of the god he or she serves, or by some other public statement. The *āpilum* has often been interpreted as an 'answerer', though we have no direct evidence to prove this Akkadian etymology.[22] An *āpilum* may often be identified with an individual god, such as the sun god Shamash, the storm god Addu, or Dagan, the chief god of the middle Euphrates valley in Syria. The second main title, *muḫḫûm*, is derived from a verb that describes some kind of uncontrolled behavior that has been compared to the 'ecstatic' performance of some biblical prophecy. In the Mari letters, untitled prophets may be said to deliver their messages by this action. In spite of both the title and the verb, the interest of the prophecy in question is always a specific coherent message, not the behavior that might signal possession by a divine power.

Like the *āpilum*, the *muḫḫûm* is frequently identified with an individual god, the god whose message is delivered. This deity may be named not simply in generic terms, but a sacred site may be added. We meet the *āpilum* of Dagan of Tuttul (ARM XXVI 209), the *āpilum* of Addu Lord of Aleppo (*FM* VII 38 and 39), and the *āpilum* of Addu Lord of Kallassu (*FM* VII 39). The expanded titles suggest that these and other titled prophets maintained a formal affiliation with temples, sometimes major ones, and did not merely work as free-lance spokespersons for the gods. Both titles have feminine forms, *āpiltum* and *muḫḫûtum*, which is unusual for Mesopotamian temple personnel. Most temple professions were gender specific, though the double forms recall words for musicians, including the Akkadian *nāru* and *nārtu*, and the Syrian *zammaru* and *zammirātu* (plural) in the ritual texts from Emar.[23]

Mari does associate prophecy with three other titles that appear less frequently. The *qammatum* is a woman whose title remains obscure. In one case, a *qammatum* is identified with Dagan of Terqa, again indicating an affiliation with the major temple there.[24] This role is not known to belong

the Written', *JNSL* 24 [1998], p. 59). He identifies 'inspiration' as the particular domain of the *muḫḫûm* and interpretation of signs as the domain of the *āpilum*, based in part on his understanding of the title as 'interpreter'. Charpin is not persuaded that dreams can be consistently separated as purely auditory (*FM* VI, p. 10 n. 35).

22. Van der Toorn considers that the *āpilum* 'interprets' rather than 'answers', insofar as the prophecies are not generally solicited ('Old Babylonian Prophecy', p. 60 and n. 27). Charpin argues that the use of the verb *apālum* with the noun *igirrûm* ('prophetic oracle') as subject should confirm the etymology, though the evidence is later (*FM* VI, p. 8 and n. 6; see *CAD* s.v. *apālu* 2a3'). It is possible that we have an Amorite term that was reinterpreted to suit the common Akkadian verb.

23. For the Emar evidence, see my *Installation of Baal's High Priestess at Emar* (Atlanta: Scholars Press, 1992), pp. 92–3.

24. ARM XXVI 199.42.

to standard Mesopotamian temple personnel. In contrast to the *qammatum*, the *assinnum* is familiar to the first-millennium cult of the goddess Ishtar (= Eshtar), where this male performer could play female roles, with a resulting ambiguity of gender identity. At Mari, the *assinnum* serves especially the goddess Annunitum and his prophecies are passed on to the king without any interest in his gender or larger ritual role.[25]

Finally, the new evidence published by Durand in ARM XXVI includes one reference to a group of *nābû* (216.7), clearly cognate with the Hebrew *nābî'*. The letter was sent to Zimri-Lim by an official posted outside of Mari, and it begins:

> The day I reached Ashmad – the very next day, I assembled the *nābû* of the tent-dwellers (*ḫana*). I had an omen taken for the safety of my lord, saying, 'If my lord stays seven days on the out[side(?)] when he performs [his] ritual bathing(?) . . .' (broken)[26]

It is clear that the *nābû* take part in an inquiry about the king's immediate future that is initiated by his official. The detailed question seems to beg a yes-or-no answer and the language of 'taking omens' applies specifically to the divination craft of finding signs in the entrails of slaughtered sheep. That specialty is called extispicy, and the specialist was the *bārûm*, or 'haruspex'.[27]

Both Durand and Sasson understand the sequence to make the *nābû* into *ḫana* (my 'tent-dwelling') practitioners of extispicy, although this skill is otherwise attributed uniquely to those holding the *bārûm* title.[28] Also, extispicy is not generally performed by massed haruspices, though one encounters the occasional collaboration of two specialists.[29] In Durand's systematic discussion of Mari divination, he cites only one reference to a larger group, as 'the *bārûm*-diviners of Hammurabi'. The diviner who wrote the letter explains that he was not summoned with the diviners as a whole, so he will not be taking any omen 'with them'.[30] This text does not appear to refer to the group performance of one extispicy rite. In the text

25.   The meaning and use of these titles is discussed in practically every article on Mari prophecy. In Durand's publication of the prophetic texts together, see *AEM* I.1, pp. 395–96.

26.   ARM XXVI 216.5–12; [5] *u₄-um a-na ṣe-er Aš-ma-a[d]* [6] *ak-šu-du i-na ša-ni-i-im u₄-m[i-im]* [7] [lú]*na-bi-i*[meš] *ša ḫa-na*[meš] *ú-pa-ḫ[i-ir]* [8] *te-er-tam a-na ša-la-am be-lí-i[a]* [9] *ú-še-pí-iš um-ma a-na-ku-ma* [10] *šum-ma be-lí i-nu-ma ra-ma-[ak-šu(?)]* [11] *i-pé-šu* U₄.7.KAM *i-na ka-[wa-tim(?)]* [12] [*ú*]*š-[š]a-ab-ma . . .*

27.   On the idiom, 'to take an omen' (*tērtam epēšum*), see Durand, *AEM* I.1, p. 46.

28.   See Durand, *AEM* I.1, p. 378; Sasson, 'Divine Messages', p. 311 and n. 42. Charpin acknowledges that this sort of question is typical of hepatoscopy (taking omens from sheep livers), but cautiously concludes that it is impossible to identify their technique without other attestations of the term (*FM* VI, p. 19).

29.   See Durand, *AEM* I.1, pp. 48–9.

30.   ARM XXVI 96.33–37.

with the *nābû*, only a single omen-sacrifice is carried out (*tērtum*). While I am not persuaded that the Mari *nābû* group perform technical Mesopotamian extispicy, they certainly work in close collaboration with those who do, in the context of inquiry initiated from the human side. In another letter, a long message from Addu Lord of Kallassu is delivered through plural *āpilū* who have spoken only when the god showed himself present by omens, evidently the work of the *bārûm*-diviner.[31]

Unfortunately, the letter that refers to the assembled *nābû* is badly broken and we cannot tell whether they spoke on behalf of some god. They are not defined by the service of any deity, and there is nothing to suggest a temple affiliation. It does appear to me, however, that they were not the specialists who were capable of performing extispicy, or who partook of the authority that accompanied that craft. As with the prophecy of the *āpilum*s, extispicy provided a control on what was considered a less secure mode of divine communication.

3. *Prophecy and the Temple*

It has long been observed that many of the episodes of prophecy in the Mari letters take place in temples. In some cases, this is explicit:

- An *āpilum* rises to speak in the temple of the goddess Hishamitum (XXVI 195).
- Shelebum the *assinnum* speaks from a prophetic trance in the temple of Annunitum (XXVI 213).
- An untitled woman does the same (XXVI 214).
- A *muḫḫûtum* rises to speak in the same place (XXVI 217).

Other episodes appear to occur in temples, but these direct descriptions all relate to goddesses, and three different prophets speak from the same base in the temple of Annunitum. Here, the temple is not merely an acceptable location but provides the entire sacred environment that inspires the experience of receiving a divine message. None of these letters refers to any special celebration, although the speeches all assume some audience, and word of them quickly reached some higher authority.[32]

---

31. *FM* VII, p. 39:13–14, 29–30. Durand proposed that the verb *paqādum* ('to look after, administer', with varied meaning) in ARM XXVI 199.8–9 refers to the obtaining of a *piqittum* oracle as a check, the work of a *bārûm*. In his recent article, however, Charpin concludes that there is no solid evidence for the use of the verb with this technical sense (*FM* VI, p. 20 and n. 113).

32. Van der Toorn even proposes that when 'a prophet delivers an oracle outside the sanctuary…it must be assumed that he repeats an oracle revealed to him in the sanctuary' ('Old Babylonian Prophecy', p. 57). This conclusion may be unnecessarily restrictive.

Occasionally, a prophet would speak at a public festival, and the references to 'rising' (verb *tebûm*) are typical of this setting. At a festival for Dagan, probably at Mari, two different *āpilum* prophets rose to denounce the Babylonians in the voices of Dagan of Tuttul and the goddess Belet-ekallim (XXVI 209). Zimri-Lim's representative at the western center of Tuttul reports that a *merḫûm* rose during a local feast for Dagan and requested pure water for the sanctuary there (XXVI 215). The goddess Ninhursag likewise makes a personal request at her own festival, where her own *āpilum* rises on her behalf (XXVI 219). All of these suggest very public displays.

It would be useful to know exactly what was the relation of the *āpilum* of Ninhursag to her temple. Could he have been considered a part of its permanent staff? At this point, we are faced with how little we know about the temple cults of the Mari archives. I would like to pursue this question beyond the limits of my current ignorance. Because standard education in cuneiform writing was based first of all on a southern Mesopotamian vocabulary, even Syrian cult personnel are ascribed Babylonian names. Some of these names would have represented genuine borrowings of southern Mesopotamian categories for temple operation, while others may have offered a more superficial scribal rendition of local customs. I am not confident that I can recognize which is which, especially outside of the Mari center.

In thirteenth-century Emar, this tension is quite sharp. There, the southern Mesopotamian title for a 'temple administrator' of an extensive staff (Akkadian *šangû*, Sumerian SANGA) could be co-opted to name the solitary 'priest' of a small shrine.[33] Already in the Mari period, most Syrian temples may have represented much smaller communities than their Babylonian counterparts, and it may be dangerous to assume that all titled temple personnel held the same status as in lands downstream. It is not clear to me who actually lived in temple-related lodgings, nor whether temple-based titles meant that all of their bearers received their full income through temple-based work.

This means that when we return to the prophets who are named by individual sacred sites, we must be careful about defining who may or may not qualify as 'temple personnel', never mind as 'priests'. If a prophet took part in feasts and held the title *āpilum*, we do not know that he lived in the temple or took even a majority of his income from service there. Unlike the *bārûm*-diviners, whose work demanded a constant monitoring of the divine atmosphere that might compare to modern weather forecasters, the prophets' activity seems to have been more intermittent. If they did not

---

33. Daniel E. Fleming, *Time at Emar: The Cultic Calendar and the Rituals from the Diviner's Archive* (Winona Lake, IN: Eisenbrauns, 2000), p. 31 n. 55.

perform daily chores in the temples, they may not have merited large-scale support. One may ask similar questions regarding performers at special festivals, such as singers and musicians, not to mention the wrestlers and other entertainers of Mari's great Eshtar festival.[34]

4. *Prophet, Temple and Defining the Elite*

In an oversimplified view of biblical priests and prophets, priests represent the elite of the temple institution, especially the one at Jerusalem, while prophecy is located further toward the margins of Israelite society. All sorts of biblical details militate against such a scheme and, in fact, it seems that people of both the priest and prophet types were found at various distances from the centers of power. If anything, it is surprising how close prophets could stand to the power of kings.

Mari also displays a great diversity, but the configurations of influence are somewhat different. This contrast mainly reflects the role of technical extispicy, the craft of the *bārûm*-diviner, both at Mari and in early Syria-Mesopotamia more broadly. In southern Mesopotamian Sumer during the centuries before the Mari archives, each central city was dominated by a massive temple complex that represented a major social and political force, even with the emergence of other powers. Upstream at Mari, as well as further west and north, the temples played a crucial social role, but their influence was much smaller.[35] By the early second millennium, power and wealth were focused in the palace and the king.[36]

When it came to understanding the designs of the gods, the ultimate authorities were the experts in extispicy, the *bārûm*-diviners. Every prophecy and every dream required some kind of confirmation as genuine by means of extispicy.[37] We do not have evidence for any outright rivalry, however, and the diviners never seem to be threatened by any sense that prophecy could gain too much prestige. At least from the restricted vantage of our letters to Zimri-Lim, neither *bārûm* nor prophet ever imagined any reversal of the diviner's power.

---

34.   *FM* III, p. 2, column iii.

35.   For a discussion of this contrast in third-millennium terms, see Piotr Steinkeller, 'Early Political Development in Mesopotamia and the Origins of the Sargonic Empire', in Mario Liverani (ed.), *Akkad: The First World Empire* (Padova: Sargon srl, 1993), pp. 107–29.

36.   I affirm this general pattern, even as I have just devoted a whole book to the alternative political forms that coexisted with the dominant kingship (*Democracy's Ancient Ancestors*, 2004).

37.   This has been widely observed. See, for example, André Lemaire, 'Les textes prophétiques de Mari dans leurs relations avec l'Ouest', *Amurru* 1 (1996), p. 436; Sasson, 'Mari and the Bible', p. 117.

As Jack Sasson has already observed, the diviners were not employed by temples but by the palace.[38] They supervised the sacrifice of sheep for extispicy, but they were not priests. Above all, the *bārûm*-diviners were royal officials with career opportunities almost without limit. During the reign of Zimri-Lim, a *bārûm* named Asqudum reached the innermost circle of trusted royal advisers.[39] Once a diviner had achieved a certain exalted political stature, he could leave the gory details of extispicy to his more junior colleagues.

So far as the responsibilities of temple personnel, prophets, and diviners touched each other, then, the diviners clearly represented the elite and stood by far the closest to the centers of power. If we search for the Mari expression of priest and prophet, with the role of 'priest' defined by temple service, then in fact both may be found together in roles farther from the political center. Divine messages sent through prophecy or dreams were diverse phenomena, capable of finding expression outside of strict institutional bounds. When prophets operated in cooperation with temples, however, they may even be understood to offer a coordinated alternative to divination, from an alternative social location.[40] In the Bible, priests could play a role in divination, as with the Urim and Thummim or the ephod. In Mesopotamia, the personnel who maintained temples and cared for their divine residents did not naturally include in their portfolios any means for finding out the plans and desires of the gods. Where prophets spoke at temples or their festivals, therefore, they served as the temples' only specialists in divine communication. The only way that a deity could advance information about the future, opinions about the present, or requests to the king for support, from their own temple homes, was to speak through an *āpilum, muhhûm*, or another participant in temple life. Far from being in competition, the priest and the prophet in the Mari letters could work in profound cooperation to speak for their gods outside the bounds of elite divination.

5. *Mari and the West*

Abraham Malamat has argued for years that what he called 'intuitive prophecy' in the Mari archives derived from 'an originally nonurban,

---

38. Sasson, 'Mari and the Bible', pp. 116–18.

39. On the career of Asqudum, who started out as a diviner in the court of Yasmah-Addu, see Jean-Marie Durand, *AEM* I. 1, 'La personnalité d'Asqudum', pp. 71–80.

40. Charpin (*FM* VI, p. 8) envisions a similar contrast between the settings for prophecy and divination: 'les deux catégories sont rattachées au culte d'une divinité et généralement mentionnées en rapport avec un temple, ce qui les distingue essentiellement des devins (*bârûm*)'.

seminomadic, tribal society'.[41] He identified this constituency with the 'Haneans', mobile pastoralists whose *ḫana* name may, according to Durand, refer to their tent camps.[42] The opposing pole of Malamat's duality would be the settled 'Akkadian' farmers and their city centers.[43] Malamat has made steady contributions over decades to the application of Mari evidence to biblical studies, but the work of Durand and his colleagues now makes this kind of social dualism impossible.

Especially under the rule of Yahdun-Lim and Zimri-Lim, Mari was the capital of the Binu Sim'al tribal people, borrowed for its prestige and its possibilities as an administrative hub. No tribal ruler worth his salt could claim the title 'king' (*šarrum*) without a settled capital, and Mari was an impressive prize. Zimri-Lim, whose reign we know best, governed his kingdom in a way that allowed town and country, farmer and pastoralist, to coexist on equal terms. With the enormous population of both Binu Sim'al tribespeople and their Binu Yamina cousins within the Mari realm, such divisions were often bridged by kinship. In terms of practical politics, the old valley districts of the Euphrates and the Habur Rivers were governed under strong central control through local branch palaces and governors. Meanwhile, the pastoralist tent-dwellers (*ḫana*) of Zimri-Lim's Binu-Sim'al tribe were allowed a completely separate political life, with only two 'chiefs of pasture' (*merḫûm*) to maintain contacts with the king. It is possible that even town-dwelling Binu Sim'al could identify themselves by their tent-dwelling relatives, so as to enjoy this greater freedom.[44]

Within this framework, few if any of the Mari institutions can be defined as the power-base of urban elites who fended off essentially foreign tribespeople, West-Semitic speakers, or pastoralists. Zimri-Lim ruled the Binu Sim'al *ḫana* as his political core. At the same time, like every Amorite

41.   A. Malamat, 'A Forerunner of Biblical Prophecy: The Mari Documents', in Patrick D. Miller *et al.* (eds.), *Ancient Israelite Religion*, Frank M. Cross volume (Philadelphia: Fortress, 1987), p. 35.

42.   Jean-Marie Durand elaborated his key argument in 'Unités et diversités au Proche-Orient à l'époque amorrite', in Dominique Charpin and Francis Joannès (eds.), *La circulation des biens, des personnes et des idées dans le Proche-Orient ancien* (CRRAI, 38; Paris: Editions Recherche sur les Civilisations, 1992), pp. 113–14; cf. LAPO 17, pp. 417–18. I discuss the *ḫana* category at length in my recent book, *Democracy's Ancient Ancestors*.

43.   Malamat, 'Forerunner', p. 33.

44.   One primary goal of my book, *Democracy's Ancient Ancestors*, is to develop an extended portrait of the political landscape of the Mari archives, which I sketch briefly here. I include a brief preliminary version in 'Mari and the Possibilities of Biblical Memory', *RA* 92 (1998), pp. 41–78, especially pp. 45–56. Durand describes the kingship of both Yahdun-Lim and Zimri-Lim in terms of their conquest of Mari when he discusses Der, the 'campement nomade' where both kings go to affirm their power, with their kingship 'définie à la fois par la possession de Mari et l'autorité sur des tribus bédouines' (Durand and Guichard, 'Rituels', p. 40).

king, Zimri-Lim embraced the achievements of southern Mesopotamian society, from the writing-based administration of a grand palace and its harem to the sophisticated calculation of future prospects by the craft of the *bārûm*. This embrace was only one expression of an Amorite royal court that mingled people and cultures of multiple backgrounds. The palace, its harem, and even diviners such as Asqudum were taken over by Zimri-Lim from another Amorite kingdom of somewhat different character, but still not as unadulterated southern Mesopotamian or essentially 'urban' institutions.[45] When rendered as the poles of social dualisms, urban and rural, kingdom and tribe, farmer and pastoralist, settled and nomadic, Akkadian and Amorite all offer little help toward illuminating the blend of cultural influences in the Amorite Mari kingdoms.

All of the players who are somehow involved in prophecy reflect this mix. The king and his court retained a strong identification with the Binu Sim'al tribal confederacy and its pastoralist components even as it took over the palace and existing patterns for governing people outside the Binu Sim'al group. The temples probably varied in their expression of old and newer customs. Dagan had been worshipped at the temples in Terqa and Tuttul, upstream from Mari, for centuries, and these settled centers would have served pastoralists and tribally defined peoples of varying identities throughout their use. Tuttul had been a capital of the Binu Yamina tribal confederacy before its capture by Yahdun-Lim.[46] The staff and the rites of such temples may have reflected a mix of cultural influences. Southern Mesopotamian categories may have colored the Mari temple culture in more than one phase, but some of this influence was probably quite recent. King Yahdun-Lim renovated the temple of the sun god Shamash with a noticeable orientation toward the lands downstream. In its dedication inscription, the pantheon of the protective curses is led by the Sumerian Enlil, not the local Dagan, and the other deities do not represent Mari's own sphere.[47] We know that Yahdun-Lim also renovated the entire palace

45. For Zimri-Lim's taking over of Yasmah-Addu's harem, see Jean-Marie Durand, 'Les dames du palais de Mari à l'époque du royaume de Haute-Mésopotamie', *MARI* 4 (1985), p. 421. Nele Ziegler has now studied this phenomenon in greater detail and finds that under Zimri-Lim, the women from Yasmah-Addu's harem tended to be kept apart from those who arrived with the new king ('Le harem de Zimrî-Lîm', *FM* IV [Paris: SEPOA, 1999], pp. 36–38 and table on p. 37).

46. See the Shamash temple dedication inscription of Yahdun-Lim, lines iii 4–9 (L'inscription de fondation de Iahdun-Lim, roi de Mari', *Syria* 32 [1955], pp. 1–28).

47. The curses in column iv invoke Enlil, the moon god Sin, Nergal as god of war, and Ea as god of fate, along with the sun god's consort Aya and his vizier Bunene. As a set, these offer an abbreviated pantheon from southern Mesopotamia.

scribal system toward the standards of Eshnunna, the powerful kingdom of southeastern Mesopotamia.[48]

Prophecy likewise cannot be ascribed to one side of a simple Akkadian/ Amorite or settled/nomadic division. It does seem to have been somehow more characteristic of Syria than southern Mesopotamia, in that we do not find the same sort of speech in third-millennium Sumer. Perhaps beause of the influence of Amorite populations in the early-second millennium, evidence for Mari-type prophecy is found across all of Syria-Mesopotamia, from Aleppo in the west to the kingdoms of Eshnunna, Babylon, and Uruk in the southeast.[49] We cannot be sure what we are missing, because of the biases in our written evidence. Even the odd concentration of references to prophecy in letters from the reign of Zimri-Lim may reflect neither personal preference nor his strong Binu Sim'al affiliation. Again, comparisons are always risky, but Zimri-Lim's huge legacy of letters seems to display an unusually intense pursuit of information control. It is possible that we have inherited this wonderful resource because this one Mari king insisted on a written record of every bit of news, every rumor, every sign of divine activity that occurred in or beyond his realm. The various loyalty oaths preserved for Zimri-Lim's reign make this an absolute requirement.[50] Finds from other sites of the same period do not allow us to know to what extent other kings matched Zimri-Lim's volume of correspondence. Insofar as they did, such correspondence may have included a similar number of references to prophecy.

One of Zimri-Lim's envoys, in fact the same Nur-Sin whom I quote at the beginning of this piece, reports two different messages from the storm god Addu, both received through an *āpilum* (*FM* VII, p. 39). Addu was the principal god of Aleppo, Mari's powerful western neighbor, and he takes credit in the first of these messages for putting Zimri-Lim on his throne. In return, the god demands the transfer of a town called Alahtum to his possession, effectively a demand from the kingdom of Aleppo.[51] Zimri-

48.   See Jean-Marie Durand, 'La situation historique des Šakkanakku: nouvelle approche', *MARI* 4 (1985), pp. 147–72, especially pp. 160–71. On Mari's relations with Eshnunna during the reign of Yahdun-Lim, see also Dominique Charpin, 'Les champions, la meule et le fleuve, ou le rachat du terroir de Puzurrân au roi d'Ešnunna par le roi de Mari Yahdun-Lim', *FM* I (1992), pp. 29–38.

49.   See Charpin, *FM* VI, pp. 32–33.

50.   See Jean-Marie Durand, 'Précurseurs syriens aux protocoles néo-assyriens: considérations sur la vie politique aux Bords-de-l'Euphrate', in Dominique Charpin and Francis Joannès (eds.), *Marchands, diplomates et empéreurs. Études sur la civilisation mésopotamienne offertes à Paul Garelli* (Paris: Éditions Recherche sur les Civilisations, 1991), pp. 13–71.

51.   More precisely, this demand is made through a specific cult of the storm god within the Aleppo kingdom, identified as that of 'Addu of Kallassu'; see Durand's discussion in *FM* VII, with the text.

Lim's representative is not entirely comfortable with this bold request, and he is moved to defend his role as the bearer of bad news:

> Previously, when I was on duty in Mari, I passed on to my lord any word that a male or female prophet (*āpilum/āpiltum*) might speak. Now I am on duty in another land – will I not send to my lord what I hear and (what) they say? If in the future any misstep is found to have occurred, will not my lord say as follows? 'The word that a prophet spoke to you so as to claim your plot (of land)(?), why did you not send it to me?' Therefore I have (now) sent to my lord.[52]

For all that Mari prophecy has been attributed to tribal Amorrites, not one of the reported episodes is communicated to the king by a leader of the mobile pastoralist *ḫana*, or especially by the chiefs of pasture (*merḫûm*). None of the dreams or prophecies takes place among the *ḫana*, nor among any group directly identified in tribal terms. This is not for want of correspondence dealing with the pastoralists of the Mari kingdom and beyond. We need not conclude from this that such prophecy was foreign to West Semitic 'Amorite' speakers, to the Syrian tribal peoples of the Binu Sim'al and the Binu Yamina, or to the communities of the steppe. The divine messages that reached the Mari king, however, did not come from settings defined in these terms.

Only one prophetic exchange includes personnel associated with the tent-dwelling *ḫana*, and these are the unique *nābû* of ARM XXVI 216. In terms of professional terminology, the one direct point of contact between biblical Israel and the distant Mari archives appears in connection with mobile pastoralists. The one other reference to the *nābû* in cuneiform evidence comes from thirteenth-century Emar, where they are located in the temple of the goddess Ishhara, inside the city proper.[53] Emar did have longstanding ties with tribal peoples from the old Binu Yamina confederacy,[54] but this use alone cautions against drawing any straight lines of tribal cultural communication that would end up in Israel. The activity of prophets called *nābû* was surely widespread. If nothing else, however, Mari's *nābû* hint that behind the generic label of ancient Near Eastern prophecy, the biblical custom may be one late descendant of the practices attested for the early second millennium.

---

52. *FM* VII, 39: 34–45 (= A.1121 + :34–45, in Bertrand Lafont, 'Les prophètes du dieu Adad', *RA* 78 [1984], pp. 7–18).

53. Emar (VI.3), p. 387, version F:11, as [lú.meš]*na-bi-i*, in the *kissu* ritual for Ishhara and Emar's city god [d]NIN.URTA. For discussion, see my '*Nābû* and *munabbiātu*', pp. 175–84.

54. See Jean-Marie Durand, 'La cité-État d'Imâr à l'époque des rois de Mari', *MARI* 6 (1990), pp. 39–92.

ADDENDUM: *On the Etymology of* nābû *and Hebrew* nābî'

Some years ago, I tried to revive the active etymology of the Hebrew noun *nābî'* as 'one who invokes' God, rather than one 'named' or appointed by God.[55] According to the active interpretation, prophecy under this name would have been characterized above all by human rather than divine initiative. More recently, John Huehnergard demonstrated systematically that Hebrew *qātîl* nouns (from earlier **qatīl-*) can only be passive in their relation to the verbal root from which they are derived, so that the *nābî'* would have to be 'one named'.[56] This conclusion would leave uncertain the etymology of the older cognate from Mari and Emar, which could be understood as either active or passive, based on form alone. The meaning of a supposed passive noun **nabû(m)* (representing West Semitic **nabi'u(m)*/**nabī'u(m)*) remains intrinsically unsatisfying to me, based on what we know of the verb *nabû(m)* from cuneiform evidence.[57] According to the passive etymology for the Hebrew *nābî'*, the prophet is 'one called' as bearer of divine messages. I still maintain the complaint from my earlier argument:

> Unfortunately, the actual use of the Akkadian word is commonly obscured in the discussion centered on the Bible. In particular, the primary meaning of the verb *nabû(m)* is 'to name', which may then indicate 'calling' on the name of a god, naming to kingship or rule, or even naming a price. Akkadian *nabû(m)* is not used for proclamation by humans, even on behalf of the gods. The Akkadian verb has no association with the concepts and language of the messenger, which currently stand as a popular model for placing the prophet in a larger Near Eastern setting. Finally, the naming of kings to royal office and destiny does not clearly apply to the prophetic 'vocation', which may involve a quite different relationship between a deity and a human being.[58]

I would like therefore to continue the dialogue with Huehnergard, who has generously responded to and corrected errors in an earlier draft of this addendum. Beginning from the lack of evidence for application of the verb *nabû(m)* to the 'naming' to any office other than royal, I propose that the Syrian noun *nabû(m)*/*nābû(m)* was more likely an active participle, 'one

55. D. E. Fleming, 'The Etymological Origins of the Hebrew *nābî'*: The One Who Invokes God,' *CBQ* 55 (1993), pp. 217–24; '*Nābû* and *munabbiātu*: Two New Syrian Religious Personnel', *JAOS* 113 (1993), pp. 175–84.

56. J. Huehnergard, 'On the Etymology and Meaning of Hebrew *nābî'*', *Eretz-Israel* 26 (1999), pp. 88–93.

57. The verb is well attested in Akkadian, though the Syrian noun *nābû(m)* indicates that the verb was probably current in early West Semitic, at least in the north.

58. Fleming, 'Etymological Origins', pp. 218–19, with citations in the notes.

who names' rather than 'one named'. If this interpretation is correct, the ancient noun would have to have changed its pattern from **qātil-* to **qatíl-* at some point before our Biblical Hebrew evidence. Some time in the mid-late second millennium, the 'Canaanite Shift' changed the long /ā/ of all active G (= Qal) participles to /ō/, so that the Hebrew word for 'prophet' would have come to be vocalized **nōbē*.

Such changes of noun pattern are widely attested across the Semitic languages and may occur by the association of a word with other nouns that share some category of meaning. Joshua Fox defines 'semantic analogy' as 'the creation of new words or the transfer of words of a given root and meaning from one form to another on the basis of an already-existing word with similar semantics which has this form'.[59] In Arabic, the word for 'raven' is *ġurāb*, in contrast to Akkadian *āribu(m)* and Biblical Hebrew *'ōrēb*, both from a **qātil-* pattern. Many Arabic nouns for birds, animals, and insects have the **qatūl-* pattern, and this noun seems to have been transformed so as to take its place among them. Several Biblical Hebrew nouns that describe agricultural activities tend to take the passive *qātíl* form, including *qāsîr* ('harvest') and *bāsîr* ('vintage').[60] Fox observes that in Biblical Hebrew, quite a few passive **qatíl-* (> *qātíl*) nouns take on meanings independent from, though still related to, the simple passive adjectives that denote only the object of a verb. Many of these refer to what Fox calls 'political roles', among which he includes the *nābî'* 'prophet' ('called'), the *māšîah* 'prince' ('anointed'), the *nāgîd* 'leader' ('set in front'), the *pāqîd* 'official' ('appointed'), the *nāśî'* 'prince' ('raised up'), and the *pālîl* 'judge' ('one who is beseeched').[61]

This cluster of leadership terms in *qātíl* form provides one basis for a 'semantic analogy' by which an originally active noun *nābû(m)*, written in Akkadian style for West Semitic *nābi'u(m)*, could have been converted to the passive form **nabî'u(m)*. Although the group of Hebrew nouns offers one possible explanation for the pattern change, we cannot know exactly when and why it would have occurred. It appears that the verb *nabû(m)*, which remained common in Akkadian, may have fallen out of use in western Syria-Palestine by the late-second millennium. Already in the thirteenth-twelfth centuries, we do not find the verb *nb'* as 'to name' in the alphabetic texts from Ugarit, and Northwest Semitic of the Iron Age offers only a secondary denominative verb in Biblical Hebrew, derived from the noun meaning 'prophet'.

---

59.   Joshua Fox, *Semitic Noun Patterns* (HSS, 52; Winona Lake, IN: Eisenbrauns, 2003), p. 32.

60.   Fox, *Semitic Noun Patterns*, p. 33.

61.   Fox, *Semitic Noun Patterns*, pp. 192–93.

In general, the *qatīl*- noun pattern seems to have been more common in early West Semitic than in Akkadian,[62] and the change of pattern could have occurred even before the thirteenth-century Emar evidence, where the syllabic spelling ^{lú.meš}*na-bi-i* would not distinguish passive *qatīlu* or *qatilu* from active *qātilu* forms. The much discussed noun *'aBiru* may have undergone a similar change from active participle to a pattern of the passive type some time in the middle of the second millennium.[63] In the late-second millennium, this word designated a social class of dangerous people who were not affiliated with the accepted political and social entities such as towns or states. Huehnergard has treated the Ugaritic expression of the word as a substantive of unknown type (*qatil-* or *qatīl-*), but not an active participle (*qātil-*).[64]

The Mari archives now offer evidence for somewhat different use of the root in the early-second millennium. It is always difficult to establish secure definitions of rare words in new settings, but the Mari references certainly involve movement of a person from one place to another. In particular, this movement seems consistently to take the person from his place of regular residence to some hope of safety or independence. Each location is outside the political entity of original residence. Compare the following abbreviated citations:

> ARM XIV 50.14 A man accused of deserting defends himself by saying, 'I left (*aḫ-Bu-ur*) four years ago for the land of Shubartu.'
> ARM XXVI 510.25 'Asdi-madar son of Sumumu, who came here (*iḫ-Bu-ra-am*, Karanâ) f[rom Mar]i', was put in prison.
> ARM XXVII 70.17 A man was wanted for questioning, but 'this man has left (*iḫ-Bu-úr*) for Kurdâ'.
> ARM XXVII 116.32 Two men are identified by residence. One is still in the Mari kingdom, settled (verb *wašābum*) at Saggaratum, but the other 'left (*iḫ-Bu-ra-am*) for Kurdâ'.
> ARM XXVIII 46.6 The king of Urgish (= Urkesh) reports that he has had to leave his residence in that city for neighboring Shinah. 'I have departed in exile' (*a-na ḫa-Bi-ru-tim at-ta-ṣi*).

Durand translates the verb as 'quiter sa résidence', and the verb is intransitive in any case, so that the substantive *ḫāBirum/ḫaBirum/ḫaBīrum* cannot easily be read as passive.[65]

---

62. For suggested examples in Ugaritic, see John Huehnergard, *Ugaritic Vocabulary in Syllabic Transcription* (HSS, 32; Atlanta: Scholars, 1987), p. 309; Josef Tropper, *Ugaritische Grammatik* (AOAT, 273; Münster: Ugarit-Verlag, 2000), p. 261.

63. Note that the upper case -*B*- represents an uncertain or variable pronunciation of the -*b/p*- labial.

64. Huehnergard, *Ugaritic Vocabulary*, pp. 161, 309.

65. Jean-Marie Durand, *Documents épistolaires du palais de Mari. Tome III* (Littératures Anciennes du Proche-Orient, 18; Paris: du Cerf, 2000), p. 552; cf. discussion on p. 205.

The active participle *ḫāBirum* would designate one who has performed the action of *ḫaBārum* (root '*Br*), leaving his home for some other, beyond the administrative reach of his native ruler. This definition of an active participle by completed past action rather than generalized present action is the less common type, but there are nevertheless a number of examples. In Akkadian, a cluster of words that define parentage usually have this nuance: *ālidu/ālittu* ('he who begot'/'she who bore'), *bānû* ('one who created, begot'), and *zārû* ('progenitor' as 'one who sowed').[66] Like the verb *nabû(m)*, which is not found in the west during the late-second and first millennia, the verb '*aBāru(m)* seems to have dropped from use some time between the early- and late-second millennium. The root survived most prominently in the substantive '*aBiru*, of uncertain noun pattern.[67]

Insofar as this noun also changed pattern from **qātil-* to **qatil-/*qatīl-*, it would seem to have been by a semantic analogy related to that which operated in the case of the word *nābû*. The **qatīl-* pattern not only served leadership terms, but also personnel and categories of people more broadly. For example, the Biblical Hebrew noun *śākîr* ('hired laborer') is already found at Ugarit, and one might compare the Hebrew '*āsîp* ('prisoner'), *yālîd* ('house-born slave'), **nātîn* ('temple slaves, bondsmen'), *sārîs* ('eunuch, court official'), *pālît* ('refugee'), and *śārîd* ('battle survivor'). These nouns stand in various relationships to cognate verbal roots, and none matches the exact sort of social class defined by the '*aBiru*, but they add to the impression that the **qatīl-* pattern was common in the west for identifying people by type. By the time the '*aBiru* had become a well-known social class, the associated verb was out of use and the relationship of noun to verb was no longer evident. Under these conditions, the noun '*aBiru* seems to have gone the way of the word *nābû* and was transformed to fit a common pattern for identifying a category of people.

---

66. Compare also (*w*)*āṣû*, 'one who has gone out'; *dā'iku*, 'murderer' ('one who has killed'); *nādinu*, 'seller' ('one who has sold,' cf. *nādinatu*, a woman who has sold property); and *rāšû*, 'creditor' ('one who has acquired'). A number of active G participles occur as substantives with the particularizing -*an*- element: *dā'ikānu*, (same as *dā'iku*); *māḫirānu*, 'buyer' (usually 'one who has bought' property); *māḫiṣānu*, 'one who has struck'; *māšiḫānu*, 'one who has surveyed' (a field); *nādinānu*, 'seller' (same as *nādinu*); *nā'ikānu*, 'one who has had intercourse'; *ṣābitānu*, 'captor' ('one who has apprehended' a criminal).

67. Huehnergard observes that in the syllabic form of the word found at Ugarit ('*apiru*, spelled *ḫa-Bi-ri*), 'The rare writing of Ugar /'/ with ḪA probably indicates a learned spelling of the Akkadianized form of the word (*ḫapiru*)' (*Ugaritic Vocabulary*, p. 161).

The Northern Voyage of Psammeticus II and its Implications for Ezekiel 44.7–9

Julie Galambush

The Problem: Strangers Guarding the Temple

The question of precisely which foreigners Ezekiel has in mind when he excoriates the Levites for having stationed 'foreigners, uncircumcised in heart and flesh' (44.7–9) as functionaries in the Jerusalem sanctuary, has never been answered satisfactorily. As Stephen Cook points out in his 1995 article on the question, 'it is difficult to clarify a monarchic-period referent' (Cook 1995: 195 n. 7); indeed, no case has been put forth for a referent from within the prophet Ezekiel's historical context. Instead, candidates for the mysterious strangers' identity have ranged from the Gibeonites of Joshua's day to the sons of the servants of Solomon, to Cook's own preference, the Korahites as portrayed in Num. 16–18. The identity of Ezekiel's בני נכר may never be established with certainty, but attempts to locate the allusion's historical referent in Israel's distant, or even its narrative past, seem to work against what we know of the impetus behind Ezekiel's writing, namely, the political, military, and religious events that shaped the years in which he prophesied.

In recent decades scholarship on Ezekiel has emphasized the prophet's social and historical context as influencing both the worldview of the exiled priest-prophet and the contents of his carefully dated oracles. This is the prophet who gives us one oracle in response to Nebuchadrezzar's siege of Tyre (26.1–21) and another in response to his failure, thirteen years later, to take the city (29.17–21). Ezekiel's references, while often obscure, are always tantalizing, precisely because we have reason to believe that he is writing in response to specific details of current Judean history.

Why, then, do scholars continue to seek Ezekiel's cultic strangers solely from among figures from Israel's distant biblical (and perhaps not even historical) past? Two factors contribute to this tendency: first, the influence of Julius Wellhausen and second, the dearth of information about the Israelite cult in the exilic and immediate pre-exilic period – the period in which we would hope to find such strangers accounted for. According to Wellhausen, 'the position of the Levites is the Achilles heel of the Priestly Code' (Wellhausen 1994 [1885]: 167), and Ezek. 44 was the key to the position of the Levites. The Levites, argued Wellhausen, functioned in the pre-exilic period as priests, pure and simple. Only with Ezekiel and the emergence of an exclusively Zadokite priesthood, were the Levites (that is, all Levites who were not considered descendants of Zadok) demoted to the status of temple servants. The P documents show the Levites as cultic support staff; hence, P reflects a post-Ezekielian view of the priesthood. Wellhausen's reading of Ezek. 40–48 has been immensely influential, as have later studies by Gese (1957) and Gunneweg (1965) that moved beyond Wellhausen to develop the theory of a post-Ezekielian 'Zadokite stratum', in which Zadokite priests put forth their case for their own cultic supremacy. Walther Zimmerli's massive commentary (Zimmerli 1979 [1969]; 1983 [1969]) further developed this view and even works such as Levenson's *Theology of Restoration of Ezekiel 40–48* (Levenson 1976), which treat the temple vision as on the whole original, still credit a 'Zadokite stratum' as a late addition to the book.

The model of Ezek. 40–48 (including its Zadokite stratum) as a late addition has come under serious criticism in recent decades, most notably with M. Greenberg's 1984 demonstration of the temple vision's high degree of coherence (Greenberg 1984), both internally and with the rest of the book. For reasons we shall not go into here, the book's substantial unity is almost a given in current scholarship. On the specific question of the Levites, R. Duke's argument that Ezek. 44 represents the Levites' *restoration* to their hereditary role as temple guards and servants, not their demotion, has found wide acceptance (Duke 1988). If most scholars now treat Ezekiel's temple vision as the work of the sixth-century prophet, a prophet intimately involved with and commenting on events of his day, why do these same scholars continue to search for Ezekiel's temple intruders among literary figures of Israel's distant past? The answer lies in the lack of known historical candidates from Ezekiel's own period. Given virtually no external data concerning conflicts or changes in 'temple management' that might have given rise to Ezekiel's charges against the Levites, we have, naturally enough, sought an answer from the source that, however ambiguous its data, is readily available – the biblical text itself. This essay will propose a new solution to the problem of the covenant-breaking foreigners that fits the details of Ezek. 44.7–9 better than the alternatives and that has the advantage of being based on external evidence related to events of Ezekiel's own day.

Previous Scholarship

Ezekiel reports in 44.6–7 that the 'house of Israel' have committed 'abominations... by bringing in foreigners (בני נכר), uncircumcised in heart and uncircumcised in flesh, to be in my sanctuary (במדקשי) and profane my house (את-ביתי) when you brought near my food (the fat and the blood).

They have broken my covenant by means of all your abominations'. He continues with a second charge, namely that 'you have not kept guard over my holy things (ולא שמרתם משמרת קדשי), but have appointed them to guard my sanctuary (במקדשי משמרתי לשמרי)' (44.8).

Ezekiel here makes several claims:

1. Foreigners (בני נכר) were brought by the 'house of Israel' into the Jerusalem sanctuary precincts (מקדשי),[1] and were present during the offering of fat and blood to YHWH.
2. The foreigners were uncircumcised.
3. The bringing of these foreigners into the sanctuary precincts constituted an act of abomination on Israel's part.
4. Through this abomination on Israel's part, the *foreigners* (reading, with MT, ויפרו) have broken YHWH's covenant.
5. These same foreigners were appointed to act as guards in YHWH's sanctuary precincts (במקדשי).

In seeking the identity of these temple intruders, scholars have combed the biblical text for any references to non-Israelites connected to the temple. Only a few options present themselves: 2 Kgs 11.4–8 (and see 2 Sam. 20.23) mentions the otherwise unknown Caraites (= Carians?) as guardians of the palace who also stand guard at the temple while young Joash is crowned; Ezra 2.43–58 mentions 'נתינים' and 'descendants of Solomon's servants', apparently among temple personnel who returned to the land following the exile; and, last but not least, Josh. 9 recounts the ruse by which the Gibeonites became 'hewers of wood and drawers of water for the congregation and for the altar of YHWH' (9.27).

Of these possibilities, the נתינים and descendants of Solomon's servants are the most easily dismissed, since we have no reason to think that they were either foreigners or uncircumcised, that they either entered the sanctuary or guarded it, or that they were involved in the breaking of YHWH's covenant.[2] What they have going for them is that they appear in a list including (but not limited to) temple personnel, and that they are mentioned in the post-exilic period – not long after Ezekiel prophesied. It is difficult to argue that the נתינים and descendants of Solomon's servants were either foreigners or uncircumcised, since they are included specifically in a list of those proving their descent in order to return to Israel from the exile. Nor are they accused of any improper conduct. If anything, it is the

1. On the מקדש as the entire sanctuary precincts, rather than the temple proper, see Milgrom (1983).

2. The term נתינים might indicate a person who has been 'given', or devoted to temple service, but without further evidence of their status, the NRSV's 'temple servants' is hardly warranted. For the case that Ezek. 44 refers to the נתינים and sons of Solomon's servants, see Abba (1978).

very *lack* of concrete information about these groups that has allowed scholars to mold them into whatever suits – in this case, covenant-breaking foreigners.

The Caraites are similarly attractive primarily because of our lack of information about them. Their origin is unknown (attempts have been made to connect them with the Carians of Asia Minor);[3] they are *palace*, not temple guards, temporarily enlisted to aid the priests in 2 Kgs 11. It is hard to extrapolate from this that they were ever 'appointed as guardians' in the sanctuary, let alone that they were present during the offering of fat and blood. Moreover, nowhere is the use of Caraite guards condemned (though it is omitted in the parallel account in 2 Chron. 23.1–11) as covenant violation, nor is it clear why anyone (including Ezekiel) would do so.

The Gibeonites, as Levenson put it, have been the 'consensus' choice for much of recent interpretive history.[4] The Gibeonites have the advantage that they are in some sense 'foreigners' (though it is open to dispute whether the term בני נכר can properly refer to native inhabitants of the land) and were appointed to supply the wood and water used in the tabernacle (and presumably, later, in the temple). So much for their advantages. We do not know whether they continued to be uncircumcised and we have no reason to think they were ever appointed guardians either outside or within the sanctuary, let alone present during offerings of fat and blood. And, perhaps most importantly, during the supposed thousand-plus years of the Gibeonites' wood-chopping service, no one seems to have objected to them – until Ezekiel, who, while not naming them, apparently considers their presence a covenant-breaking 'abomination'. All in all, the available options are simply not very strong.[5]

Stephen Cook approaches the problem from a different angle. Cook (1995) reads the passage as deriving from an early Persian-period 'Ezekiel school'. This school, argues Cook, is engaged in promulgating a renewed and purified cult in anticipation of the rebuilding of the temple. Such a modification of the Zadokite hypothesis allows one to read the text as reflecting a time close to the prophet's own socio-historical context and viewpoint, without insisting that a literal 'Ezekiel' was responsible for every line. On the basis of numerous linguistic connections between Ezek. 44 and the story of Korah's rebellion in Num. 16–18, Cook argues that the reference to the בני נכר in the sanctuary is an allusion to the Korahites as portrayed in Num. 16–18.[6] The verbal links (phrases such as 'רב-לכם' and

---

3. For arguments in favor of the Caraites, see Allen (1990: 261).

4. (Levenson 1976: 135) For the argument in favor of the Gibeonites, see König (1901).

5. For a detailed review of the literature, see McConville (1983), who remains agnostic on the question of the foreigners' identity.

6. Additional discussions of these similarities can be found in Fishbane (1985: 138–143) and Milgrom (1983: 10–16).

the stipulation in both texts that the Levites shall both perform משמרת for the sanctuary, and shall 'bear their guilt') are indeed striking. Cook makes a strong case that an exilic or early post-exilic author is using these verbal links self-consciously to argue that some more contemporary abomination should be understood as tantamount to Korah's rebellion. Having, however, concluded that imagery drawn from the Numbers narrative is being reworked in order to depict a more recent incident, Cook has thereby come no closer to solving the problem we wish to address: who perpetrated the *recent* trespass? Working from the fact that בני נכר are being kept from temple service, Cook turns to the promises made to בן הנכר in Isa. 56.1–8 as the source of the problem addressed in Ezek. 44. Trito-Isaiah makes an open offer to 'strangers' who 'minister' to YHWH, that they will be made joyful 'in my house of prayer'; in 66.21 we find a list of foreigners who will be made into priests and Levites. It is precisely this broad inclusivity, argues Cook, that an Ezekielian, Zadokite school would seek to counter. Ezekiel 44 argues, in effect, that once before, 'outsiders' – the Korahites – attempted to arrogate too much cultic authority to themselves, with disastrous results. Only the Levites – home-grown Levites, not newly-made, foreign Levites – have been authorized to provide maintenance and security for the temple, as Num. 16–18 clearly says.

Cook's analysis of the literary relationship between Ezek. 44 and Num.16–18 is compelling, but the attempt to draw a connection between the בן הנכר of Isa. 56 and those of Ezek. 44 is strained. Regardless of when it was composed, Ezek. 44 clearly says that in the *first temple*, uncircumcised בני נכר were both posted as guards and present during the offering of fat and blood. Trito-Isaiah's post-exilic promise that בני נכר who have become 'joined to YHWH' (and so are presumably circumcised) will one day be welcome to bring offerings to and even to serve in the (second) temple seems to belong to an entirely different setting. Even if one were to conclude that a Persian period author wished to oppose Trito-Isaiah's program of welcoming בני נכר, one would still have to address the claim made by that Ezekielian author: that this sort of thing has caused us trouble before – not only with Korah's rebellion, but also before the destruction of the first temple, when uncircumcised בני נכר were given extraordinary access to the temple, thus breaking YHWH's covenant. No number of connections to the past via Korah, or to the future via Trito-Isaiah, helps to answer the original question of who it was that was appointed guard in the *first* temple, allowing Ezekiel or his followers to insist that such a thing not be allowed to happen again. And so we are back to the search for suitable sixth-century strangers.

The Strangers Who Broke the Covenant: A New Reading

One of the least examined aspects of Ezekiel's complaint about the foreigners in the temple is the fact that they are said to have broken YHWH's covenant. Two questions arise; first, does the presence of the foreigners constitute a *de facto* covenant violation, and second, how can foreigners break a covenant (YHWH's covenant) to which they are not a party? It is not at all clear that the mere presence of any foreigners in the sacred precincts would constitute a violation of any kind. Foreigners (גרים, not בני נכר), like native Israelites, are expected to offer their sacrifices at the entrance to the tent of meeting (see, for example, Lev. 17.8–9, 22.18–19). The presence of the foreigners במקדשי, in the sacred precincts, then, does not necessarily constitute an offense. On the other hand, in Num. 3.38 (and cf. 1.51, 18.4), the priests are to guard the sanctuary (שמרים משמרת המקדש), and any זר who 'draws near' is to be killed. In this case, however, the זר is anyone, including an Israelite, who encroaches without authorization upon the sancta (Milgrom 1983: 8–18). Thus, foreigners had roughly the status of lay Israelites in regard to the sanctuary; they enjoyed limited access. In fact, it is only in response to the abuse cited in 44.7–9 that Ezekiel in 44.9 forbids foreigners from entering the envisioned new temple compound. Ezekiel's charge that the foreigners had been assigned as guardians over temple sancta (לשמרי משמרתי במקדשי) is certainly surprising – this is the responsibility of the Levites and seems to describe guardianship between the areas permitted to the Israelites and those permitted only for the priests (the sacrifice altar and the temple proper). The second objection, to the foreigners' presence during the offering of the fat and blood, is ambiguous, since those who brought their sacrifices were ordinarily able to look on while the priests made these offerings (Milgrom 1983: 18). The fact that these foreigners are uncircumcised (unlike the גרים who ordinarily participate in the cult) is presumably part of the objection, as is their function as guards – a role Ezekiel (like P) reserves for the Levites. Even if the foreigners' actions constitute sancta trespass (מעל), however, the language of covenant violation is puzzling.[7]

In fact, it is difficult to see how foreigners *could* break YHWH's covenant in any event, unless they were party to it. The logistical difficulty involved in foreigners breaking YHWH's covenant has led interpreters almost

---

7. The charge of covenant violation (פרר ברית) usually refers to idolatry (as in Deut. 31.16; Jer. 11.10), but sometimes describes a wholesale abandonment of the commandments (Lev. 26.15; Isa. 24.5). In Ezekiel, references to the broken covenant are always to the treaty between Nebuchadrezzar and Zedekiah, with the exception of 16.59 which is ambiguous. Attempts have been made to connect Ezek. 44 to the 'covenant with Levi', mentioned in Jer. 33.21, Mal. 2.4–9, but the contents of such as covenant, let alone the means of breaking it, are unknown.

universally to prefer LXX ותפרו over MT, ויפרו (Block 1998: 621 n. 40; Zimmerli 1983: 448). This is, however, an occasion for preferring the harder reading. LXX, being functionally as far removed as we are from Ezekiel's historical context, could easily have despaired of imagining any foreigners capable of breaking YHWH's covenant, and would therefore have 'corrected' the text to read that it was Israel, not the foreigners, who broke it. More recent interpreters have simply accepted the resolution to this problem already provided by the versions.[8] Before emending the text, however, it is appropriate to ask whether it is in any way plausible that Ezekiel could have considered that foreigners had in fact broken, or were instrumental in breaking, YHWH's covenant.

The only foreigners surmised to have been in any covenant relationship with YHWH in the early-sixth century are the Babylonians. The evidence of 2 Chron. 36.13, that Nebuchadrezzar made Zedekiah take his vassal oath 'in the name of YHWH' is generally understood to mean that YHWH had entered into the role of guarantor of the vassal treaty between Judah and Babylon. If this were the case, then it would be theoretically possible for the Babylonians, as Judah's covenant partners, to break a covenant identified by YHWH as 'mine'. In fact, of course, Ezekiel reflects the opposite situation. YHWH *does* claim the covenant between Zedekiah and Nebuchadnezzar as 'my covenant', but it is Zedekiah, not Nebuchadrezzar, who has broken it. The allegory of the great eagle in 17.1–21 spells out the situation: Zedekiah has 'despised the oath and broken the covenant' by seeking out a military alliance with Egypt. The oath Zedekiah has broken by consorting with Egypt, says YHWH, is 'my oath', and the covenant 'my covenant' (v. 19). This illicit relationship between Judah and Egypt forms a constant undercurrent in the book of Ezekiel: Oholah and Oholibah seek the sexual favors of the Egyptians (23.3, 19–21, 27); already before the Exodus the Israelites preferred the idols of Egypt to the promises of YHWH (20.7–8). Fully seven chapters of the oracles against foreign nations are directed against Egypt because of its overinflated pride and its role in causing Judah to rebel. Other nations are condemned for rejoicing in Judah's downfall; Egypt, for luring Judah into disobedience. Egypt, says YHWH, will ultimately be destroyed so that 'the Egyptians shall never again be the reliance of the house of Israel'. As for Judah, 'they will recall their iniquity, when they turned to [Egypt] for aid' (29.16). Of all the nations Ezekiel condemns, Egypt alone is condemned on the basis of having facilitated *Judah's* sins rather than for its own sins against Judah.

---

8. An exception is G. R. Driver (1954), who argues that the foreigners, while not parties to the covenant, have caused it to be broken (p. 309). Driver adduces Jer. 32.20–21 as a similar usage.

Ezekiel repeatedly argues that Judah has broken YHWH's covenant, but
that Egypt has caused it to do so. The foreigners whom Ezekiel links most
closely with Judah's covenant violation are thus the Egyptians. Is it
possible, however, that it was the Egyptians who 'broke my covenant in
addition to all your [Israel's] abominations' in 44.7? Is there any sense to be
made by positing that Egyptians were brought into the מקדש at the time
when blood and fat were offered, and who thereby defiled the holy
precincts (את-ביתי)?[9] Could Egyptians, further, have been posted as guards
over the sanctuary? Certainly, if Egyptians had been brought into the
Jerusalem sanctuary precincts, it would become easy to explain why their
presence would merit the label 'abomination' and constitute a violation of
YHWH's covenant. It was, after all, precisely Judah's continued alliance
with Egypt that had constituted the breaking of YHWH's covenant decried
in Ezek.17. The problem in Ezek. 44, then, would no longer be that
foreigners had been brought into and even posted as guards in the temple
precincts, but that *these* foreigners, by their very presence, signified
rebellion against Nebuchadrezzar and thus against YHWH as well. *These*
foreigners defile the holy realm, since their very presence violates the oath
taken in YHWH's name.

In light of Ezekiel's insistence in ch. 17 that Zedekiah's overtures to
Psammeticus constituted a violation of YHWH's covenant, the presence of
Egyptians in the Jerusalem temple area would also seem to constitute such
a violation. While the Egyptians seem good candidates as 'covenant
breakers', however, it is more difficult to reconcile the Egyptian option
with Ezekiel's charge that the foreigners were 'uncircumcised in heart and
uncircumcised in flesh' (44.7). The fact that the strangers are 'uncircumcised' forms the strongest argument against the case that the intruders were
Egyptian, since many Egyptians, particularly those of high rank, were
circumcised (Sasson 1966). Ezekiel clearly assumed, for example, that
Apries, Psammeticus II's son, was circumcised, since he taunts him no
fewer than nine times with the threat that after death he will be laid in
Sheol '*with the uncircumcised*'. The taunt assumes that the pharaoh is
circumcised; only because of his affronts to YHWH will he suffer the
disgrace of being paired with the uncircumcised.

Ezekiel's description of the strangers as 'uncircumcised of heart and
uncircumcised of flesh' is unique in the Hebrew Bible, and merits further
discussion. Deuteronomy, Leviticus, and Jeremiah all employ the metaphor
that Israel must be 'circumcised in the heart' as well as in the flesh (Deut.
10.16, 30.6; Lev. 26.41; Jer. 4.4, 9.25–26); that is, they must embody the
covenant in their attitudes and actions as well as in their physical persons.

---

9.   On Ezekiel's distinction between the בית, or temple enclosure generally, and the היכל, or
temple proper, see Milgrom (1983: 14).

While most of these references state either that Israel or Judah is uncircumcised of heart, or that it must soon undergo such circumcision, only Jer. 9.25–26 deals with uncircumcised foreigners as well as Israelites. In Jer 9.25 YHWH announces that he will deal with all who are circumcised 'only in the foreskin: Egypt, Judah, Edom, the Ammonites, Moab, and all those with shaven temples who live in the desert'. YHWH goes on to make a very peculiar claim: 'For all these', YHWH says, 'are *uncircumcised*, and the house of Israel is uncircumcised in heart'. Thus, Jeremiah places the Egyptians among those who are at once circumcised *and* uncircumcised – though only Judah is accused of being uncircumcised in the heart. How, then, can the circumcised Egyptians also be uncircumcised? The simplest answer is that foreigners' circumcision did not count as 'real' circumcision, since it was not part of the covenantal rite practiced by the Israelites.[10] Another, quite fascinating possibility has been proposed by R. Steiner (1999),[11] who discusses the evidence that the Egyptians practiced 'partial circumcision', that is, a form of circumcision in which the foreskin is cut but not entirely severed. Egyptians, then, who considered themselves well and truly circumcised, would have been liable to the insulting claim lodged by Israelites, that they were not circumcised at all – either physically or attitudinally. Whether Jeremiah is referring to the Egyptians' alternative style of circumcision or to the irrelevance of circumcision that is not part of the Israelite covenant, he claims in 9.25 that Egyptians, whom he first admits are circumcised, are in fact not circumcised. It is entirely possible that Ezekiel, who follows Jeremiah in so much of his imagery, has taken over this perspective. Ezekiel repeatedly expresses his opinion that Pharaoh belongs among the uncircumcised, where he will ultimately reside after death. It would thus not be surprising if he were to express a similarly derisive view in 44.7 – that the foreigners admitted to the temple were not only uncircumcised of heart, but uncircumcised even in their flesh.

We have argued thus far that the foreigners who best fit the description of Ezek. 44.7–9 are the Egyptians. The next question is, simply, were the Egyptians there? Do we have any evidence that would place Egyptians in Jerusalem in such a way as to break Zedekiah's covenant with Nebuchadrezzar? The presence of Egyptians in Palestine during the late 590s is, of course, confirmed by the mention in Rylands Papyrus IX of Psammeticus II's voyage in 592 BCE.[12] While comparatively little is otherwise known about Psammeticus II's rule, the story of his 'victory tour' into Palestine after his successful Nubian campaign is described in a

10. For this reading of Ezek. 44, see Cook (1995: 200).

11. See also the discussion in Sasson (1966: 474).

12. The exact date of Psammeticus' voyage to Palestine cannot be ascertained with certainty, but see the extensive discussions in Redford (1992: 462–64), Spalinger (1978: 21–24), and Redford and Freedy (1970).

legal brief by an Egyptian of priestly lineage, whose grandfather, Pediese, accompanied Pharaoh on the journey:

> In the 4th year of Per'o Psammetk Nefebre messengers were sent to the great temples of Upper and Lower Egypt, saying 'Per'o goeth to the land of Khor [southern Palestine]: let the priests come with the bouquets (?) of the gods of Kemi to take them to the land of Khor with Per'o'. And a message was sent to Teuzoi, saying, 'Let a priest come with the bouquet of Amûn to go to the land of Khor with Per'o'.[13]

Pediese is chosen and goes, along with a servant and a guard, to join Psammeticus' retinue. A problem arises, however, upon Pediese's return from his voyage: during his absence his hereditary share in the priestly duties (and income) at Teuzoi has been given to a competitor. Pediese immediately goes to Pharaoh to seek redress, but is told that 'Per'o is sick, Per'o cometh not out' (Griffith 1972 [1909]: 97). Pediese next appeals to local judges, but after 'many days' his claim is rejected. He then sets out to take his case to other priests of Amun, in Thebes, but upon his arrival he learns that Psammeticus has died, thus complicating any appeal the priests might have made on Pediese's behalf.

This colorful vignette has often been mined for details concerning Psammeticus' movements and the extent of his control over territories along the eastern Mediterranean seaboard. What concerns us, however, is a topic closer to Pediese's heart – the experience of the priests. Pediese is called, together with other priests, to accompany Pharaoh in 'the 4th year', or 592 BCE.[14] Pediese does not say when he returned to his home, though clearly he was gone long enough for mischief to have developed during his absence. More importantly, by the time Pediese arrives home and learns of his misfortune, Psammeticus is already on his deathbed; by the time the priest has concluded his first round of appeals, the pharaoh has died. Psammeticus II died in February, 589, more than two years after his voyage into Palestine. Although we do not know when Psammeticus returned to Egypt, we can assume that he did not spend two full years on his 'victory tour' (following a war of a year or less!). On the other hand, the fact that Pediese did not return home until Psammeticus was on his deathbed suggests that considerable time elapsed between Psammeticus'

13. Griffith (1972 [1909]: 95–96).
14. Yoyotte (1951) notes that the text does not specify when Psammeticus actually left for the Levant, but given that his Nubian campaign, begun in 593, was not concluded until the spring of 592 (though it is not certain that the pharoah stayed with the army throughout the campaign), the entourage probably would not have gone forth into the Levant until later in 592, or possibly early in 591. (Yoyotte's chronology places Psammeticus' fourth year in 590 BCE and his death in 587. We are using the chronology employed by Redford [1992], in which Psammeticus' fourth year is 592 and the year of his death, 589.)

return and that of his priest. While the Egyptian ruler probably spent considerably less than a year traveling to advertise his Nubian success, his priest seems to have spent closer to two years in the Levant. Of Pediese's timeframe, we know only that he was gone long enough for opponents to have taken over his post, and that after returning and learning of Psammeticus' illness he spent 'many days' pleading his case before hearing that the pharaoh had died. Even allowing some months for Pediese to spend pressing his suit in Teuzoi, at least a year seems to have passed between Psammeticus' return from Palestine (in 592 or early 591) and the return of Pediese his priest (probably late in 590, a matter of months before Psammeticus' death in February, 589). It is therefore highly probable that after his 592 visit to Palestine, Psammeticus left behind a delegation that included cultic personnel.

The connection – presumably both temporal and causal – between Psammeticus' visit to Palestine and Zedekiah's revolt against Nebuchadrezzar (and, consequently, Ezekiel's condemnations of Zedekiah) has long been noted. The very presence of Psammeticus in Babylonian territory was tantamount to revolt against Babylon.[15] Greenberg (1983: 10) and others associate Psammeticus' presence with Ezekiel's temple vision in chs. 8–11 (both of which he dates to 592), but the connection is uncertain. In order for Psammeticus' tour to coincide with or precede the vision, which is dated to September, 592, one must assume that the royal entourage set out from Egypt almost immediately upon arriving home from the Nubian campaign earlier that same year. The timing is not impossible, but it is tight. A greater problem is raised by the apparent lack of references to Egypt in the very vision Greenberg correlates to Psammeticus' arrival in Palestine. While occasional details of the vision, such as the animal pictures outlined in red, have been taken to suggest Egyptian inscriptions, the abominations Ezekiel condemns seem to be overwhelmingly drawn either from Mesopotamian or Canaanite ritual. But whereas the temple vision seems unconcerned with illicit dealings with Egypt, beginning in ch. 16 the lure of Egypt, and Zedekiah's broken covenant begin to dominate Ezekiel's prophecy. In 16.59 YHWH first claims that Judah has broken his covenant, and the allegory of the two great eagles in ch. 17 is entirely taken up with condemnation of Zedekiah's unholy alliance with Egypt.[16] Ezekiel's oracle delivered to the elders in ch. 20, dated to August, 591, continues to express YHWH's anger over Judah's

---

15. As Greenberg put it (1983: 10), 'even a nonmilitary assertion of the Egyptian royal presence in territory claimed by Babylonia to be within its orbit was calculated to promote anti-Babylonian forces in Palestine and Phoenicia'.

16.   The fact that the vine in 17.7 stretches out toward the second eagle has often been read as suggesting that Zedekiah sent a delegation to Psammeticus. While such recourse to Egypt is undocumented, it is significant that, according to the Letter of Aristeas, Judeans 'had been

unwillingness to let go of 'the idols of Egypt', and the oracle in ch. 23 against Oholah and Oholibah asserts that a continued longing for Egypt is at the root of Judah's 'whoredom'.[17] Ezekiel's most direct condemnations of Judean dependence on Egypt begin in precisely the period when Psammeticus was 'on tour' in Palestine.

How then, does the visit of Psammeticus II, along with the continued presence of the unfortunate Pediese, contribute to the question of strangers in the temple in Ezek. 44.7? Clearly, the Egyptians qualify as בני נכר, and their presence during the sacrificial offerings would, in light of the treaty violation implied, constitute a breaking of YHWH's covenant. Of all possible foreigners, it is the Egyptians who might best be said, by their very presence, to violate YHWH's covenant. But *were* the Egyptians present in the temple during Psammeticus' visit, or, as 44.8 charges, posted as guards there? Here we come to the limits of what can be argued with certainty. Were visiting monarchs generally allowed unusual access to the temple precincts? We simply do not know. We *do* know that Psammeticus was accompanied on his visit by priests of the gods of Egypt, and that these had brought along cultic paraphernalia (the bouquets of the gods) as well as guards to protect the sacred objects. Presumably, the priests performed some liturgical functions as part of the official visit of state. And, remarkably, judging from the experience of Pediese, at least some priests (with their accompanying servants and guards) were left behind as part of an official delegation after the pharaoh's departure. Were these Egyptian priests and their guards ever present during offerings made to YHWH? Were they or their guards ever stationed in a way that could be understood as being 'in charge' of temple sancta? The questions takes us beyond the realm of what is known about diplomatic practice in the ancient Near East generally, or about Psammeticus' voyage in particular. Certainly, if Ezekiel's vision of 8–11 is accurate, the leaders in Jerusalem had no compunctions about syncretistic or non-Yahwistic rites taking place in the temple! Still, the question of whether these foreigners, directly engaged in breaking Zedekiah's covenant with Nebuchadrezzar ('my covenant' cited

---

sent to Egypt to help Psammetichus in his campaign against the king of the Ethiopians' (Charlesworth 1985: 13). Assuming that the letter refers to Psammeticus II, we here see Judah in a military alliance with Egypt already in 593 BCE.

17. Ezekiel in 23.36–42 also accuses Oholah and Oholibah of defiling YHWH's sanctuary, with the explanation, 'This is what they did in my house: They sent for men to come from far away, to whom a messenger was sent, and they came'. YHWH's adulterous wives then entertain the foreign men with 'my incense and my oil'. The connection between this accusation of foreigners, invited into the temple, which they then defile, and the accusation in 44.7–9, is tantalizing. While the allusion in ch. 23 is too vague to serve as evidence for identifying the strangers of ch. 44, the combination of the two passages argues strongly that Ezekiel has a specific, recent violation in mind in both cases. For a more detailed discussion of 23.36–42, see Galambush (1992: 72–78, 117–123).

in 17.19), who left priests and cult objects behind after their diplomatic visit, were the foreigners whose presence Ezekiel condemns in 44.7–9 (and cf. 23.36–42), cannot be answered with certainty.

The evidence offered by the story of Pediese the priest is suggestive, rather than conclusive. Evidence internal to Ezekiel would lead us to expect that the covenant violated in 44.7 is the same covenant referred to elsewhere in the book of Ezekiel – the vassal treaty between Zedekiah and Nebuchadrezzar. Psammeticus was present in Palestine and instrumental in Zedekiah's breaking of the covenant. Was he, or were his representatives, ever present in the temple? The story of Pediese contributes only the tantalizing detail that Egyptian priests were included in Psammeticus' entourage, and that they continued to serve in some official capacity in Palestine even after the pharaoh's return. The possibility that in 44.7–9 Ezekiel is referring to a specific offense that occurred during his lifetime has much to recommend it, since the passage would then be consistent with the prophet's intense engagement with the events of his day. Egyptians, arriving in conjunction with Psammeticus' 592 tour of the Levant, are the strongest candidates available to fit the role of the strangers in YHWH's temple.

BIBLIOGRAPHY

Abba, R.
  1978   'Priests and Levites in Ezekiel', *VT* 28: 1–9.
Allen, L.
  1990   *Ezekiel 20–48* (Word Biblical Commentary, 29; Dallas: Word Books).
Block, D. I.
  1998   *The Book of Ezekiel: Chapters 25–48* (NICOT; Grand Rapids: Eerdmans).
Charlesworth. J. (ed.)
  1985   *The Old Testament Pseudepigrapha*, II (New York: Doubleday).
Cook, S.
  1995   'Innerbiblical Interpretation in Ezekiel 44 and the History of Israel's Priesthood', *JBL* 114: 193–208.
Driver, G.
  1954   'Ezekiel: Linguistic and Textual Problems', *Bib* 35: 145–59, 299–312.
Duke, R.
  1988   'Punishment or Restoration?: Another Look at the Levites of Ezekiel 44:6–16', *JSOT* 40: 61–81.
Fishbane, M.
  1985   *Biblical Interpretation in Ancient Israel* (Oxford: Oxford University Press).
Galambush, J.
  1992   *Jerusalem in the Book of Ezekiel: The City as Yahweh's Wife* (SBLDiss, 130; Atlanta: Scholars Press).

Gese, H.
1957   *Der Verfassungsentwurf des Ezechiel (Kap. 40–48) traditions-geschichtlichen Untersucht* (Beiträge zur historischen Theologie, 25; Tübingen: J. C. B. Mohr).

Greenberg, M.
1983   *Ezekiel, 1–20* (AB, 22; New York: Doubleday).

1984   'The Design and Themes of Ezekiel's Program of Restoration', *Int* 38: 181–208.

Griffith, F. (ed.)
1972 [1909]   *Catalogue of the Demotic Papyri in the John Rylands Library*, III (Hildesheim: G. Olms).

Gunneweg, A.
1965   *Leviten und Priester* (Forschungen zur Religion und Literatur des Alten und Neuen Testaments, 89; Göttingen: Vandenhoeck und Ruprecht).

König, E.
1901   'The Priests and Levites in Ezekiel xliv.7–15', *ExpTim* 12: 300–303.

Levenson, J.
1976   *Theology of the Program of Restoration of Ezekiel 40–48* (Harvard Semitic Monographs, 10; Missoula, MT: Scholars Press).

McConville, J.
1983   'Priests and Levites in Ezekiel: A Crux in the Interpretation of Israel's History', *Tyn Bull* 34: 3–31.

Milgrom, J.
1983   *Studies in Cultic and Levitical Terminology*, I (SJLA, 36; Leiden: Brill).

Redford, D. B.
1992   *Egypt, Canaan, and Israel in Ancient Times* (Princeton: Princeton University Press).

Redford, D. B, and K. S. Freedy
1970   'The Dates in Ezekiel in Relation to Biblical, Babylonian, and Egyptian Sources', *JAOS* 90: 462–85.

Sasson, J.
1966   'Circumcision in the Ancient Near East', *JBL* 85: 473–76.

Spalinger, A.
1978   'The Concept of the Monarchy during the Saite Epoch – an Essay of Synthesis', *Or* 47: 12–36.

Steiner, R.
1999   'Incomplete Circumcision in Egypt and Edom: Jeremiah (9:24–25) in the Light of Josephus and Jonckheere', *JBL* 118: 497–526.

Yoyotte, J.
1951   'Sur Le Voyage Asiatique de Psammetique II', *VT* 1: 140–144.

Wellhausen, J.
1994 [1885]   *Prolegomena to the History of Israel* (Atlanta: Scholars Press).

Zimmerli, W.
1979, 1983 [1969]   *Ezekiel* (Hermeneia; Philadelphia: Fortress Press).

A Priest Is without Honor in his Own Prophet: Priests and Other Religious Specialists in the Latter Prophets

Lester L. Grabbe

The biblical prophets are real curmudgeons. It seems as if there is not very much – nor very many people – they like. They appeared to cock a snook at just about everything in society. If they condemned a particular group or profession, this should occasion no surprise since they condemned most groups and professions at one time or other. In the past two centuries many scholars have found significance in the fact that priests are condemned in a number of passages in the prophetic books. Yet such passages raise a variety of issues. Priests are hardly the only ones condemned by the prophets: indeed, prophets are especially good at condemning other prophets. What we need to do is consider the full range of prophetic pronouncements and prophet messages about particular groups in order to understand better their concerns and the social context in which they carried out their calling.

This article is in two parts. The first deals with individual texts in the Latter Prophets about priests, and also about other religious specialists especially as they are associated with priests. The second part then engages with these texts and other data to ask broader questions about the priestly *gestalt* and the situation of priests in society.

Texts

This section focuses on the more important texts in the Latter Prophets. It does not attempt to cite every passage where the word 'priest' occurs, especially those where the word is part of a list of members of society or of society leadership. Brief note is also taken of references to prophets and other religious specialists, though this will hardly be a thorough survey (for a more complete survey, see Grabbe 1995).

Hosea

Among the many references to priests and the cult in Hosea, in no case is the reference clearly positive, but the place of priests in society is recognized (e.g. 5.1–2). Priests and the royal house are called on to take responsibility for the right conduct of the nation (5.1–2). The priests are like murdering bandits because they have carried out depravity (6.9). In what is a rather difficult passage, Hos. 4 condemns both Judah and Israel for their sins. The first few verses (4.1–3) address the 'people of Israel' and detail their sins. Then at v. 4 the focus shifts to the priests. The priests will stumble both by day and night, along with the prophets, because they have withheld knowledge from the people and have forgotten God's law (תורה). The people are destroyed for lack of knowledge.

A number of passages seem to criticize the cult, but the exact connotation of this criticism is disputed (cf. 5.6; 6.6; 8.11, 13, 14; 10.1–2, 8; 14.3). Some commentaries, especially but not entirely older ones (Mays 1969; Wolff 1974; Andersen and Freedman 1980), take the view that Hosea is opposed to the cult *tout court*; a number of commentators take the view, however, that the criticism is of a 'baalized' cult (Emmerson 1984: 120–45). But are the references to 'Baal' (2.10, 15, 18–19; 11.2) anything more than just a way of condemning what the writer does not like? One passage (13.1) seems to refer not to the god as such but to the events at Baal-peor (cf. 9.10; Num. 25.1–3). If the cult of Baal was still alive by Hosea's time, it may well have been in decline. References to the cult of Baal rapidly diminish after the days of Jehu (2 Kgs 10). What is clearly criticized is the worship at Bethel (cf. 4.15; 8.5; 10.5, 8, 15; 13.1–2). Both the people and priests mourn over the 'calf' (ironic reference to the bull which represented YHWH) of Beth-aven, which in turn is probably a deliberate twisting of the name Bethel (10.5). The word here for priests is *kĕmārîm*, a term usually explained as a term for priests of other nations, which suggests that the Bethel priests are being lumped in with the pagan priests of foreign cults. Uehlinger (1995: 77–79) argues, however, that the term is not just a generic one for priests outside Jerusalem, but a specific class of priests functioning exclusively for astral deities.

Of particular interest is Hos. 3.4 which states that Israel will go a long time without king, officials, sacrifice, pillar, ephod, and teraphim. All but the pillar and teraphim are approved institutions, in the view of most OT texts. Does this passage show a situation in which teraphim were *also* generally accepted as legitimate, perhaps even by Hosea himself? Sacrifices, pillars, the ephod, and the teraphim were especially associated with priests and the cult. The mention of the ephod is noteworthy. The ephod was a priestly instrument of divination (cf. 1 Sam. 23.9–12; 30.7–8). Hosea 4.12 may also refer to divination, though the exact meaning is disputed. A general statement is made that the prophets and the men of the spirit (איש הרוח) are mad (9.7–9). On the other hand, God spoke through prophets in olden days, apparently during the period in the wilderness, when he gave them visions (חזון) and spoke in parables through them (12.10–11 [Eng. 12.9–10]). Verse 14 (Eng. v. 13) suggests the reference is to Moses as a prophet.

Amos

The only priests referred to in Amos are those relating to the cult site of Bethel, specifically the episode described in 7.10–17. The Bethel (high?) priest Amaziah first sends a message to King Jeroboam (II) that Amos is conspiring against the king by saying that he would be slain and Israel exiled (7.10–11). He then confronts Amos directly, addressing him as a 'seer' (חוזה) and telling him to cease prophesying at Bethel but to go back and prophesy (nif. נבא) in Judah for a living. Amos responds by one of the most enigmatic statements in the prophetic corpus: אנכי ולא בן נביא אנכי לא־נביא (7.14). Several hundredweight of scholarly discussions have arisen out of this one verse but without any clear consensus of what it means (see the discussion in Paul 1991: 244–47). In any case, Amaziah's point seems to be that Amos is a professional prophet who earns his living by prophesying, which Amos denies (7.12–15).

Amos then prophesies that Amaziah's wife would be ravaged, his children slain, and he himself exiled to die in a foreign land (7.16–17). Nothing further is said about Amaziah or whether he in fact suffered this appalling fate. Apart from his opposition to Amos (with whom the text obviously sides), there is nothing unusual about Amaziah. He is a family man, conscientiously carries out his duties at a royal shrine by passing relevant information to his patron the king, and maintains the sanctity and tranquillity of the temple by trying to drive away one whom he regards as a troublemaker and fraud.

Amos has several visions which are interpreted by YHWH (7.1–2; 8.1–3; 9.1). Several favorable statements are made about prophets. When God raised up prophets and Nazarites, the people made the Nazarites drink wine and told the prophets not to prophesy (2.11–12). YHWH will do nothing without revealing it to his servants the prophets; God has spoken: who can but prophesy? (3.7–8).

Micah

Two points of interest arise from this book. One concerns a possible dialogue between Micah and his opponents (ch. 2). The other is the diatribe against 'the prophets' (3.5–8). Although there does seem to be a dialogue in ch. 2, it is not clear that the opponents are meant to be prophets (van der Woude's 'pseudoprophets' [van der Woude 1969]); they could simply be those who refuse Micah's message (vv. 6–7). In 3.5–8 the prophets, along with the seers (חזים) and diviners (קסמים), are condemned for leading the people astray. How they do this is not clear since the passage states that their efforts are ineffectual. However, the prophets are not alone in being criticized: much of the chapter is a denunciation of the rulers and leaders in Israel (vv. 1–4, 9–12); note especially v. 11: 'Her rulers judge for a bribe, her priests teach [or give Torah] for profit, and her prophets divine for silver.' This seems to be a general condemnation of the leaders and authorities of society and includes the civil, community, judicial, and religious leaders, among whom the prophets are also numbered (cf. Carroll 1992).

Zephaniah

Already in 1.4, the statement is made that YHWH will wipe out, in Judah and Jerusalem, every vestige of Baal and the name of the כמרים along with the priests. If taken literally, this suggests that even in the final decades of the kingdom of Judah, Baal worship was still extant (if Zephaniah is to be dated about the time of Josiah, as is frequently assumed). It is unlikely, however, that Baal worship was a major endeavor at this point in Judah's history. All indications are that Baal worship was a thing of the past in Palestine by this time, though it was normative in Phoenicia (cf. Sweeney 2003: 67–68). Another passage states that the prophets are reckless, while the priests profane what is holy and do violence against the Torah (3.4).

Jeremiah

In the book of Jeremiah, priests are often coupled with prophets, as spiritual leaders, though this is frequently to condemn both for corruption, pandering, greed, and the like (5.31; 6.13–14; 8.10–11; 14.18; 18.22). Yet Jeremiah himself is not only a prophet but also of a priestly family centered in Anathoth (1.1). Although he is not said to have served as a priest at the altar, many of his activities take place in or around the temple. He is able to give a message to the Rechabites in a chamber in the temple (35.2–4), and Baruch the scribe reads Jeremiah's words in the temple chamber of Gemariah son of Shaphan the scribe (36.10). He is once told to perform a sign before the priests and elders (19.1), to preach to worshipers coming to the temple (26.2), and at another time is ordered to be flogged by Pashhur the priest and temple overseer (20.1–2). A letter from Babylon calls on Zephaniah the (high?) priest to control Jeremiah (29.24–27). The message of the text is that the priesthood and temple are very important to Jeremiah, that he carries on many of his activities around the temple, and that some priests oppose him but others are his supporters (see further Long 1982: 42–49).

Jeremiah 23.33–40 is a passage about asking messages from YHWH, making a wordplay on Hebrew משׂא which can mean 'burden' in the sense of 'oracle' and 'burden' in the sense of something weighty or difficult to be carried. The passage speaks of 'this people' who ask about 'the burden of

YHWH', but then goes on to say, 'or priest or prophet'. The basic point seems to be that the ordinary Judeans or their spiritual leadership – priest or prophet – might ask about an oracle from YHWH. But the suggestion is also that a priest or prophet might claim to have received such an oracle (explicit in the case of prophets but also implicit with regard to priests).

Several passages speak disparagingly of divination (14.14; 27.9–10; 29.8–9), lumping it together with false prophecy. However, one reference is quite interesting: the king sends two individuals (one of them Zephaniah the priest) to inquire (דרש) of YHWH (21.1–2). 'To inquire' is the language of divination. The book of Jeremiah also seems to condemn those who receive messages from dreams (23.25–32; 29.8–9), but this interpretation is problematic (on dreams, see Grabbe 1995: 145–48).

This book has much to say about prophets. They are often mentioned together with the king and/or other leaders, priests, and the people as a way of representing the totality of society (2.8; 4.9; 8.1–2; 13.13; 29.1; 32.27–35; 34.19). Prophets and priests are also referred to together, usually to condemn them (5.31; 6.13–14; 14.18; 29.1), indicating that both had important leadership roles in society. Much of what is said about prophets is negative, including major oracles against them (23.9–40): The prophets of Samaria prophesy by Baal (23.13), but the prophets of Jerusalem practice adultery and other wickedness and lead the people astray (vv. 14–15). They speak a vision of their own hearts (חזון לבם ידברו) rather than having stood in YHWH's council (vv. 16–18, 21–22). The word of YHWH comes to Jeremiah in visions (1.11–13; 31.26). Just as he accuses others of being false prophets, Jeremiah himself is similarly accused (17.14–18; 26.7–8; 28; 29.27–28).

Ezekiel

Ezekiel is himself a priest (3.1), although his main function is as a prophet. Several important references are found in the temple vision of 40–48. Priests are divided into two categories. Only one group serves at the altar; these are the descendants of Zadok (40.45–46). They are referred to as Levitical priests (הכהנים הלוים) from the seed of Zadok (43.19). The reason for this distinction is that the Levites as a whole followed Israel when it went astray and were punished by being allowed to do only menial duties in the temple (44.10–14). They are to be watchmen and in charge of the gates, to slaughter the sacrifices for the people and serve them (cf. 46.21–24), but they are not to have anything to do with the actual offerings. They are also to have different areas of settlement from the priests (45.3–5).

The Levitical priests descended from Zadok are the only ones to offer the fat and blood on the altar and to go into the temple itself (44.15–31). They are to wear special linen priestly garments, not to shave their heads,

not to drink wine when going into the inner court, and to marry only
Israelite virgins or widows of priests. In addition to service at the altar,
they are to pronounce on sacred and profane and on clean and unclean.
They are to act as judges in lawsuits. They are to preserve the teachings
(תורות) and laws relating to holy convocations and to preserve the sanctity
of the Sabbath. Because they have no inheritence, they are to receive
portions of sacrifices and the firstfruits and sacred gifts. They have special
chambers in the temple where these offerings are prepared and eaten
(42.13; 46.19–20).

The book of Ezekiel has a number of passages of relevance for the
question of divination. The prophet's reception of divine messages is
described in more detail in Ezekiel than in many other books. He has
visions and is seized by YHWH's spirit. In a number of passages, the elders
come to 'inquire' (דרש) of YHWH through him (14.1–4; 20.1–3). YHWH
predicts that there will no longer be false vision or 'smooth divination'
(חלק מקסם) in Israel (12.21–24). Ezekiel's reactions to God's inspiration are
graphically described by such phrases as 'the hand of YHWH was upon
him' (3.14, 22; 8.1), the spirit seizes him and carries him away (3.12), and
he prophesies when the spirit falls on him (11.4–5). Ezekiel himself
experiences a number of visions, including being taken to Jerusalem in a
vision (מראה) after the hand of YHWH fell on him (8.1–3; 11.24). Of
particular interest is the use of the the term 'vision' (חזון) for revelations
which are usually classified as auditions. For example, the 'word of YHWH'
comes in a vision (7.13). When the hand of YHWH comes on him and
YHWH tells him to go out into the valley where he sees God's presence
(3.22–23), this is later referred to as a 'vision' (8.4). Ezekiel castigates those
who say the vision will fail, because it is about to be fulfilled (12.21–28).

These references to visions and the language of divination are interesting
in the light of Ezekiel's own polemic against the 'false prophets' in ch. 13.
They are said to prophesy out of their own hearts without having seen
anything (vv. 2–3: לבלתי ראו). They see empty or lying visions (v. 7:
מחזה־שוא חזיתם; v. 8: חזיתם כזב; v. 9: החזים שוא). They prophesy (nif. נבא) to
Jerusalem, seeing a vision (החזים חזון) of well-being when there is none (v.
16). This clearly associates prophecy and prophets with visions. They are
said not only to give false prophecies and and false visions but also to utter
'lying divinations' (קסמ/מקסם כזב: vv. 6, 7, 9). Whether divination is being
associated with prophecy as a normal thing, as visions seem to be, is a
matter of debate. The references to divinations might be a gratuitious
slander. On the other hand, it could be recognition that some sorts of
divination were a normal accompaniment of prophecy. Exactly who these
prophets are is not said, though one can assume they are regarded as being
in a different class from Ezekiel. Why these prophets are condemned is also
left vague. They are said to prophesy out of their own hearts or spirits and
have not received a message from YHWH; also they do not provide the

support which Israel needs (vv. 4–5, 10–16). The only specific charge is that they prophesy well-being when there is none (v. 16).

Haggai and Zechariah

These two books are considered together here because they seem to be closely related and are ostensibly associated with the Persian period. A number of references are made to priests. Haggai 2.11–19 seeks a ruling from the priests with regard to a cultic matter. The purpose of this is to introduce a prophecy, but it shows the convention that priests made rulings on such matters.

Of particular importance to both Haggai and Zechariah is the high priest Joshua. He and Zerubbabel the governor are the leaders of the restoration and the ones credited with the responsibility for the rebuilding of the temple. They are the recipients of, or the central actors in, various prophecies and visions. They hear and heed the prophecies of Haggai about rebuilding the temple (Hag. 1.12–13; 2.1–4). Several of Zechariah's visions relate to Joshua, often in conjunction with Zerubbabel or with a messianic figure called the Branch. In Zech. 3 Joshua is cleansed from impurities of the exile, clothed in priestly garments, and given charge over God's house. In a subsequent vision, he is one of two olive trees who represent God's anointed, the other being Zerubbabel who would finish building the temple (ch. 4). Finally, 6.9–15 describes how Zechariah is to take members of the community, make crowns, and place a crown on Joshua's head. One called the Branch would rebuild the temple and sit on a throne to rule; alongside him would also sit a priest. Joshua is obviously intended to be the priestly leader of the community, though the identity of the Branch is debated.

In ch. 7 certain men ask the priests of God's house and the prophets whether to continue to mourn in the fifth month as was their custom, after which the word of YHWH comes to Zechariah to speak to the people and the priests. He says that YHWH had proclaimed a message to earlier prophets (v. 7) to practice justice and not to oppress the widow and orphan (vv. 9–10), but they refused to hear the instruction (התורה) and words which YHWH sent by his spirit (רוח) through the earlier prophets (vv. 11–12). This suggests not only the existence of cultic prophets alongside the priests, but also that Zechariah was himself numbered among them.[1]

In Second Zech. 10.2, teraphim, augurs, and dreamers are all said to be false and lead the people astray. Whether all such modes of inquiry were automatically considered to be wrong by the author or only certain types is

---

1. Pola (2003: 45) argues that Zechariah served as a priest as well as a prophet but denies that he was a cult prophet.

difficult to know. In Second or Third Zech. 13.2–6 YHWH says that he will make the prophets and the unclean spirit pass away from the land. Then those who prophesy (nif. נבא) would be condemned by their own father and mother (v. 3). Each prophet would be ashamed of his vision (חזיון), would cease to wear the hairy mantle characteristic of prophets (cf. 2 Kgs 1.8), and would deny being a prophet (Zech. 13.4–6). This passage takes a rather negative view toward prophets.

Malachi

Malachi 1.6–2.9 is a concerted critique of the priesthood, charging the priests with allowing defective animals to be offered on the altar, thus defiling it. Whereas YHWH's name is honored among the other nations with incense and a pure offering, YHWH's table in Jerusalem is defiled (1.1–14). God made a covenant with Levi who gave proper instructions (תורת אמת), because the lips of a priest guard knowledge (דעת), and instruction (תורה) is sought from them; he is the messenger (מלאך) of YHWH (2.6–7). Unfortunately, the Levites corrupted that covenant and disregarded God's ways (vv. 8–9). Malachi's identity is not given in the book; however, there is a good chance that he was himself a priest. Indeed, this is suggested by the name Malachi ('my messenger') which seems to be evoked by the reference to the priest as God's messenger in 2.7. If so, this passage represents an internal critique of the priesthood by one of its own members.

More difficult to answer is Malachi's view of the organization of the priesthood. Is it a two-tier priesthood? Julia O'Brien has argued that Malachi makes no differentiation between priests and Levites (1990: 47–48, 111–12). Since no clear distinction is made in the few references to priests, Levites, and 'sons of Levi', she may be correct; however, the book is a very short one. Since priests are also 'sons of Levi', even in sources which separate the Aaronites from the rest of the Levites, the writer of Malachi may be using 'Levites' and 'sons of Levi' loosely (cf. Glazier-McDonald 1987). None of the passages seems to be decisive. It would be unusual – and interesting – if a late text like Malachi regarded all Levites as altar priests. J. Schaper (pp. 177–88 below) has now also argued that Malachi knows the distinction between altar priests and Levites, though it does not suit Malachi's purpose to discuss it.

Textual Analysis

The Latter Prophets have some harsh things to say about priests. There are many negative statements about those serving at the altar; however, before we jump to the conclusion (which was once common) that the prophets were anti-priest and anti-cult, we need to consider the nature and context of the negative statements. In order to do that, it would help to consider some of the main themes that arise from the individual texts just looked at.

1. *Priests are included in general condemnation of the nation's leaders.*
A number of passages lump priests together with other professions or office holders who would exercise some sort of leadership role (though the general inhabitants of the land are sometimes also included): king and officials/leaders (Jer. 2.8; 4.9; 8.1; 13.13; 19.1; 32.32; 33.18–22; 34.19; Ezek. 22.26–27; Hos. 5.1–2; Mic. 3.1–4, 9–12), prophets (Jer. 2.8; 4.9; 5.31; 6.13–14; 8.1, 10–11; 13.13; 14.18; 19.1; 23.11; 32.32; Ezek. 13.1–16; 22.25–28; Hos. 4.5; Mic. 3.5–6; Zeph. 3.4).

2. *The priests and the cult are criticized.*
Not only the priests but sometimes even the cult itself seems to be criticized. First, there are some accusations of Baal worship (Hos. 2.10, 15, 18–19; 11.2; Jer. 23.13; Zeph. 1.4), but that is probably all they are – only accusations, since it seems that Baal worship had either ceased or was moribund by the mid-eighth century. No such accusations are made in Amos, for example, which seems strange if they were extant. It seems clear that the main worship at Bethel was Yahwistic, with the bulls a traditional symbol of YHWH. For whatever reason, though, both Hosea and Amos criticize the Bethel place of worship (Hos. 4.15; 5.8; 8.5; 10.5, 8, 15; 13.2; Amos 4.4; 5.5; 7.10–17; cf. Jer. 23.13). Yet Hosea also has a number of passages that have been interpreted as condemning or dismissing all cult practice (cf. 5.6; 6.6; 8.11, 13, 14; 10.1–2, 8; 14.3). Whether this interpretation is correct is not relevant for this point here (though see pp. 79–80 above and 115–33 below): the important issue is that popular and widespread practices are condemned in Hosea.

3. *Priests and the cult are also an accepted part of religious practice.*
Perhaps this point no longer needs to be made in the way it was once required, at a time when some saw the prophets as anti-priest and anti-cult. A number of passages refer positively to the priests or at least seem to take them for granted (Hos. 5.1–2; Joel 1.9, 13; 2.7; Jer. 18.18; 33.18–22; Ezek. 40–48).

4. *Priests are associated with some sorts of 'mantic wisdom'.*
We do not have many statements about the priests and mantic wisdom. The main priestly mantic devices the Urim and Thummim are not referred to in the Prophets; however, the ephod is mentioned in such a way that it might still exist (Hos. 3.4; cf. Jer. 23.33–40). (It is possible that the Urim and Thummim are just another way of referring to the ephod, or *vice*

versa.) The priests thus have a mantic way of inquiring of YHWH (cf. Grabbe 1995: 120–21).

One issue that needs to be considered, however, is the question of cultic prophets who had what was essentially a mantic role. It was common in older works to speak of the office of cultic prophet in the temple, though this topic seems to have been rather muted in more recent discussion. The difficulty is that no such office is described in any extant biblical passage; it is, rather, an inference from a number of hints in a variety of texts (for discussion and references, see Grabbe 1995: 112–13). One of the passages considered here seems to refer to such prophets, among whom Zechariah himself was numbered (Zech. 7.1–7). The indication is that they gradually became assimilated to the Levitical singers and perhaps other groups among the temple clergy.

5. *Division of the priesthood into the altar priests and the lower clergy.*
The priests are generally referred to in an undifferentiated sense simply as 'the priests'. One lengthy passage is an exception to this lack of data: Ezek. 40–48 (specifically 40.46; 43.19; 44.15; 48.11). Here is clearly laid down that the 'the priests the Levites the sons of Zadok' are the only ones to serve at the altar (Ezek. 44.15–16), as opposed to the 'sons of Levi', who are to carry out other tasks in the temple. This is an important passage because it seems to conform to the actual situation in the temple no later than the Persian period, but probably at least as early as the time of Josiah. Another reference in Mal. 2.1–9 is too uncertain to add anything. The suggestion that Malachi continued to believe in an undifferentiated priesthood is possible, but seems unlikely.

6. *Priests as scribes, teachers and interpreters of the law.*
Several passages mention or allude to the priestly activities relating to the written word. The priests are recognized as the ones to give rulings about the Torah and its meaning, as well as all cultic matters (Mic. 3.11; Zeph. 3.4; Ezek. 44.24; Hag. 2.11–13). These laws may have been traditional unwritten laws at one time, but they eventually became written down and incorporated into developing scripture which was in priestly custody.

7. *Priests as political leaders.*
There seems to have been a 'chief priest' or 'high priest' throughout much of the period of the monarchy (cf. Grabbe 1995: 60–62; 2000: 144–45). Although this figure was always under the control of the king – who was regarded as the chief cultic figure – it is not surprising that an office of 'chief priest' existed. Sometimes this individual is involved in the national politics (cf. 2 Kgs 11–12). In the books of Haggai and Zechariah, however, we find a new development. Joshua is not just the head of the priests but

also takes his place alongside the provincial governor Zerubbabel (Hag. 1.1, 14; 2.2). This is probably primarily because of the importance of the temple and cult to the Persian province of Judah, but it may already suggest the shouldering of some civic duties by the high priest. We probably already see the beginning of the path to national office that came to fruition in subsequent centuries (see below).

Socio-Historical Analysis

So far, so commonplace: this survey has not turned up any major surprises. I now want to ask some socio-historical questions, and to do so will mean going further afield than just the Latter Prophets, though these remain our focus. The prophetic books give an interesting perspective because they cover such a lengthy historical period and such a wide range of views. As we have just seen in the textual analysis, there is no single point of view in the Prophets, but the various attitudes may give some clues to historical developments: they may be diachronic as well as synchronic.

The first thing we need to be aware of is our point of view from the twenty-first century. It was once common to read the Bible with a particular religious prejudice taken in part from the Bible itself, and I am not sure much has changed. We need to be careful how we handle this issue. Too often in the past, scholars have approached the question with the same bias as the biblical writers. Centuries of scholars have been content to follow the biblical bias and refer to 'pagan' worship. Of course, it was once the custom to attach the term 'pagan' to any non-Christian religion. Few Christians today would use the term anymore for Judaism or Islam, yet the attitude that there are 'false' forms of religion still persists. Recent study of the development of Israelite religion makes very problematic the use of such derogatory terms as 'pagan worship', 'Baal worship', 'Canaanite religion', 'fertility cult', and even 'sacral prostitution'. It has now been well established that YHWH was probably once a storm god with many characteristics in common with Baal, that YHWH has absorbed the identity and character of several other deities, that YHWH once had a consort, that Israelite religion originated only as a type of Canaanite religion, and that some of the features most important to moderns (such as monotheism) developed only at a late state in Israelite and Judean religion (see the discussion and bibliography in Grabbe 2000: 210–15, to which should be added Zevit 2001). This includes those priests who are designated as כמרים (Hos. 10.5; cf. Uehlinger 1995: 77–79, who argues that they are specialized priests of astral deities).

What does seem questionable is whether a Baal cult was a major feature of Israelite religion by Hosea's time in the mid-eighth century BCE. The picture in the present book of Hosea – without worrying about redactional questions – is fairly anti-cultic. There are some references to Baal worship, but it is difficult to know how seriously to take them. Hosea 11.2 speaks of worshiping בעלים, which is a strange term for the traditional storm god who is not known to have said, 'My name is Legion, for we are many' – at least, in any of the texts I am aware of. Most of Hosea's more specific references seem to be to the bull cult at Bethel (4.15; 5.8; 10.5, 8, 15; 13.2; cf. Amos 4.4; 5.5), and this was a cult of YHWH. It has been argued that Hosea is anti-cultic as such (see above, p. 80). I personally would be surprised if he is. We do eventually find those who deny the need for physical temples in later Judaism and early Christianity, such as the *4th Sibylline Oracle* or Acts 7, but this is unusual and many centuries after Hosea. Although what Hosea does not like is clear, it is not so easy to say exactly what sort of worship he might have approved of.

Similarly, in Amos we find evidence of another prophetic critique of the cult at Bethel, including a confrontation between Amos and Amaziah the (high?) priest of Bethel. Even recent commentaries on Amos are happy to take a partisan point of view and picture the Bethel cult site in negative terms. That this should be the case in a scholarly context should astonish us, but it doesn't for some reason. The really puzzling thing about this criticism is that Bethel seems to have been the center for the Aaronite priests. This is not a new idea, but several recent studies have emphasized this point – the most thorough treatment being that of J. Schaper (2000: 167–68). There is little evidence that the Jerusalem priesthood was seen as Aaronite in the pre-exilic period (Schaper 2000: 269–79; Grabbe 2003: 207–8).

The prophetic critique of priests and the cult is often quoted, usually with approval, but this is by no means the whole story. It is hardly surprising that a certain amount of professional rivalry would be found between priests, prophets, diviners, and other religious specialists. Each group regarded itself as having a unique means of access to the divine. The priests usually held their office by heredity; prophets felt they had a unique calling from God; diviners would also have seen their skills as God-given; and the wise would have felt they had special insights gained by long dedication to study and wisdom. This seems to be summarized in the statement, 'For Torah will not perish from the priest nor counsel from the wise nor a word from the prophet' (Jer. 18.18; cf. Ezek. 7.26).

What we need to realize is that what might seem to be separate roles or offices in theory are sometimes rather entangled in real life (cf. Grabbe 1995: 220–21). Priests may receive a prophetic call. Prophecy is really a form of spirit divination, at least for most purposes. An important category of wisdom is mantic wisdom, which is or has affinities with divination and prophecy. Certain forms of divination are associated with the priesthood, namely the Urim and Thummim and/or the ephod. Even if one wishes to keep the roles apart, the same individual may practice or fulfill more than one such role. Whatever ideal types one might construct in theory, real life is much more complicated.

At least two biblical prophets were themselves priests, though we have no evidence that either actually carried out priestly duties. One of these was Jeremiah. The interesting thing about Jeremiah is that he seems to have used the temple as the base for attacking the establishment, including the priests. It is hardly surprising that we read that Shemaiah wrote to the high priest from the Babylonian captivity to take Jeremiah in hand. We are normally encouraged to see the incident from Jeremiah's point of view, but we should be willing to see it the other way round: how did the priests in question look at the prophet? We get a hint of how Amaziah, the priest of Bethel, viewed Amos because we are told something of what he reported to King Jeroboam. Amaziah and perhaps even Zephaniah would have raised a cry of, 'Who will rid me of this turbulent prophet?' They would no doubt have had a point. Why must we always side with the prophet?

As already suggested above, some important clues to the development of the Jerusalem priesthood are found in the Prophets. Perhaps one of the most important of these occurs in Ezek. 40–48. A clear distinction is made between the 'sons of Zadok' who are allowed to preside at the altar and 'the Levites' who have other duties in the temple. The content of the passage suggests that this is a fairly recent situation since a point is made as to why the Levites are not allowed to be altar priests: it was because of a grave sin (Ezek. 44.10–14). An explanation would hardly be needed if the division between altar priests and lower clergy was a long and accepted hereditary ranking. The explanation that it has to do with country Levites who expected to be given a place in an undifferentiated priesthood at the time of Josiah's reform or perhaps earlier is not found anywhere in the Prophetic literature.

The term 'sons of Levi' is also used in the book of Malachi which was probably written rather later than Haggai and Zechariah. Malachi gives a critique of the priests but also speaks of the 'covenant with Levi' (2.4). Does this mean that there is no differentiation between priests in the writer's mind? To think so is intriguing, but it is unlikely that at this late stage there was any serious thought that the Levites might become full altar priests. Considering that there are several hints within the book that 'Malachi' is himself a priest, what we most likely have here is a a critique of the priesthood from the inside.

The divine oracles of the Urim and Thummim belong to the priests (Exod. 28.30; Lev. 8.8; Num. 27.21; Deut. 33.8). These are not mentioned in the Prophets, but one statement associates the priesthood with the ephod (Hos. 3.4). We know from some passages (such as 1 Sam. 23.6–12; 30.7–8) that the ephod also had a divinatory function. (Whether the ephod and Urim/Thummim are simply two different ways of describing priestly divinatory devices is a question, though no passage formally equates them.) In any case, at some point these oracles seem to have ceased being used. The lack of the Urim and Thummim is specifically commented on in Ezra 2.63 and Neh. 7.65, but nothing is said about what happened to the ephod. Perhaps it was lost in the destruction of the temple. Hosea 3.4 may be an attempt to explain something whose loss was already known and needed an explanation.

The next role of the priests to be considered is that of scribe and teacher. Although this is often mentioned in passing, its significance is usually overlooked. Scribal activity was not, of course, limited to priests. Yet a number of passages suggest that the scribal profession included a strong contingent of clergy, including Levites (see the survey in Grabbe 1995: especially chapter 6). For example, the books of Chronicles emphasize the judging and teaching functions of the priests. 2 Chronicles 15.3 states that during the reign of Asa, Israel had gone many days without the true God and without a priest to teach (מורה) and without teaching (תורה). According to 2 Chron. 19.5–11, Jehoshaphat appointed Levites and priests among the judges in Judah. The high priest Amariah was to be in overall charge of judgments relating to God, with the Levite officers to assist (2 Chron. 19.11; cf. 1 Chron. 23.4). Levites also filled the office of scribe (2 Chron. 34.13; cf. 1 Chron. 26.29). A Levitical scribe had the responsibility of registering the priests when David organized the temple personnel (1 Chron. 24.6). Among the various temple offices held by Levites during the repair of the temple under Josiah was that of scribe (2 Chron. 34.13). In the context of reciting Caleb's genealogy, 1 Chron. 2.55 mentions the 'families of scribes that lived at Jabez'. Like much in Chronicles, this may well reflect the situation in the Persian period but, regardless, it does seem to suggest a hereditary occupation.

Two basic points are that (a) the priesthood as a whole had custody of the Torah and performed many judgment functions, (b) the priesthood was a group who had the opportunity for education and the leisure for intellectual pursuits. It is often assumed that priests had no concerns beyond the cultic. On the contrary, with a secure income and plenty of spare time when not serving directly in the temple, they were the ideal group to be concerned with preserving the tradition and composing theological and other works. The temple had need of scribal skills, and it was likely to be priests or Levites who were taught these rather than laymen. The analogy from other Near Eastern peoples is that literary activity was highest in the context of the temple and priesthood.

This may also be tied up with the reason for the decline in the use of the divine lots of the Urim/Thummim and/or the ephod. What we find over time is a shift to the use of the written Torah as a source for ascertaining the divine will – even as an oracular source. Priestly divination did not cease; it only changed mode. This is especially attested toward the end of the Second Temple period in the claim of Josephus that prophecy and prediction of the future is associated with the interpretation of scripture. The Essenes have those who foretell the future because they are educated (ἐμπαιδοτριβούμενοι) in the holy books and the sayings (ἀποφθέγμασιν) of the prophets from an early age (*War* 2.8.12 §159). Josephus himself is able to foretell the future, which in some way is associated with the written prophecies (*War* 3.8.3 §§351–53):

> ...suddenly there came back into his [Josephus's] mind those nightly dreams, in which God had foretold to him the impending fate of the Jews and the destinies of the Roman sovereigns. He was an interpreter of dreams and skilled in divining the meaning of ambiguous utterances of the Deity; a priest himself and of priestly descent, he was not ignorant of the prophecies in the sacred books. At that hour he was inspired to read their meaning, and, recalling the dreadful images of his recent dreams, he offered up a silent prayer to God.

Josephus notes particularly that John Hyrcanus had the gift of prophecy (*War* 1.2.8 §§68–69; *Ant.* 13.10.7 §299). He also refers to the use of the ephod by the high priests to determine the future as prophecy or prophesying (*Ant.* 6.6.3 §115; 6.12.4–5 §§254, 257; 6.5.6 §359; 7.4.1 §76).

This view is paralled in the *pĕšārîm* and related literature at Qumran. Scripture – or at least some passages in Scripture – is assumed to contain God's messages for the future in coded form. One of the best known and best attested examples is the *Habakkuk Pesher* (1QpHab), particularly the statement that the prophet Habakkuk himself did not know the meaning of his prophecy but only the Teacher of Righteousness to whom it was revealed at the endtime (2.5–10; 7.1–9). Here we have a coming together of the priesthood and priestly knowledge, together with prophecy and mantic wisdom.

The final role of the priests is one known but often forgotten in the context of discussing priestly roles: the priests as civil leaders. This is a role already well advanced in the books of Haggai and Zechariah where Joshua the high priest is bracketed with Zerubbabel the provincial governor. The term 'diarchy' has been used of this joint government and, despite some recent criticisms, is still an appropriate one.[2] According to Zech. 3.1–5, however, Joshua has to be cleansed of his 'filthy garments' and his guilt. Why is this? Various explanations have been given, one of the recent ones being that Zechariah is responding to criticism of the Zadokites by the Levites or other priestly groups (Schaper 2000: 178–84). This is one possibility, but only one. The passage is not very specific. There are passages that suggest those who returned from exile were ritually unclean (Amos 7.17; Ezek. 4.13). The passage could be no more than a means of

---

2.   Challenges to this designation have come from Rose (2000: 251) and Rooke (2000).

resolving what might seem to us a trivial problem but was by no means trivial for the the temple-based religion of the Jewish community. The high priest was ritually impure, but how could he be rendered pure to initiate the renewed cult if a functioning cult was needed to purify the unclean high priest? The passage could be resolving a theological problem rather than a political one. In the books of Haggai and Zechariah Joshua's duties still seem to involve mainly those relating to the temple and cult, but since these were central to the province of Judah – which was in many ways a 'temple state'[3] – the duties of the high priest were already starting to overlap with those of civil leader. This seems to have progressed during the Persian period, with the possibility that the high priest was sometimes also the governor of the province.[4]

We know from sources other than the Latter Prophets how the priesthood went on to develop. Better documented than the Persian period is the Hellenistic. Although a recent study has argued against the civic powers of the high priest, it seems to me that this argument is achieved only by a rather one-sided reading of the sources.[5] The eventual culmination was high priest as king of the nation under Hasmonean rule. The most information we have is on the office of high priest; however, there are indications that at least a section of the priesthood functioned as a sort of aristocractic leadership (as well as priestly support group). Reference is sometimes made to the 'Sanhedrin' or governing council. We have to be careful how we describe such a group, since the term is often used either of a rabbinic body that never existed or perhaps to a body ascribed powers of control that it seldom or never had. Yet we must recognize that the sources support the existence of some sort of advisory body to the high priest which may have varied in its powers over time, depending on the character and position of the current high priest.[6] Priests were an important constituent of this body.

3. See the discussion of this question in Grabbe 2004, ch. 8.
4. Some coins have the inscription 'Hezekiah the governor'; this individual has been widely identified with Ezekias the high priest known from Josephus, *Ag. Apion* 1.187–89. The data are too skimpy to be certain, but it must be accepted as a possibility. For a further discussion, see Grabbe 2004, ch. 3.
5. Rooke (2000).
6. See the criticisms of the concept in Goodblatt (1994), who does a good job of demolishing the theory of a rabbinic council during the Second Temple period. On the other hand, his attempt to deny the existence of any sort of body is unsuccessful, as I point out (Grabbe forthcoming).

Conclusions

The references to the priesthood in the Latter Prophets was never likely to give us a full picture of either the priesthood itself or attitudes toward it. Surprisingly, though, the individual writings show a wide variety of approach and attitude toward the priesthood. We find criticism and condemnation, but we also find support and approval. The polemic against the non-Jerusalem priestly establishments gives an important insight into the real religious scene in ancient Israel and Judah, one differing in significant ways from the one that the final editors tried to impose on the text. The long diachronic sequence covered by the Latter Prophets is very useful in trying ascertain the development of religion, cult, worship, and the priests in ancient Israel and Judah.

We also have some glimpse of the way in which priests were involved in mantic wisdom, including divination. This is better attested in sources other than the Latter Prophets, but the overlap between some activities of the priesthood and those of prophecy and mantic wisdom is one of the most intriguing questions to which a full answer is not possible. This is not to be disassociated from the priestly role as preservers and interpreters of the Torah, for the view of the written scripture as oracles from God led at some point to a priestly concern to dig out the hidden meanings there. The scriptures themselves become the containers of mantic wisdom which can be tapped for knowledge about the future with the proper techniques. (This may be one of the reasons why the priestly oracles ceased to be used.) Once again, the full description of this is only isolated and late, but like the periscope rising briefly above the waves, it is an indicator of a large submerged body of mantic speculation and endeavor waiting to be forced to the surface.

The priests were the educated class, having the resources both of freedom from having to work fulltime at their occupations and the opportunity to engage in intellectual pursuits. Writings such as *I Enoch* and the *Book of Giants* might well be the product of temple priests trying to address and resolve theological issues, cosmic problems, or insights into the future. It is not at all certain, of course, but the possibility cannot simply be dismissed. The priests may have been efficient butchers, but they were much more: both the altar priests and the Levites or lower clergy had the same opportunities for education and activity apart from serving in the temple and the sacrificial cult.

We also see in the Latter Prophets the beginnings of a new role for the priests, especially the high priest but not him alone: the duties and opportunities for leadership of the nation in a civic sense. Developments along this line are already indicated in the time of Joshua and Zerubbabel, and other sources show that it eventually led to the short-lived but very significant Hasmonean dynasty of 'priest-kings'. This was the height of priestly power and influence but a situation already presaged in the Latter Prophets.

BIBLIOGRAPHY

Anderson, Francis I., and David Noel Freedman
  1980   *Hosea: A New Translation with Introduction and Commentary* (AB, 24: Garden City, NY: Doubleday).
Auld, A. Graeme
  1984   'Prophets and Prophecy in Jeremiah and Kings', *ZAW* 96: 66–82.
Carroll, Robert P.
  1992   'Night without Vision: Micah and the Prophets', in Florentino García Martínez, *et al.* (eds.), *The Scriptures and the Scrolls: Studies in Honour of A. S. van der Woude on the Occasion of his 65th Birthday* (VTSup, 49; Leiden: Brill): 74–84.
Davies, Graham I.
  1992   *Hosea* (NCB; London: Marshal Pickering; Grand Rapids, MI: Eerdmans).
  1993   *Hosea* (OTG; Sheffield: Sheffield Academic Press).
Emmerson, Grace I.
  1984   *Hosea: An Israelite Prophet in Judean Perspective* (JSOTSup, 28; Sheffield: Sheffield Academic Press).
Glazier-McDonald, B.
  1987   *Malachi: The Divine Messenger* (SBLDS, 98; Atlanta: Scholars).
Goodblatt, David
  1994   *The Monarchic Principle: Studies in Jewish Self-Government in Antiquity* (TSAJ, 38; Tübingen: Mohr[Siebeck]).
Grabbe, Lester L.
  1995   *Priests, Prophets, Diviners, Sages: A Socio-historical Study of Religious Specialists in Ancient Israel* (Valley Forge, PA: Trinity Press International).
  2000   *Judaic Religion in the Second Temple Period: Belief and Practice from the Exile to Yavneh* (London/New York: Routledge).
  2003   'Were the Pre-Maccabean High Priests "Zadokites"?', in J. Cheryl Exum and H. G. M. Williamson (eds.), *Reading from Right to Left: Essays on the Hebrew Bible in Honour of David J. A. Clines* (JSOTSup, 373; Sheffield: Sheffield Academic Press): 205–15.

  2004   *A History of the Jews and Judaism in the Second Temple Period, vol. I; Yehud: A History of the Persian Province of Judah* (London/New York: T & T Clark International).

Forthcoming 'Sanhedrin, Sanhedriyyot, or Mere Invention?' (in preparation).

Long, Burke O.
  1982   'Social Dimensions of Prophetic Conflict', in Robert C. Culley and

Thomas W. Overholt (eds.), *Anthropological Perspectives on Old Testament Prophecy* (*Semeia*, 21; Chico, CA: Society of Biblical Literature): 31–53.

Macintosh, A. A.
1997   *A Critical and Exegetical Commentary on Hosea* (ICC; Edinburgh: T & T Clark).

Mays, J. L.
1969   *Hosea* (OTL; London: SCM).

O'Brien, Julia M.
1990   *Priest and Levite in Malachi* (SBLDS, 121; Atlanta: Scholars).

Paul, Shalom
1991   *Amos* (Hermeneia; Minneapolis: Fortress).

Pola, Thomas
2003   *Das Priestertum bei Sacharja: Historische und traditionsgeschicht-liche Untersuchung zur frühnachexilischen Herrschererwartung* (FAT, 35; Tübingen: Mohr Siebeck).

Rooke, Deborah W.
2000   *Zadoks's Heirs: The Role and Development of the High Priesthood in Ancient Israel* (Oxford Theological Monographs; Oxford University Press).

Rose, Walter H.
2000   *Zemah and Zerubbabel: Messianic Expectations in the Early Postexilic Period* (JSOTSup, 304; Sheffield: Sheffield Academic Press).

Schaper, Joachim
2000   *Priester und Leviten im achämenidischen Juda: Studien zur Kult- und Sozialgeschichte Israels in persischer Zeit* (FAT, 31; Tübingen: Mohr[Siebeck]).

Sweeney, Marvin A.
2003   *Zephaniah: A Commentary* (ed. Paul D. Hanson; Hermeneia; Minneapolis: Fortress Press).

Uehlinger, Christoph
1995   'Gab es eine joschijanische Kultreform? Plädoyer für ein begründetes Minimum', in Walter Gross (ed.), *Jeremia und die 'deuteronomistische Bewegung'* (BBB, 98; Beltz: Athenäum, 1995): 57–89.

Wolff, Hans Walter
1974   *A Commentary on the Book of the Prophet Hosea* (Hermeneia; Philadelphia: Fortress, 1974); ET of *Dodekapropheton 1 Hosea* (2te Auflage; BK 14/1; Neukirchen-Vluyn: Neukirchner Verlag, 1965).

Woude, A. S. van der
1969   'Micah in Dispute with the Pseudo-Prophets', *VT* 19 (1969): 244–60.

Zevit, Ziony
2001   *The Religions of Ancient Israel: A Synthesis of Parallactic Approaches* (London/New York: Continuum).

The Day of Yahweh and the
Mourning of the Priests in Joel

James R. Linville

This article employs a synchronic approach to explore how the book of
Joel affirms the legitimacy and centrality of Judah's Persian-era priesthood.[1] This date reflects the majority view of the book's provenance: see,
for instance, the recent commentaries by Richard Coggins (2000: 13–17),
James L. Crenshaw (1995a: 21–29) and John Barton (2001: 1, 7).[2] What
interests me, however, are the symbolic constructions employed in the
book and what Robert Carroll may have called its 'word-world'.[3]
Residents of this literary world include priests. Oddly, however, they
only appear in the first half of the book, in which they mourn the defunct
sacrifices and are exhorted to institute rites of lamentation and fasting (1.9,
13–14; 2.15–17). In the oracles of salvation that begin at 2.18, the priests
are not mentioned, but everyone gets to wear the prophet's mantle (3.1–2).
The question of how the book as a whole imagines the role and status of
the priesthood, then, is an important question.

Hans Walter Wolff (1977: 12–13) sees Joel advocating a spiritual path
that concentrates on eschatological prophecy instead of empty priestly
devotion to ritual and Torah. Many have criticized Wolff for this,
including Barton (2001: 55–56, 65–66). Typically, commentators say that,
for Joel, the liturgical rites are an acceptable and important vehicle to
express an inner-felt spirituality, even if the rites are not an end in
themselves. Often cited in this regard is Joel 2.13, which demands the
sufferers tear their hearts and not their garments (Allen 1976: 79; Garrett
1997: 327, 346). The book at least draws on liturgical forms (Barton 2001:
21–22; Coggins 1982: 89; 1996: 81–82), although some commentators
maintain that Joel was a cult-prophet or that his book (or parts thereof)
was intended to be used in a liturgy (Kapelrud 1948; Carroll 1982: 49;
Mathews 2001: 161). Even so, the conceptual significance of the temple,

---

1. A much briefer version of this paper was read at the Israelite Prophetic Literature
section of the annual SBL meeting in Toronto on 24 November, 2002.

2. On the other hand, a date as early as the late-ninth century BCE is defended by Hailey
(1972: 40). Garrett (1997: 286–94) tentatively proposes the seventh century BCE, while Stuart
(1987: 226–27) thinks any of the invasions of Judah in 701, 598 or 588 BCE are likely settings.

3. He made frequent use of this expression in a brilliant series of lectures in the autumn of
1999 at the University of Alberta, Edmonton, Alberta, Canada.

priesthood and ritual in Joel is sometimes minimized. Arvid Kapelrud (1948: 182–84) thinks the priests are accorded no particular importance, even if they are not denigrated. While Duane Garrett (1997: 298, 304–309) observes that the prophet Joel saw repentance inseparable from temple lamentation (as in 1 Kgs 8.37–40), the cult and its functionaries hardly merit mention in Garrett's overview of seven main theological points of the book, other than in juxtaposing repentance with ritual penance (1997: 308). These points include: 'The Covenant'; 'The Day of the Lord'; 'A Biblical Worldview'; 'Natural Calamity and the Will of God'; 'Ethical Questions and the Issue of Repentance'; 'Prophecy and the Gift of the Spirit'. Even in Garrett's comments on 'The Future of Zion' (1997: 306–307), there is no mention of the temple or priesthood. I will demonstrate, however, that Joel employs a strategy which allows for the priests to be all but taken for granted as it depicts ritualization as having the capacity to overcome great social stresses.

It does this by reaffirming the structure of society and its power-relations through a dual portrayal of the 'Sacred' as the numinous 'Other' and as the ordered structures of human life. Therefore, the priests have an importance in this word-world wholly out of proportion to the actual amount of text devoted to them. By extension, then, the text affirms the status of the priesthood in the writer's society by reinforcing the view that they are essential players in the divine/natural/human economy of the cosmos.

Joel's literary world is marked by fantastic descriptions of catastrophe, but the exact nature of these crises is famously indeterminate. Most see the locusts of Joel 1.4 as referring to a real infestation, with either an accompanying drought or a figurative description of the insect-ravaged landscape suffering in the typical summer heat (Joel 1.10–12, 16–20). In Joel 2.1–11 a fantastic image of an invasion is found and some commentators, including Crenshaw (1995a: 122), Barton (2001: 70) and Willem Prinsloo (1985: 47–48), argue that this invasion should be seen as either a hyperbolic description of the same insect infestation of Joel 1 or a subsequent one.[4] On the other hand, Garrett (1997: 298–301, 333–39) finds real locusts in Joel 1, but human armies depicted figuratively in Joel 2. For Wolff (1977: 41–42), the real locusts of Joel 1 were the trigger for the prophet's envisioning of an apocalyptic army in the next chapter. A number of interpreters, however, say all actual and apparent references to locusts are metaphors for human armies (Ogden 1983; Andiñach 1992).[5] In this paper I will privilege none of the historical rationalizations of Joel's

---

4. For another way of reading Joel in terms of locusts and weather patterns, see Nash (1989: 74–80).

5. Stuart (1987: 233–34, 241–42) agrees, and compares Joel's stereotypical descriptions of locust infestation, drought, and invasion with Deut. 4 and 28–32. This, however, actually undermines his own argument that one can identify invasion as the real issue in Joel.

descriptions of disaster. Ferdinand E. Deist's view is that Joel's calamities are entirely hypothetical or the product of the imagination. He writes that Joel, 'was merely creating a *literary* world of calamities to serve as metaphors' to illustrate the Day of Yahweh (1988: 64, emphasis in original). Perhaps the prophet Joel did have some real-world catastrophe in mind, but the book presents a *literary* world, and it is only to the latter world that the modern critic has any direct access.

Another difficulty the interpreter of Joel faces is in determining what, if anything, the writer thought the people had done to deserve their fate. As noted already, Wolff (1977: 12–13) thinks the cult itself was displeasing to the prophet. Gösta Ahlström (1971: 69) sees Joel justly decrying the syncretistic state of early Persian-era worship in Jerusalem.[6] Paul Redditt (1986) finds Joel was initially not opposed to the priesthood *per se*, but to their lack of leadership or devotion to their duties. Douglas Stuart (1987: 230) relates Joel to the covenant curses in Deuteronomy and writes of a 'general national disobedience to Yahweh, regardless of whatever particular sets of violations may have been foremost in Joel's day'. James Nogalski (1993: 17–22) views Joel in the light of 1 Kgs 8.35–39 (= 2 Chron. 6.26–30) in which plague, invasion, illness, drought and famine are attributed to human guilt. Nogalski also argues that Joel is employing Hosea's images of guilt, interpreting Joel from the perspective of the book that immediately precedes it in the Book of the Twelve.[7]

Joel's own purposes and ideas, however, cannot *a priori* be considered identical to those expressed in other components of the Twelve.[8] Coggins (2000: 23, 24) argues that Nogalski's key words linking the end of Hosea with the beginning of Joel are too common to demonstrate the claimed connection. Ehud Ben Zvi (1996: 155–56) notices that there is no superscription for the whole collection, but each book has individual superscriptions and each offers its own 'plot' that can be considered self-contained. Variations in the order of the books exist in the versions and intertextual connections can be made between non-adjacent prophetic books and even with literature in other parts of the Hebrew Bible. Ben Zvi concludes that the components of the Book of the Twelve were most likely intended to be read for their own uniqueness within their shared ideological focus as parts of the Twelve. To my mind, one should be careful of building too much on Stuart's (1987: 230) discovery of Joel's allusions to covenant curses: these allusions are only one part of Joel's complex symbolic web, a web that nowhere unambiguously says the

---

6. Deist (1988: 69) also suggests that Joel 1.2–20; 2.18–27 serves an anti-Canaanite polemic.

7. For a summary of work on the Book of the Twelve, see Redditt (2001: 47–80).

8. Still, Coggins sees Joel addressing some inadequacies in the cultic practice of the day.

Judeans had broken the covenant. Presumably, the writer(s) and editors of Joel were familiar with literature that questioned why the righteous suffer. The story of Job immediately comes to mind as something of which they may have been aware. Barton (2001: 35–36), developing observations of Crenshaw (1995a: 18n.6; 1995b: 185–86), raises the question of whether the finished book of Joel is more a work of theodicy than a work of prophecy. As such, both scholars find Joel comparable in some respects to Job and even Jonah (Barton 2001: 35; Crenshaw 1995b). Graham S. Ogden (1983: 105) compares Joel to Ps. 59.3–4 in which a lament includes assertions of innocence. The expression, 'return שוב to me [Yahweh]' (Joel 2.12–13), is often taken as indicating that the people are urged to 'repent', implying they have sinned (e.g. Stuart 1987: 252). This word, however, needs not imply repentance, but a renewed and heightened devotion to the deity (Barton 2001: 35, 36, 76–80). Isaiah 44.22 can be referred to as a proof-text in this regard (Crenshaw 1995a: 40–41; 1995b: 188).[9] Joel's silence on the people's sins must not be drowned out by importing into its word-world the emphasis on guilt found in other literature and having this dominate our thinking about the book.

Joel's conceptual world is shaped more by cosmic themes of chaos and the restoration of creation than by themes of guilt or, for that matter, innocence. Ronald Simkins (1991) argues convincingly against recognizing a separation in biblical thought between human and natural history, a dichotomy he traces back to Hegel. Instead, God, nature and human life are inextricably linked. Simkins says that interaction between the deity, nature and humanity are key motifs of the 'combat myth' which is the model for the book of Joel. This familiar motif sees a divine warrior march against forces which threaten his sovereignty. The earth and nature convulse in a violent response to the champion's struggle. The victorious warrior returns to be enthroned and to speak from the temple. Nature, in turn, responds with its bounty as the heavens fertilize the earth, making it a fit home for living beings. Citing many biblical passages, including Pss. 96, 114 and 68.8–9, Simkins argues that nature is often portrayed as animate, active and conscious (1991: 58–75; 1993). Even though he takes a very unique approach to Joel, like most interpreters he historicizes the depictions of disaster. Joel 1 and 2 describe a real infestation while the drought imagery stems from the arid summer of Israel, all happening at a time when Judah was harassed by foreign enemies. The locusts of Joel 2 and the foreign nations in Joel 4 represent to Joel the same threat to divine sovereignty and the created order. The conflict myth is, therefore, a strategy which accords cosmogonic significance to real situations as the fulfillment of prophetic tradition. Moreover, the relieving of the threat

---

9. On the various meanings of 'return', see also Wolff (1977: 49).

symbolically re-creates the world (1991: 101–20, 225, 235–76).There is much to commend in Simkins's work, but I am not convinced that the mysterious invaders of Joel 2.1–10 are so unambiguously the opponents of Yahweh and his army who are described in Joel 2.11 (Simkins 1991: 160, 167). As I see it, the role of Yahweh in this combat myth is ambivalent. In 1.6–7, a 'nation' גוי assaults God's land destroying his vines and trees. Yet the Day of Yahweh in 1.15 is likened to destruction from the Almighty. In Joel 2.1–10 the terrible and mysterious invaders attack, while v. 11 overtly describes Yahweh's armies. I see little reason to understand v. 11 as talking about a divine opponent to the hordes described earlier. Indeed, in 2.25, the great locust army is said to have been unleashed by Yahweh, not against him. As the sole divine power, God can be both enemy and champion. The combat myth motifs are only part of a greater mythic complex which centres on the transformation of the earth *and* Yahweh.

The book of Joel ascribes natural and/or political crises (real or imagined) to divine action, especially as instances of the 'Day of Yahweh' (Joel 1.15; 2.1–2, 11; 3.3; 4.14). Many scholars have built on this awareness, among them Barton (2001: 59–60). This understanding recalls Mircea Eliade's (1959) thoughts on hierophany, the manifestation of the numinous 'Sacred' within the 'profane' world.[10] William E. Paden (2000) holds that such an understanding of the sacred, which he calls the 'mana model', has great explanatory power. This is especially so regarding the structured ways in which societies interact with select objects which they have empowered as focal points of the 'Sacred'. Yet, Paden also holds that the mana model needs to be complemented by another model he calls 'sacred order'. Herein sacrality is not alterity, but a perception of the inviolable order of society and its environment. Paden writes that Eliade developed the mana model in terms of world-making: the establishment of a fixed centre with links to the divine which grounded the world in the midst of chaotic non-being. Eliade's focus was on how this world-making employed cosmic myth rather than on the maintenance and defence of the system. Paden's 'sacred order' model describes this maintenance as 'a dynamic process of self-maintenance in the face of threatened or actual impurity, wrongness, or guilt' (2000: 211). It is in the sharp reaction to such disruptions that the sacrality of order really becomes easy to identify. Paden, therefore, categorizes various social aspects of sacred order and various human threats and infractions against it. He does not discuss at any length the threat posed by natural catastrophes, although his theoretical basis can accommodate such crises: he mentions demon-

---

10. Simkins (1991: 3–30) includes Eliade among those who artificially imposed a dichotomy between human history and nature in their characterization of ancient Israelite religion.

induced illness along with a more general sense of 'failures' of order and 'chaotic anomy' and the like (2000: 209–11). With this understanding, however, the profane is not merely the secular, that which is 'outside the temple, but rather what subverts it' by threatening order (Paden 2000: 209). When we use this model as a tool to understand Joel, therefore, one is confronted with an ambivalent Yahweh acting as the 'profane' enemy subverting sacred order! But resolving this existential nightmare seems to me to be what Joel, as a theodicy, is all about.

That resolution is initiated in the call to public lamentation and fasting in Joel 1.14; 2.12, 15. Interpreters often explain this as a public means of expressing anguish and submission to God (e.g. Garrett 1997: 326; Barton 2001: 56; Wolff 1977: 33). But what is the point of *communal* lamentation? Are the people not already in anguish? And by what perverse irony are the people asked to fast? *Are they not already starving?* Why does everything have to be turned into a ritual?

An answer might be found in the work of Catherine Bell, who writes that the power of ritualization has more to do with social power relationships than a perception of manipulated external reality. She describes ritualization as embracing a misrecognition or blindness. The ritualized body sees itself as responding naturally and appropriately to a situation, event or problem. What it does not see is how the ritual redefines those situations by imposing its own conceptual schemes. Even social power relations in the ritualization are not obvious to the participants, who largely assume them unconsciously. The ultimate authority is therefore identified as being beyond the ability of the community itself to control: in other words, from tradition or a god, thereby representing the structure of the cosmos. In the end a sense of social and cosmic reintegration is experienced as personal redemption becomes dependent upon communal redemption (1992: 98–100, 108–16, 197–223).

> Indeed, in seeing itself as responding to an environment, ritualization interprets its own schemes as impressed upon the actors from a more authoritative source, usually from well beyond the immediate human community itself. Hence, through an orchestration in time of loosely and effectively homologized oppositions in which some gradually come to dominate others, the social body reproduces itself in the image of the symbolically schematized environment that has been simultaneously established (Bell 1992: 108–109).

It should be possible to extrapolate from work done on real rituals to Joel's *literary* representation of calls for ritual responses to pressing circumstances. One can see a similar 'blindness' at work, as the ritualization imposes a collective scheme on suffering and implies the affirmation of the status of those lead the ritual. Moreover, one can also see the ambivalent

Yahweh redefined, a (re)creative act of the ritual body which is imagined as having a positive effect on the fortunes of the worshippers.

Bell's thoughts intersect with Paden's, and the sacred order model has some important points of contact with Simkins' views on Joel. Both of the latter require acknowledging a close relationship between the human world and nature, and this is indeed found in Joel. In 1.9 the offerings or libations have been 'cut off' הכרת from the temple, as was the wine from the drinkers in v. 5. In Joel 1.13, offerings are 'withheld' (מנע. A few commentators accuse the priests of abandoning the sacrifices (Allen 1976: 53; Simkins 1991: 145). Barton (2001: 55) rightly advises, however, that this cessation is part of the divine assault and is not merely the desperate measures of a starving people. Barton can be supported by reference to Joel 2.12–14 in which the people are admonished to 'return' to Yahweh in the hope that the deity will leave a blessing behind him: an offering and libation for God himself. In 1.9–12, this reciprocal relationship is played out in the phraseology. In vv. 9–10, the priests 'mourn' אבל the lost rites, as does the ground its destroyed fields.[11] The oil is 'exhausted' אמלל and the wine is 'dried up'. This last word is הוביש, from the root יבש. In v. 11 הבישו from the root בוש describes the agriculturalists' disgrace over the failed crops. In v. 12, הובישה describes the desiccation (and perhaps shame) of the vine.[12] Here too, the joy of cultic celebration dries up or is ashamed הביש, 'from humanity'.[13] Moreover, joyless 'humanity' בני אדם evokes the mourning ground of v. 10 אבלה אדמה, while the withered אמללה fig recalls the exhausted wine of that earlier verse. These word-plays and associations articulate a *symbiotic and organic relationship* between the land, the people and its priesthood.[14] Its attribution of painful emotions to the land and later to animals (cf. 1.18, 20) is not a mere personification. It expresses a closeness between humanity and the natural world that has parallels in other religions (Ebersole 2000: 214–22). This part of Joel recalls the

11.   Clines (1998) writes that אבל may connote dryness when its denotation, mourning, is a reaction to drought. Barton (2001: 53) follows Clines.

12.   The parallelism with אמללה suggests 'dry up', as noted by Crenshaw (1995: 101) although I disagree that 'be ashamed' lessens the poetic force.

13.   הביש ששון מן־בני אדם is difficult. I follow Wolff (1977: 32) who asserts that a dual association is probably intended, joy is withering, which results in shame. Simkins (1991: 139–41) says מן־בני אדם should be read 'by the sons of men' referring to foreigners, since 2.23 speaks of joy for the 'sons of Zion'. Crenshaw (1995: 102) refutes this interpretation. On the one hand, I link 'sons' in 1.12 to the successive generations of 1.2–3. On the other hand, 'sons of man' has a certain nuance of autonomy to it. In 2.23, however, the people are called the 'sons of Zion', i.e., the people of the sacred shrine. This lexical transformation follows the flow of the narrative as it turns from grief and separation from God to a happy reconciliation with the deity.

14.   For a fuller discussion of the richness of the language in this passage, see the insightful study of Hayes (2002: 189–96).

ambiguous and rich Hos. 2.23–25. Here Yahweh answers the sky as the earth responds to 'Jezreel' (*God sows*) and provides its rich bounty that heals the wounded relationship with which the book is concerned (Landy 1995: 25, 46–47). In Joel, however, the language merges Israel and the land to highlight the rupture between them and God.

These textual features along with the bizarre imagery of invasion in Joel 2.1–11 are interpretable according to Paden's (2000: 215) view that territory is a sacred quantity because it is the very basis of a sustainable life. We can see the successful defence of sacred territory in Joel after 2.17. In 2.19–26, the enemy is driven into the sea and nature explodes with her bounty. In v. 27, God is in the midst of his people, Israel. In 4.16, he roars from Zion and is a shelter to his people. In v. 17, he resides in Zion. The holy city is inviolable: never again will a stranger pass through it. Verse 20 predicts that Judah will forever be inhabited.

Maintaining tradition is also important in maintaining sacred order. This 'system allegiance' replicates social scripts, to break with it is to 'rupture the world's a priori coherence' (Paden 2000: 216). In Joel, tradition has been broken with the cessation of sacrifice. Of course, the fast and lamentation are traditional forms of public expression that can be seen to replace the defunct sacrifices. It is also interesting how other themes of tradition reinforce this. Elders, those with the strongest connections to traditional knowledge, figure in the text, and not kings and governors (Joel 1.2, 14; 2.16). Even though Joel 1.2 and 2.2 affirm that no parallel to the crisis has ever happened, or will happen again, Joel 1.3 demands that the story become the content of a *new* tradition, passed on from generation to generation. Joel's well-known reliance on motifs and ideas found elsewhere in biblical literature may also be a device that affirms the validity and survivability of tradition in the face of unholy chaos.[15] This is especially so regarding Joel 2.13–14, in which the speaker raises the hope that a gracious, compassionate and long-suffering deity will relent. This passage, with its echoes of a number of biblical texts, including Exod. 34.6–7; Num. 14.18; Pss. 86.15; 103.8, 145.8 and especially Jon. 4.2, asserts a traditional conception of the relationship between God and his people (Crenshaw 1995a: 135–37; Dozeman 1989). In Bell's terms (see 1992: 108–109), a ritual affirmation of a merciful god would confront and eventually dominate the participants' experience of a capricious and violent god. It does the same for the reader of our text: God is now defined by his mercy, not his violence.

---

15. Joel's borrowings, quotes and/or allusions to other traditions are well known, see Coggins (1996). Simkins (1991: 267) explains this as Joel possessing a general familiarity with a shared 'prophetic tradition'.

Sacred acts in sacred places take place in sacred times. In Joel, all other times and places are negated. The regular ritual calendar is wiped away. Regardless of what day of the year that might be, it is dry season: the earth is scorched and burned. More terrifying, the sun is darkened and every place is a place of suffering and death. This is the 'Day of Yahweh', unlike any other (Joel 1.15; 2.1–2, 11). Joel's use of the concept may be far removed from its original setting (Prinsloo 1985: 36). In general, however, it refers to any of numerous historical and future days associated with dramatic acts of God.[16] In Joel the 'Day' sees the reformulation of liturgical gatherings. Thus, even with the cessation of the sacrificial rites, the text opens a sacred time and place: a sanctuary on Yahweh's day in the midst of chaos. The priests who can no longer maintain their status as officiates of the sacrifices retain their leadership role as organizers of the rituals that are left open to the beleaguered people: mourning and fasting. The personal has become collective. And, equally important, the cosmos becomes cohesive again as the rituals reassert that the ultimate source of power and cosmic integrity lies with God and, regardless of his apparent enmity, he is merciful, as tradition teaches.

The proposed ritual in Joel resists the idea that the system of exchange between God, nature and humanity is entirely extinct. An excellent example of this exchange, not to mention the 'recycling' of gifts, is found in Deut. 14.22–23, in which the tithe offered to God is to be eaten in the presence of Yahweh. God gives prosperity to the people, the people give back to God, the people eat what they have given (Burkert 1996: 148). In Joel 1.9, 13; 2.15–17, the priests bewail the failed sacrificial exchange system and the hope is expressed that God himself would restore it (2.14) by leaving an offering. They are to spend the night in sackcloth and convene a solemn assembly at the temple. Young and old must all gather: even the newly-weds must come (2.16). The people must 'sanctify' themselves קדשׁו (2.16). There is no other place to be but in the assembly. Even so, the priests, the ministers of Yahweh and his altar (1.9, 13; 2.17), have nothing to offer. Yet, a solution can be found.

Leviticus 5.1–13; 12.1–8; 14.19–22 describe a number of situations in which those of modest means are allowed to make less expensive sacrifices than those more well-off. In Joel, however, the people are left without the resources to make any kind of material gift at all. The belief that a deity is actually concerned with a worshipper's 'heart' and not his or her ability to provide expensive offerings or conduct ritual (cf. Joel 2.13) is not rare in biblical texts (e.g. Hos. 6.6; Pss. 40.7–8, 50.1–15, 141.2; Prov. 21.3) or those of other religious traditions (Burkert 1996: 143). In one sense, it allows

16. The bibliography on the 'Day's' tradition history is huge. See the brief review in Crenshaw (1995: 47–50) and the influential essays by Everson (1974), and Hoffmann (1981).

those with nothing at all to offer something acceptable to God: the inner purity upon which all effective sacrifice depends can sometimes be enough. Yet, in Joel this inner transformation is accompanied by a symbolic sacrificial substitution that reflects the actual 'economy' of the crisis. Such an attempt to placate an angry deity by offering symbols of the divine wrath itself is found elsewhere in the Hebrew Bible. 1 Samuel 6.1–17 describes how the Philistines appease Yahweh with five golden models of the mice and five more of the haemorrhoids with which the Israelite god plagued them. The number five corresponds to the number of Philistine cities and lords. In a less humorous vein, other biblical texts refer to various effects of divine action as a form of ritual. The exile of Judah in 2 Chronicles is imagined as a 'Sabbath' for the land. Isaiah 34.5–7 and Jer. 46.10 describe God's violence against the nations as a sacrifice, as does Zeph. 1.7–8. Sacrificial and ritual concepts, then, provide a way of imagining the entire divine-human encounter: its breakdown and its restoration.

God used to give food, but now in Joel the deity gives starvation. Yet, the recommended ritual fast and lamentation assimilates even this suffering to the exchange system which grounds creation, tenaciously rejecting defeatism. Thus, the hunger and grief is symbolically returned to its source in ritual time and place on behalf of the people and, presumably, nature itself. The specification that the priests 'sanctify' the fast קְדְּשׁוּ־צוֹם (Joel 1.14; 2.15) seems almost redundant, as Crenshaw (1995a: 104) notices: fasts are inherently religious. Yet, this sanctification symbolically transforms the hunger: it is not destruction from, but communion with the numinous 'Other'. So, too, the lamentation. Ritualized tears in many non-Western societies are not empty formalisms and are no less real than the spontaneous crying acknowledged as 'true' emotional responses in the West (Ebersole 2000: 213–15). In Joel, the ritual weeping is part of the communalization of private grief which Bell (1992: 217–18) argues can be personally empowering, despite the complex relationship between the individual and hegemonic order that exists in ritual. Moreover, on a literary level the demand in 2.13 that the people rend their hearts and not their garments adds an image of symbolized violence closely following the invasion imagery of 2.1–11. In that passage, one can imagine hearts, along with other significant body parts, being physically torn. It is no wonder that the text demands that the ritualization of suffering take place at the temple, between the portico and the altar (2.17, cf. 1.14). Yet, what is transformed is not only the human and natural suffering and the cosmos, but the deity as well. He is no longer the enemy but the saviour. After 2.17 the transformation is complete: nature is restored as God gives the rain and sweeps the locust army away. Starvation gives way to full bellies, disgrace is ended and God is with his people once more (Joel 2.18–27). In 2.20, the destroyed enemy is called the זְפוֹנִי 'northerner', echoing traditions of a mighty northern enemy, or even the name of Mt Zaphon: the mythical home of the Canaanite gods.[17] In Joel, God the champion has disowned his threatening insect/military/supernatural horde. The dangerous, profane 'Other' is once again part of the sacred order.

Paden (2000: 215–16) treats the maintenance of social hierarchy, role, status and group loyalty as essential elements in sacred order. In Joel, there is no overt condemnation of traitors, false prophets or the like: instead, group solidarity underlies the assemblies. Other than the elders mentioned in a few places (1.2, 14; 2.16), the priests are the *only* authority figures mentioned in Joel 1–2. They are accorded their special status as ministers of Yahweh and his altar (Joel 1.9, 13; 2.17). The ritualization process depends on them: their status is without rival or overt criticism. To accept the mercy of God affirmed in the ritual is to accept the social standing of the priests as orchestrators of the rites. On the other hand, role differentiation and status after 2.17 becomes ambiguous. The בני ציון 'Sons of Zion' are told to rejoice (2.23). Everyone will become prophets (Joel 3), but no priests are mentioned. If sacred order is most easily seen in the reaction to transgression, perhaps the priests need not appear in the salvation oracles because their social status has never really been challenged in the book: prophecy and priesthood are not conceived of as rivals to each other. Even without mention of priests, there remain allusions to priestly functions and temple imagery in the final half of Joel. The expression 'Sons of Zion' in 2.23 does not name the priesthood specifically, but it does call attention to the temple-site as a focus of Judean identity. In Joel 4.17, the people will know that Yahweh their god dwells in Zion, his holy mountain. No foreigner will transgress its boundaries. In one sense, the priesthood has become assimilated to the collective, presumably because the collective is the more important theme. Similarly, in 1 Kings 8, it is 'Solomon and the whole community of Israel' who offer sacrifice (vv. 3–5) at the new temple. After being forced to abandon the sanctuary by the divine cloud in vv. 10–11, the priests are not mentioned again. In v. 62, 'the king and all Israel' sacrifice once more, not the priests. Joel 3 seems to embody Moses' wish that all Israel could be prophets (Num. 11.29). But, taken together, Joel 2.18–4.21 also suggests the fulfillment of Exod. 19.6 that Israel is a kingdom of priests and a holy nation. Even the destiny of Judah's enemies is predicted in priestly terms: the battle that will destroy them must also be 'sanctified' קדשו, just like Judah's fast (4.9).

Much of this suggests that Joel reflects quite strongly two other categories of Paden's sacred order, that of 'high definition membership' and honour as the maintenance of integrity (2000: 218–19). Joel does not

17. Many commentators recognize this, e.g., Crenshaw (1995: 151).

develop themes of identity based on the exodus, the covenant or patriarchal traditions. Yet, the land is God's in 1.6 and so are the people in v. 14. Judah is called God's 'possession' נחלה in 2.17, and later in the chapter they again are his people (2.17, 18, 19, 23, 26, 27). Simkins (1994) holds that if there is any sin implied in Judah's actions, it is in Judah hiding the shame of having their land ravaged. They hide their disgrace by abandoning the worship of an apparently absentee divine protector. As noted already, however, it is God who abolished the sacrificial exchange. The symbiotic nature of the cosmos, however, implies that God's honour is linked to that of his people. This is evident in Joel 2.17 which directs the priests to ask Yahweh not to surrender Judah to the mockery and/or dominion of the nations.[18] The final rhetorical point they are advised to make is to ask, 'why should the nations say, "Where is their God?"' This implies that Yahweh is defensive about his own honour, as noticed by Barton (2001: 83–84). After raising the question, however, the text does not pause to say that the priests did what they were commanded. The prophetic voice immediately turns to describe how God has changed his mind (2.18) and that the shame of the land and the people will be put away (2.19, 27). This gap, however, is not fatal to the integrity of the text. Rather, it speaks volumes about how the text's producers relied on the reader making the necessary conceptual leaps from Judah's agony to God's potential dishonour, from prophetic demands to priestly *and divine* action. This involves the reader acquiescing and accepting the hierarchical order of God, the priests, and the populace, as the basis for the eventual restoration of the cosmos. As Joel 2.18–4.21 depicts, the reintegration displaces any discomfort over the unexplored causes of the disasters onto the oppressive foreign powers, who are belatedly identified as the enemy to all that is sacred.

Without exploring the issue, Paden (2000: 222) wonders how sacred order relates to ideological insecurity. Biblical scholars would do well to consider it too. In Joel, it seems as if tradition is used creatively to solve real or imagined crises which call into question accepted beliefs about God. We might label this literary process with Wendy Doniger O'Flaherty's term, 'metamyth', a transformation of earlier mythology through the telling of a new narrative. She employs it in discussing the evolving Hindu myths of Rudra/Pashupti and Prajapati as 'nightmares' of sacrifice. These myths posit surrogates for human, and eventually animal, sacrificial objects. Finally, in some texts, prayers are said to a satisfactory substitute (1988: 88–89, 112–14). In Joel we do not have 'nightmares' of human

---

18. משל may be read as 'to rule' or as indicating mockery in parallel with חרפה. Some suggest a possible *double entendre*, e.g. Crenshaw (1995: 183), who still affirms 'to mock' is the stronger possibility. I think the word play should not be discounted at all.

sacrifice. We have instead a nightmare of a failed environmental, economic and ritual system. The book of Joel imagines how even this fear can be brought into the transformative world of sacred time and place and, in so doing restore hope. Joel's word-world provides a central image to describe the collapse of the stable universe 'outside the temple' that is predicted for the 'Day of Yahweh'. Yet, the reciprocity between God, nature and humanity, spoken of in images of withheld and hoped for sacrifices, casts human life itself as a liturgical process. The strategy which discovers a surrogate offering upon which recreation depends is at once traditional, ad hoc and integrative. Starvation and anguish become fasting and lamentation, torn 'hearts' symbolize shock and torn bodies. In the end, the foreign nations to be defeated in Joel 4 are the true surrogates: like the fast they are to be 'sanctified' for the war that will destroy them (4.9). In response to the cut-off wine of 1.5, the nations find themselves crushed in a winepress (4.13), symbolically reinstituting the previously withheld libations (1.9, 13, cf. 2.14). The nations are harvested as ploughs and pruning hooks become weapons (4.10, 13), and here is the symbolic return to cereal offerings. The nations' defeat is the prelude to the recreation of the primal paradise (4.14–21) as heaven and nature respond to one another again.

Because we have taken a synchronic view of the book of Joel, we have said little of the real priests of Joel's time, whatever time that may have been! The text articulates a functioning social hierarchy, the necessity of the control of territory, the numinous power behind the basics of life, and rituals that seek to address the rupture in the sacred order. This rupture, however, is addressed in terms which reaffirm social hierarchies, even if the structure of that hegemony is not addressed directly. Neither is that hierarchy challenged in Joel: the eventual invisibility of the priests in the oracles of salvation does not really constitute a charter to replace priests with a new focal point for religious life. As Bell (1992: 197–223) suggests, we should recognize how social power-relationships can be taken for granted in ritualization, although resistance to hegemony can never be fully suppressed. There is no indication of resistance to the priesthood, however, even if the fantasy of the restored earth means that everyone, young and old, will share in the prophetic gift (Joel 3.1–2). The priests, of course, are not excluded, but merely subsumed within this greater group. Indeed, it is the prophetic voice which directs the priests to act: 'The words of Yahweh which came to Joel' (1.1). The reader at least gives a hypothetical approval to this concept before reading further and, with that nod of acceptance, the role, social status, and efficacy of the literary priesthood are easier to accept, since that voice never openly criticizes the priests. It is easy to see this as a legitimatization strategy which served the purposes of ancient Judah's actual priests. Any crises that can be seen in the hyperbolic descriptions of Joel 1–2, then, have their solution in the efficacy of the priestly leadership of the people validated by prophecy.

In articulating the dual aspect of the 'sacred', alterity and integrity, the 'prophetic' (or mythic) imagination can sometimes be seen to revolve around a conception of the temple and its liturgies as a microcosm of the cosmos and society.[19] A conceptual temple should be understood as being as real an influence on biblical writers as any actual building. Indeed, the two temples depend on each other! The prophet Joel and other writers and editors whose work is represented by the book bearing his name would only have needed awareness of the temple's cosmic significance and common rituals to produce the text. This awareness was probably shared by many of the literate in ancient Judah. It is, therefore, difficult to assert with any confidence that the prophet Joel was an actual functionary in the sacrificial religion. Of course, the reverse is also true: it is impossible to prove he was *not* a temple official! Similarly, we still cannot be sure if the book of Joel was meant to be read in a liturgy. But what we can be confident about is that the book easily serves the interests of the liturgical institutions and that it suggests no replacement for the temple itself as the centre of Judean religious life. Indeed, the book affirms that the temple is necessary to the very stability of the cosmos and its relationship with its creator.

BIBLIOGRAPHY

Ahlström, G. W.
 1971 *Joel and the Temple Cult of Jerusalem* (VTSup, 21; Leiden: Brill).
Allen, L. C.
 1976 *Joel, Obadiah, Jonah, and Micah* (NICOT; Grand Rapids: Eerd-mans).
Andiñach, P. R.
 1992 'The Locusts in the Message of Joel', *VT* 42: 433–41.
Barton, J.
 2001 *Joel and Obadiah: A Commentary* (OTL; Louisville, KY: Westmin-ster/John Knox Press).
Bell, C.
 1992 *Ritual Theory, Ritual Practice* (Oxford: Oxford University Press).
Ben Zvi, E.
 1996 'Twelve Prophetic Books or "The Twelve": A Few Preliminary Considerations', in J. W. Watts and P. R. House (eds.), *Forming Prophetic Literature: Essays on Isaiah and the Twelve in Honor of*

19. Cf. Mic. 1.2–3, in which Yahweh is in his 'holy temple' then 'comes down' from his place to tread on the earth's 'high places'.

112 *The Priests in the Prophets*

John D. W. Watts (JSOTSup, 235; Sheffield: Sheffield Academic Press): 125–56.

Burkert, W.
1996   *Creation of the Sacred: Tracks of Biology in Early Religion* (Cambridge, MA: Harvard University Press).

Carroll, R. P.
1982   'Eschatological Delay in the Prophetic Tradition?', *ZAW* 94: 47–58.

Clines, D. J. A.
1998   'Was there an 'bl II "be dry" in Classical Hebrew?' in D. J. A. Clines, *On the Way to the Postmodern: Old Testament Essays 1967–1998*, II (JSOTSup, 292; Sheffield: Sheffield Academic Press): 585–94.

Coggins, R. J.
1982   'An Alternative Prophetic Tradition', in E. J. Coggins, M. A. Knibb, and A. Phillips (eds.), *Israel's Prophetic Tradition: Essays in Honour of Peter Ackroyd* (Cambridge: Cambridge University Press): 77–94.
1996   'Interbiblical Quotations in Joel', in J. Barton (ed.), *After the Exile: Essays in Honour of Rex Mason* (Macon GA: Mercer University Press): 77–84.
2000   *Joel and Amos* (NCBC; Sheffield: Sheffield Academic Press).

Crenshaw, J. L.
1995a   *Joel: A New Translation with Introduction and Commentary* (AB, 24; Garden City, NY: Doubleday).
1995b   'Who Knows What Yahweh Will Do? The Character of God in the Book of Joel', in A. B. Beek, A. H. Bartelt and C. A. Franke (eds.), *Fortunate the Eyes That See: Essays in Honor of David Noel Freedman in Celebration of His Seventieth Birthday* (Grand Rapids: Eerdmans): 185–96.

Deist, F. E.
1988   'Parallels and Reinterpretation in the Book of Joel: A Theology of the Yom Yahweh?', in W. Classen (ed.), *Text and Context: Old Testament and Semitic Studies for F. C. Fensham* (JSOTSup, 48; Sheffield: Sheffield Academic Press): 63–79.

Doniger O'Flaherty, W.
1988   *Other People's Myths: The Cave of Echoes* (Chicago: University of Chicago Press).

Dozeman, T. B.
1989   'Inner-Biblical Interpretation of Yahweh's Gracious and Compassionate Character', *JBL* 108: 207–23.

Ebersole, G. L.
2000   'The Function of Ritual Weeping Revisited: Affective Expression and Moral Discourse', *History of Religions* 39: 211–46.

Eliade, M.
1959   *The Sacred and the Profane: The Nature of Religion* (trans. W. R. Trask; New York: Harcourt/Brace/Jovanovich).

Everson, A. J.
  1974   'The Days of Yahweh', *JBL* 93: 329–37.
Garrett, D.
  1997   *Hosea, Joel* (NAC, 19a; Nashville: Broadman & Holman).
Hailey, H.
  1972   *A Commentary on the Minor Prophets* (Grand Rapids MI: Baker Book House).
Hayes, K. M.
  2002   *"The Earth Mourns": Prophetic Metaphor and Oral Aesthetic* (Academia Biblica, 8; Atlanta: Society of Biblical Literature).
Hoffmann, Y.
  1981   'The Day of the Lord as a Concept and a Term in the Prophetic Literature', *ZAW* 93: 37–50.
Kapelrud, A. S.
  1948   *Joel Studies* (Uppsala: Almqvist & Wiksell).
Landy, F.
  1995   *Hosea* (Readings; Sheffield: Sheffield Academic Press).
Mathews, V. H.
  2001   *Social World of the Hebrew Prophets* (Peabody, MA: Hendrickson).
Nash, K. S.
  1989   'The Cycle of the Seasons', *The Bible Today* 27: 74–80.
Nogalski, J.
  1993   *Redactional Processes in the Book of the Twelve* (BZAW, 218; Berlin: de Gruyter).
Ogden, G. S.
  1983   'Joel 4 and Prophetic Reponses to National Laments', *JSOT* 26: 97–106.
Paden, W. E.
  2000   'Sacred Order', *Method & Theory in the Study of Religion* 12: 207–55 m
Prinsloo, W. S.
  1985   *The Theology of the Book of Joel* (BZAW, 163; Berlin: Walter de Gruyter).
Redditt, P. L.
  1986   'The Book of Joel and Peripheral Prophecy', *CBQ* 48: 225–40.
  2001   'Recent Research on the Book of the Twelve as One Book', *CR:BS* 9: 47–80.
Stuart, D.
  1987   *Hosea-Jonah* (WBC, 31; Waco TX: Word Books).
Simkins, R.
  1991   *Yahweh's Activity in History and Nature in the Book of Joel* (Ancient Near Eastern Texts and Studies, 10; Lewiston/Queenston/Lampeter: Edwin Mellen Press).
  1993   'God, History, and the Natural World in the Book of Joel', *CBQ* 55: 435–52.
  1994   '"Return to Yahweh": Honor and Shame in Joel', *Semeia* 68: 41–54.

Wolff, H. W.
    1977   *Joel and Amos: A Commentary on the Books of the Prophets Joel and Amos* (trans. W. Janzen, S. D. McBride Jr, C. A. Muenchow; Hermeneia; Philadelphia: Fortress Press).

Priestly Purity and Prophetic Lunacy:
Hosea 1.2–3 and 9.7

Richard D. Nelson

1. *The Social Role of Prophets*

The stories about prophets in Samuel and Kings, taken together with indications in the Latter Prophets, permit us to make persuasive generalizations about the social role of prophets. In function and social location, Israelite prophecy may be compared to similar institutions reflected in the Mari archives, Neo-Assyrian texts and, less directly, to the phenomenon of intermediation found in many other cultures. Some prophets may be seen as peripheral intermediaries who advocated more or less radical social, religious, or political change and gave voice to the concerns of marginal or disaffected elements in society. Other prophets may best be described as central intermediaries who helped maintain and legitimate the social order. All prophets, however, would have been supported by some societal groups and opposed by others.[1]

It seems reasonable to expect discord between priests, whose interests would often correspond to those of the elite establishment, and peripheral prophets representing the interests of marginalized social groups. Such conflict is apparent in Amos and Jeremiah. Nevertheless, it is important not to overstate this opposition. Prophets and priests had similar vocations as 'intermediary religious specialists'. Both played roles in facilitating the people's relationship with the national deity, and their interests sometimes coincided.[2]

1.1. *Stereotypical Behaviors*

Israelite religious specialists, both prophets and priests, relied on stereotypical behaviors to attain and maintain their distinctive roles in society. Religious intermediaries from many cultures exhibit socially defined stereotypical behaviors in order to authenticate their roles and maximize their influence. Such stereotypical behavior is important for achieving validation in the struggle for public opinion and acquiring

---

1. Standard studies on the social role of prophets are Grabbe (1995); Overholt (1989, 1990); Wilson (1980).
2. Long (1981) stresses that conflict between intermediaries is to be expected.

influence in the public arena. The legitimacy of any intermediary is open to dispute on the part of the public and may be assailed by opposing and competing groups. The audience of a biblical prophet would need to be convinced of the authenticity of that prophet's divine communication and encouraged to listen to and act on it.[3]

Even if such stereotypical behaviors seem to be beyond the conscious control of the intermediary, they are not arbitrary, but are generated by cultural expectations about how an intermediary is supposed to behave. Through its behavioral expectations, society exerts control, sometimes subtle, sometimes overt, over the intermediary. Stereotypical behaviors tend to be flamboyant and eccentric, in accord with their function of demonstrating the super-normal reality of being a mediator between the human and divine worlds. Stereotypical behaviors enhance the role of the intermediary and may be performed or enacted at different levels of psychological and physical involvement (Petersen 1981: 25–34). But their unconventional nature also means that such behaviors are open to contradictory assessments on the part of the public. An intermediary's potential audience may take the very same behavior as validation of an authentic vocation or as evidence of physical or mental illness (Overholt 1986: 11–13).

1.2 *Ecstasy as Stereotypical Behavior*

Much recent study has focused on the stereotypical behavior of ecstasy. The terms ecstasy, trance, or possession behavior are used to describe overt actions on the part of an intermediary that sometimes accompany the reception and delivery of a communication from the divinity. The precise nature of such trance behavior varies according to the expectations of different societies and cultures. Observers are intended to recognize these performances as indications of valid intermediation. One example of trance behavior in the Hebrew Bible is provided by Balaam, who 'falls down' with 'his eyes uncovered' (Num. 24.16).[4]

---

3. For stereotypical behaviors in anthropological reports, including trance behavior, distinctive costume, and 'patterned public performance', as well as the process of public evaluation, see Overholt (1986).

4. The physical symptoms described in Jer. 4.19 and 23.9 may describe trance behavior but also reflect literary conventions about the way one reacts to the reception of bad news. On trance behavior, see Grabbe (1995: 108–12); Michaelsen (1989); Overholt (1986: 165–80); Uffenheimer (1988: 257–69); Wilson (1979). Parker (1978) denies that Israelite prophets exhibited possession behavior. Etymology indicates that the *muḫḫûm* at Mari engaged in trance behavior. The Phoenician intermediary described by Wen-Amon exhibits violent physical activity as part of his prophetic performance (*ANET* 26; cf. n. 13). On Mesopotamian prophecy, see Huffmon (2000).

Such trance or possession behavior is denoted by the verbal root *nb'* in Hitpael, to 'act like a prophet'. Those who exhibit such '*hitnabbē'*-behavior' in 1 Sam. 10.5–6, 10–13 can still walk and play instruments. However, in 1 Sam. 19.18–24 this distinctive behavior incapacitates Saul's messengers in their mission to capture David and involves stripping off one's clothes. Trance behavior is 'contagious' for Saul and his messengers. In 1 Sam. 18.10–11 it is connected with Saul's aggressive violence against David. For the Baal prophets on Mount Carmel, such ecstasy was expected as stereotypical behavior ('as was their custom') and involved self-harm (1 Kgs 18.28–29). The Hebrew Bible connects *hitnabbē'*-behavior to the activity of spirit: the spirit of Yahweh in Num. 11.26–27, an 'evil spirit' in 1 Sam. 18.10, and the return of the spirit of life in Ezek. 37.10. One must be careful to note that nowhere in the Hebrew Bible is there an explicit connection between ecstatic behavior and the reception or delivery of a divine message, although this is strongly suggested by Elisha's use of music in 2 Kgs 3.15.

Recent scholarship has tended to bypass the question of whether trance behavior involves any sort of extraordinary psychological state (or pathology) and instead treats it phenomenologically, as an objectively visible activity evaluated in various ways by those who observe it. For prophets, the option of exhibiting trance behavior was socially expected and determined, functioning to authenticate the prophet's role, authority, and message. That *hitnabbē'*-behavior was performed in order to gain role recognition and validation is apparent in the story of Eldad and Medad (Num. 11.26–27). This same concern is visible in 1 Kgs 22.10, 12, where the prophets of Ahab perform trance behavior 'before' the kings in a context of a dispute over the legitimacy of their oracle. One notes that Micaiah undercuts their prophecy, not by attacking their ecstatic performance, but by attributing their message to a lying spirit (vv. 22–23). When Saul acts in this way, onlookers recognize (or deride) him as a potential prophet: 'Is Saul also among the prophets?' (1 Sam. 10.11; 19.24).

A stereotypical *hitnabbē'* performance could lead to conflicting positive and negative evaluations. Thus Saul's trance behavior seems to be evaluated positively in 1 Sam. 10.11–12, but clearly negatively in 18.10–11 and 19.18–24. Such eccentric and uncontrolled conduct might be disapproved of as a symptom of madness. The opposition prophet Shemaiah associates Jeremiah's *hitnabbē'*-behavior with madness in order to counter Jeremiah's proclamation and undermine his prophetic office (Jer. 29.26–28). 2 Kings 9.11 reflects a popular evaluation of prophetic speech in terms of insanity.[5]

---

5. Müller (1969: 363–63) proposes ecstatic glossolalia.

1.3 *Other Prophetic Stereotypical Behaviors*

Biblical prophets also exhibited other sorts of non-normal, eccentric behavior intended to authenticate their role and validate their communications. For example, the patterned and standardized poetic speech characteristic of prophets served as a sort of stereotypical behavior (Wilson 1980: 141–44, 257–63). Audiences expected prophets to speak like prophets, just as priests were expected to utilize stereotypical forms of priestly speech such as blessings, declarations, and predictably formatted torah teaching.

Another sort of stereotypical behavior was the performance of miraculous acts of power intended to validate a prophet's role and message (Deut. 13.2–3 [E 1–2]; 1 Kgs 17.24; Isa. 7.11, 38.7–8). Prophetic legends preserved in the Hebrew Bible suggest that wondrous deeds were popularly expected from an authentic prophet (cf. 2 Kgs 5.3, 8.4–5; Overholt 1982; 1989: 86–111).[6]

Other distinctive stereotypical behaviors included wearing characteristic clothing and following an idiosyncratic diet (2 Kgs 1.8; cf. Zech. 13.4). Those who recounted the stories of Elijah expected that a prophet might habitually withdraw from human contact and then suddenly turn up again (1 Kgs 17.3, 18.10–12, ch. 19; 2 Kgs 2.16). Prophets might be itinerants, leaving home and performing their calling in alien places (Amos and the Judahite prophet of 1 Kgs 13 in Bethel, Elijah in Zarephath, Elisha in Damascus).[7] Sometimes prophets engaged in special avoidance behaviors. The Judahite prophet in 1 Kgs 13 refrained from eating or drinking while on his mission and avoided returning by the same road. Jeremiah shunned the normal contacts of marriage, mourning, and social interaction (Jer. 16.1–9), and Ezekiel failed to mourn his wife's death (Ezek. 24.15–24). Ezekiel's period of muteness provides another example of conspicuous avoidance behavior (Ezek. 3.25–26).

Thus a wide range of unconventional behavior supported prophetic claims and sought public recognition of a prophet's role. Somewhat paradoxically, much of what was stereotypical about these behaviors was their oddity, their eccentricity, and their abnormality. With prophets, one expected the unexpected!

---

6. For the confirming corroboration of an effective cure, see Overholt (1986: 25–58).

7. The hometowns of Assyrian intermediaries did not always coincide with the places where they delivered their prophecies (van der Toorn 2000: 73). Assyrian intermediaries for Ishtar took special names reflecting their prophetic role and message (Parpola 1997: il-lii). Perhaps something similar is involved with Elijah ('Yahweh is God') and Malachi ('My messenger').

1.4 *Priests and Stereotypical Behavior*

Priests also engaged in stereotypical behavior to enhance their role as religious specialists and intermediaries connected to the sphere of the divine. They would need to authenticate their status with the public, especially when under attack from those representing other, peripheral or marginalized interests. Thus priests engaged in special actions and gestures (that is, 'patterned public performance'), spoke in distinctive formulas, and wore distinctive costumes. They also practiced long term, 'life-style' stereotypical behavior in diet, choice of marriage partners, sexuality, and other aspects of everyday life. These behaviors sought to keep them and their families in a state of ritual purity so that they could engage the holy effectively and safely (cf. Lev. 21; Ezek. 4.14–15; Nelson 1993: 17–38, 83–88).

1.5 *Negative Evaluations of Prophetic Behavior as Madness and Folly*

Much stereotypical behavior on the part of prophets could be labeled as dramatic or even as histrionic. Elisha's show of weeping at the import of his message to Hazael (2 Kgs 8.11) and Ezekiel's moaning (Ezek. 21.6–7) are paralleled by Balaam in the text from Deir Alla (I 3–4; Dijkstra 1995). The anonymous prophet in 1 Kgs 20.35–38 becomes so deeply involved in his dramatic role as a wounded veteran of battle that he seeks out real wounds to hide behind his bandage disguise. The wounds that divulge one's prophetic status in Zech. 13.4–6 may have been the result of eccentric, self-harming behavior (cf. 1 Kgs 18.28).

As in the case of *hitnabbē'*-behavior, these other abnormal behaviors were liable to be judged as folly or madness by those who did not accept a supposed prophet's status or message. Madness was diagnosed on the basis of unconventional behavior such as scratching on doors and drooling (1 Sam. 21.13–14), a lack of control like that of swiftly driven chariots (Nah. 2.5 [E 4]; Jer. 46.9), or disorientation like that of drunks (Jer. 25.16) or terrorized warriors (Zech. 12.4). The overlap in bizarre public behavior between the mentally ill and the practicing prophet could easily lead to an accusation of madness. Perhaps a hostile observer of Elijah's hyper-athletic feat of running at chariot speed from Carmel to Jezreel (1 Kgs 18.46) might associate this with the sort of abandoned craziness exhibited by Jehu at the reigns of his chariot (2 Kgs 9.20).

2. *Symbolic Acts as Stereotypical Behavior*

Biblical prophets performed acts connected to their proclamation. These are frequently called symbolic acts because they often served as metaphorical or analogous illustrations of the prophet's verbal communication. These prophetic acts also had a causal aspect. By mimicking what was to happen, such behavior was seen as helping predicted events proceed to their inevitable fulfillment. In this way they corresponded to what has traditionally been called sympathetic magic (Fohrer 1953; cf. Stacey 1990: 260–82). Nevertheless, not all symbolic acts were about the future. For example, the names given to Hosea's children are initially linked to present realities, not future phenomena.

Over and above their illustrative and causative purpose, however, these prophetic acts should also be understood as social mechanisms for establishing and maintaining a prophet's role in society. Symbolic acts functioned as extraordinary and bizarre stereotypical behaviors intended to legitimate a prophet and authorize the prophetic word.[8]

2.1 *Symbolic Acts as Eccentric and Abnormal*

The mimetic nature and dramatic effect of symbolic acts depended on their being eccentric and abnormal to some degree. We call such a prophetic performance 'symbolic' because of the perceived relationship between the act and the present or future reality that it communicated and initiated. This necessity for analogy required that prophetic acts be mimetic. Moreover, the goal of effective public communication necessitated that they be dramatic. As behaviors with a communicative function, prophetic acts naturally called attention to themselves. At times, prophets needed to shock and disturb their audiences in order to maximize effectiveness in communication (Amsler 1980). As a result, prophetic acts were quite often striking and outrageous, involving novel and imaginative elements. Prophetic acts needed to attract public attention and to be seen as behaviors inherently laden with numinous and paranormal power.

The striking element of a prophetic act sometimes aimed to encourage a course of action (1 Kgs 19.19, 22.11; Isa. 7.3–9; Hab. 2.2). An abnormal act could also create puzzlement that would encourage the audience to listen attentively to the prophetic word (Jer. 16.1–13; Ezek. 12.1–16, 21.11–12 [E 6–7], 24.15–24, 37.15–23). Unsettling prophetic acts could also lead to hostility (Jer. 28). Moreover, prophetic actions sometimes seem to have a subtext of undermining the orderly and expected. Tearing cloth or breaking a jar attacks the very fabric of a kingdom and the integrity of a society (1 Kgs 11.29–39; Jer. 19). Digging through walls undermines security (Ezek. 12.5, 7). Sinking a scroll sinks a nation (Jer. 51.63–64). Provocative sexual conduct like that of Hosea could be construed as destabilizing social and moral boundaries.[9]

---

8. Overholt (1989: 87–88) touches on prophetic symbolic action in terms of stereotypical behavior, but his interest centers on miraculous acts of power.

9. Assyrian prophets engaged in non-standard sexual behavior, transvestism, and activities indicative of gender confusion (Nissinen 2000: 94–95).

There are overlaps between stereotypical prophetic behavior in general and prophetic acts in particular. Saul is labeled as a potential prophet not just by his *hitnabbē'*-behavior, but by its end result of being stripped naked and lying on the ground (1 Sam. 19.23–24). Saul's stereotypical behavior is a short-term counterpart to Isaiah's three-year public nakedness (Isa. 20) and to Ezekiel's compulsory lying on the ground for weeks and months (Ezek. 4.4–8). Zedekiah's fabrication of iron horns is also portrayed as an outcome of *hitnabbē'*-behavior (1 Kgs 22.10–11). Like other prophetic stereotypical behaviors, prophetic acts had much to do with expecting the unusual. Different proclamations required different acts, ranging from Ezekiel's pantomimes to Isaiah's nudity to the sexual involvements of Hosea. What was stereotypical about symbolic acts was not a limited menu of typical behaviors, but rather their dramatic, striking, and unconventional nature.

2.2 *Symbolic Acts as Madness and Folly*
Like ecstasy, prophetic acts could give rise to allegations of madness. Indeed, few symbolic acts could be characterized as normal behavior, and some edge over into the grotesque and offensive. Some are just odd, such as eating a scroll (Ezek. 3.1–3). Many seem to reflect a regression to childhood play. In this category one might place the elaborate playacting of Ezekiel in chs. 4–5 and 12, fooling around with sticks (Ezek. 37.15–20; Zech. 11.7–14), and acting out animal roles with horns and yokes (1 Kgs 22.11; Jeremiah 27–28).[10]

Hostile opponents would easily judge certain other prophetic acts as examples of folly. Destroying a newly purchased jug (Jer. 19.10–13) or a new cloak (1 Kgs 11.29–30) violates common sense and financial logic. The purchase of a field in the face of military defeat or futilely offering wine to Rechabites (Jer. 32 and 35) would certainly be open to the accusation of foolishness. Putting up a signpost to mark the road for an invader is hardly a rational act (Ezek. 21.24–27 [E 19–23]). To pay a price to enter into a love relationship with a woman and then not to have sex with her (Hos. 3.1–3), would likely have been deemed eccentric at best. Understood literally, some prophetic acts involved excessively long journeys to do things such as burying a loincloth at the Euphrates or stones near Pharaoh's palace or taking a scroll to Babylon to read and then sink in the Euphrates (Jer. 13.1–7; 43.8–13; 51.60–64). Of course, some of these prophetic acts may be only literary constructs, especially those that

---

10. Hermann Gunkel: '*Dergleichen tun in Israel die Kinder, die Narren und die P[rophet]en*'. – (*RGG*[2] 4: 1541) ['In Israel children, fools, and prophets do such things']. ARM 26.206 describes a bizarre symbolic act in which a *muḥḫûm* of Dagan 'tears asunder' a lamb and eats it raw, connecting this act to the threat of pestilence. For other peculiar behaviors on the part of intermediaries, see Grabbe (2000: 22).

transcend what seems humanly possible. However, even literary constructs indicate what Israel would have considered to be within the expected parameters of prophetic behavior.

Some prophetic acts entailed public shame, such as going about naked and barefoot (Isa. 20.2–3; cf. 'shame' in v. 4 and Mic. 1.8). The priest Ezekiel narrowly avoided the unclean action of baking on human dung (Ezek. 4.12–15), although cutting his hair and beard would also seem to be a violation of priestly conventions (Ezek. 5.1; Lev. 19.27, 21.5). It is easy to see how Jeremiah's anti-social behavior of celibacy, childlessness, and the avoidance of mourning or feasting (Jer. 16.1–9) – or Ezekiel's omission of expected mourning and his refusal or inability to speak (Ezek. 3.25–27; 24.15–18) – could have been taken as evidence of an unbalanced personality.

One can distinguish between momentary prophetic acts (Jer. 19; 25.15) and long-term performances or enduring changes in life style (Isa. 8.1–4, 20.1–6; Jer. 16.2; Ezekiel 4, 24.15–24). The latter would have an even greater potential to be judged as mad and foolish by the prophet's public. One such long-term act would be giving non-standard and outrageous names to one's children, such as Lo-ami or Mahar-shalal-hash-baz.[11] The charge of folly and madness made against Hosea (Hos. 9.7) could quite believably have been occasioned by his marriage to Gomer, a 'promiscuous woman'. Hosea's shocking behavior finds its closest parallel in a symbolic act of Isaiah that entailed him having sex with some anonymous fellow intermediary ('the prophetess') to produce a portentously named sign child (Isa. 8.3).[12]

To summarize, there was a clear overlap in function between prophetic symbolic acts and other stereotypical prophetic role behaviors. Many of these behaviors were eccentric enough to be labeled as folly and madness by a prophet's opponents.[13]

3. Hosea's Marriage: An Outrageous Stereotypical Act[14]

Comparison with Isa. 8.1–4 shows that Hos. 1.2–9 is a prophetic sign act report (*prophetische Zeichenhandlungsbericht*). Unlike the Isaiah parallel,

---

11. The context in which the inauspicious name Ichabod is given indicates the radical nature of such an action (1 Sam. 4.19–22).

12. There is no reason to see this 'prophetess' as Isaiah's wife (Jepsen 1960; cf. Exod. 15.20; Judg. 4.4; 2 Kgs 22.14; Neh. 6.14).

13. Earlier scholars sometimes evaluated prophets in terms of mental illness. Sellers (1925) diagnosed Hosea with an inferiority complex, sadism, and exhibitionism.

14. I presuppose that the book of Hosea contains, to a greater or lesser degree, words spoken by the eighth-century prophet himself, along with narrative materials that point in some way toward actual incidents in his life. For the danger of confusing Hosea's factual biography with the literary shaping of the book, see Vogels (1984).

however, Hosea's prophetic act is presented as communicating a present reality rather than future events. Another difference is that in Hos. 1.2 the specific act of taking a wife is emphasized as something important in and of itself, and not simply as a preparation for the birth of sign children. Information about Gomer's name and family background, along with her characterization as a promiscuous woman, goes far beyond what would be needed simply to introduce her childbearing role. In fact, outside of vv. 2–3 the 'promiscuous woman' motif plays no role in the remainder of 1.2–9. Hosea 1.4–9 connects to vv. 2–3 by way of the children and not through Gomer's promiscuous nature. Thus the wording of the text indicates that the specific action of taking her as wife is intended to have its own self-contained significance as a prophetic act.

However, the independent significance of Hosea's prophetic act in marrying Gomer is immediately obscured because the following vv. 4–9 focus on their children. It is further eclipsed by the way that ch. 2 utilizes the figure of the children's mother as a personification of Israel and then by a second sign act involving Hosea and an adulterous woman in ch. 3. However, if one reads Hosea ch. 1 on its own, apart from chs. 2 and 3, it becomes apparent that Hosea's act of marrying Gomer simply cannot not work as a metaphor for Yahweh's relationship to Israel. Certainly this analogy is not present in ch. 1 itself.

Marriage to a promiscuous woman would surely have been a shocking and shameful deed, an outrageous stereotypical act comparable to Isaiah's nakedness. Yahweh commands Hosea as to what sort of woman to marry, but the choice of the particular woman Gomer seems to be the prophet's own. As *'ēšet zĕnûnîm*, Gomer is presented as a woman characterized by promiscuity in an intensive and repetitive sense. Construing *zĕnûnîm* as a plural of intensity suggests habitual, repeated actions and a variety of sexual partners: 'a promiscuous woman' (cf. 'days of embalming', Gen. 50.3; *IBHS* 7.4.2 c). Taken as a plural of abstraction it would imply a personal quality: 'a woman inclined to lewdness' (cf. 'wife of contentiousness' [Prov. 21.9; 25.24; 27.15] and 'wife of one's youth' [Prov. 5.18]; *IBHS* 7.4.2 a, b). Hosea marries a sexually active woman, who indulges or has indulged in loose sexual behavior without regard to any strictures that might be imposed on her by a father or husband.[15]

3.1 *Isolating Chapter 1 from Chapters 2 and 3*
As already mentioned, Hosea's marriage to Gomer takes on the character of an analogy describing Yahweh's relationship to Israel *only* when the

---

15. For the origin and impact of this language, Bird (1989); Törnkvist (1998: 25–29, 96–115); Wacker (1996: 39–43). Other recent studies of Hosea's marriage include Abma (1999); Bitter (1975); Hornsby (1999); Leith (1989); Sherwood (1996); Snyman (1993).

reader subsequently encounters this comparison in chs. 2 and 3. However, there are good critical reasons for treating ch. 1 separate from its continuation in chs. 2 and 3. To state these briefly:

- There is a sharp contrast in genre and style between chs. 1 (prose report) and 2 (poetic prophetic speech).
- The imperative address shifts suddenly from singular (Hosea) to plural (the nation) between 1.9 and 2.1 [E 1.10].
- Hos. 2.1–3 [E 1.10–2.1] abruptly reverses the sense of 1.1–9.
- An *inclusio* created by the children's names in 2.1–3 [E 1.10–2.1] and 2.25–26 [E 22–23] sets off ch. 2 as a self-contained section.
- In ch. 1, interest in the children centers on their promiscuous nature and negative names, but in 2.3–4 [E 2.1–2] they move beyond being the objects of the actions of Gomer and Hosea to become active characters who are called upon to speak and accuse.
- In ch. 1, Yahweh's problematic relationship with Israel is expressed through the children's names; ch. 2 instead describes the relationship in terms of husband and wife.
- Chapter 3 is linked in shape and genre to ch. 1 but in topic to ch. 2: adultery (2.4 [E 2]; 3.1), lovers (2.7, 9, 12, 14, 15 [E 5, 7, 10, 12, 13]; 3.1), divine restoration (2.18–19 [E 16–17], 21–22 [E 19–20]; 3.2, 5), deprivation (2.10–11, 13 [E 8–9, 11]; 3.3–4).

The usual understanding of the marriage between Hosea and Gomer as a symbolic act signifying Yahweh's role as Israel's husband is purely a function of its *present* literary location as the first element in the larger context of chs. 1–3. That is to say, a marital and parental prophetic act has been converted into an extended metaphor about Yahweh as the victimized husband and Israel as the faithless wife. Taken on its own terms, however, Hos. 1.2–9 is a tightly constructed and self-contained narrative, one that contains its own explanation of the prophetic acts it reports. It is structured by four cycles of command and explanation. The children Hosea is to acquire in v. 2 materialize one by one in vv. 4–9.

3.2 *Not an Analogy of Election Followed by Infidelity*
Hosea's marriage does not work as an analogy describing divine election followed by national infidelity. As it is presented within the limits of ch. 1 itself, Hosea's act of marrying Gomer can scarcely be a metaphor for Yahweh's relationship to Israel. Wedding a woman who was already promiscuous would provide an exceedingly clumsy parallel to Yahweh's previous election of Israel. Debauched bride and shamed bridegroom are hardly proper roles for Israel and God to play in a drama of election or initial covenant making. This contradicts Hosea's own picture of Israel being found like grapes in the wilderness in 9.10, the tender romanticism of 2.16 (E 14), or Israel's youthful receptivity in 2.17 (E 15). An allegory of marital infidelity would seem to require an originally innocent bride who

subsequently 'goes wrong' (cf. Ezek. 16). The call for Israel to return to its pure beginnings made in 2.16–25 (E 14–23) would be undermined by a denial of Israel's pure starting point in the relationship. Moreover, marriage to a woman already known to have a penchant for sexual adventure would seriously undermine any claim that Yahweh has been betrayed by Israel. One would expect instead that an allegory describing Israel's disloyalty to Yahweh in terms of Gomer's activities would focus on her specific behavior while married to Hosea, not on her general character as demonstrated by her previous behavior.

To save the analogy, commentaries regularly take the statement of her promiscuous nature in 1.2 as something proleptic, as a characteristic that actually only emerged after her married life had begun. However, understanding Gomer's promiscuity as a future reality contradicts the most normal understanding of the text. The children's 'promiscuous' quality and their names in vv. 4–9 undoubtedly relate to the present state of affairs rather than to whatever may unfold in the future, as does the accusation in v. 2b that the land 'commits great whoredom'.

Both grammar and context force the reader to understand the expression 'promiscuous woman' as an indicator of Gomer's present character based on her past behavior. On its own, her promiscuous nature may not suggest anything about her future behavior. Indeed, if Gomer is understood to be a blameless bride who only *later* became unfaithful, v. 2 would be a remarkably misleading and peculiar introduction to the story told in 1.2–9. Yahweh commands marriage to a promiscuous woman and the production of children whose promiscuous quality relates to or derives from that of their mother. And this is precisely what takes place in the following verses. The bearing and naming of children is commanded and is obediently performed. What emphatically does *not* unfold is a story about any dysfunction in the marriage brought about by Gomer's behavior.

The use of the term 'promiscuous woman' rather than the vocabulary of adultery is another indication that the prophetic act commanded in 1.2 is not intended to express any sort of analogy involving Yahweh's covenantal relationship to Israel under the figure of the relationship between Hosea and Gomer. If her problematic behavior is to be thought of as something happening *within* their marriage, then the language of adultery should have been used. That is the appropriate language for describing the disloyal actions of a woman sexually accountable to a husband (cf. 2.4 [E 2]; 3.1) and of a nation violating its exclusive covenant relationship with its God (7.4). The children Gomer and Hosea produce are 'children of promiscuity', pointing to the transgression of people and land, but since they are legitimately Hosea's children ('bore him a son'), they do not point to any analogy about Yahweh and a faithless wife or to Yahweh's relationship to Israel thought of in marriage terms. Moreover, if Hosea were supposed to represent Yahweh in 1.2, there would be an unbearable internal tension between 'take a wife' and 'the land [goes] away from Yahweh'. How can an image of bringing the two parties *together* into a relationship by marriage be intended to represent the reality of their moving further *apart*?

In short, Hos. 1.2–9 does not correlate Hosea with Yahweh, or Hosea's wedding with election, or his marriage with the covenant in any way. The notion of promiscuity leads into the birth of the sign children, not into any sort of drama about marital problems. Yahweh's problematic relationship to Israel focuses on the names of the children, not on the marriage of Gomer and Hosea.

3.3 *The Real Focus of Hosea 1.2–3*

Taken on its own terms, Hos. 1.2–3 concentrates on the initial act of contracting a marriage rather than on living out any sort of problematic married life. The comparison is narrow: a wife of promiscuity and children of promiscuity point to the land that engages in promiscuity by distancing itself from Yahweh. Such an image comparing the land to a woman with a sexually dubious character corresponds nicely to Hosea's penchant for shocking metaphors (cf. 5.12; 8.9). The *sole* point of mimetic comparison in Hosea's prophetic act is Israel's behavior over against Yahweh. Then vv. 4–9 set forth this deteriorated relationship in terms of the children's names.

From a methodological perspective, the explanation of Hosea's prophetic act given within the bounds of 1.2–9 should be taken as primary, in contrast to concepts imported from outside the unit. Hosea's four prophetic actions are explained by the 'for' clauses that immediately follow (vv. 2, 4, 6, 9). Self-evidently, the interpreter should concentrate on the explanation within v. 2 itself to understand the import of Hosea's act of marrying.[16] The 'for' clause explicates the 'promiscuous' quality of Gomer and the children in terms of the land's disloyal activities. The land is engaging in conduct that distances it from Yahweh, a transgression analogous to illicit sexual behavior. Gomer is a 'first stage' sign of the land's transgression, who then births three 'second stage' sign children whose 'promiscuity' derives (in an unexplained way) from their origin from her. She points to the *fact* of transgression; they point to the *punishment* that results (Sherwood 1996: 126–27).

However, there is a problem. The text does not really need Hosea to engage in a wedding in order to compare the promiscuous woman and the land. That is to say, the explanation given in v. 2b does not provide any sort of rationale for the act of getting married itself. Absolutely no association is made between Gomer's promiscuous nature and Hosea's act

---

16. An explanatory 'for' clause also follows the command to perform a prophetic act in Isa. 8.3–4; Jer. 16.5; Ezek. 21.24–26 [E 19–21]; Hab. 2.2–3; Zech. 11.4, 6, 15–16.

of wedding her. The only explicit analogical correlation is that drawn between the promiscuous nature of wife and children and the behavior of the land. Why then is a wedding to a promiscuous woman the first element of Hosea's prophetic act?

Gomer herself is the subject of numerous active verbs and obviously plays an indispensable role as an associate performer in this extended prophetic act. However, her contribution to the story has nothing to do with promiscuity, but only with motherhood. Chapter 1 says nothing about any failure of hers to meet the obligations of marriage. On the contrary, she acts quite properly in conceiving, bearing, and weaning her three sign children. If anything, Gomer seems to be described as a model wife in spite of her promiscuous character.[17]

At every turn, ch. 1 resists being forced into the analogy: 'Hosea the husband stands for Yahweh'. As already mentioned, this pattern emerges only when the reader subsequently encounters chs. 2 and 3. It is only reading under the influence of chs. 2 and 3 that constructs the metaphorical relationship: Hosea is to Gomer as Yahweh is to Israel. A comparison with the very different prophetic act reported in ch. 3 is instructive. There the analogous connection between Hosea and Yahweh is unavoidable: 'love a woman . . . just as Yahweh loves the people'. There Hosea clearly performs a prophetic act pointing to Yahweh's future action. In contrast, in ch. 1 Gomer and the children correspond to the land, but neither Hosea nor his act of getting married seems to correspond to anything.

3.4 *Shame, Folly and Madness*

Hosea's marriage was a stereotypical act open to being attacked by opponents. In its original context, his prophetic act of marriage to Gomer did not have any symbolic or analogical function beyond pointing to the promiscuous behavior of the land. However, it also must have functioned as an outrageous bit of stereotypical behavior. Like the bizarre conduct of other prophets, part of its intent would have been to solidify Hosea's status as a prophet to be taken seriously. Such an astonishing marriage fell within the parameters of what might be expected in a stereotypical prophetic act, as the similar behavior reported in Isa. 8.3–4 suggests.[18]

Like other prophetic stereotypical behaviors of an extreme nature, marriage to a woman with a promiscuous background would have involved Hosea in public shame and opened him up to charges of foolishness and mental illness. Hosea 9.7 quotes the opponents of Hosea

---

17. Perhaps Gomer herself was a 'prophetess' like Isaiah's sexual partner in Isa. 8.1–4. This could explain why she is fully identified by name and paternity.

18. Jeremiah seems to have been outraged by similar actions by his prophetic opponents: 'in the prophets of Jerusalem I have seen a more shocking thing: they commit adultery' (Jer. 23.14).

charging him with folly and madness. It is highly likely that this related to his reputation in regard to Gomer and the woman of ch. 3 (if she is not Gomer). Proverbs 12.4 could easily describe Hosea's situation in the view of many: 'A good wife (*'ēšet ḥayil*, contrast *'ēšet zĕnûnîm*) is the crown of her husband, but she who brings shame is like rottenness in his bones'. Fools lack self-control and fall under the spell of dangerous women (Prov. 7.6–23).[19]

4. *Marriage to Gomer as a Prophetic Act*

By taking Gomer as his wife, Hosea performed a prophetic act intended to undermine priestly claims of purity and mimic the nation's apostasy. In spite of its lack of any analogical connection to Yahweh's relationship to Israel, there is no reason to suppose that Hosea's prophetic act of marrying Gomer would have been completely unrelated to his prophetic message. I am suggesting that Hosea married this sexually active woman in order to imitate the trespasses that the priests and people were committing and to undercut the public standing of his priestly opponents by undermining their claims of priestly purity. A ritually pure lifestyle functioned as stereotypical behavior for priests. An important element of this purity was the priesthood's exceptionally restricted patterns of marriage. Hosea's prophetic act directed a mocking attack on the priesthood's commitment to a life of ritual purity as expressed in their choice of marriage partners. Hosea's marriage also imitated and thus assailed the entire people's penchant for 'promiscuous' behavior in the realms of both sexuality and religion.

4.1 *Hosea's Criticism of the Priests*
Hosea condemned priests and the worship they managed. As a peripheral prophet, Hosea criticized the priestly establishment. His attack on the Yahwistic cult was extensive: the gold calf image (8.5–6; 10.5–6; 13.2; 14.3), pillars, altars and sacrifice (4.19; 6.6; 8.11, 13; 9.4; 10.1–2, 8; 12.11), shrines (4.15; 5.1–2; 9.15; 10.8; 12.12 [E 11]), and the cult in general (2.13 [E 11]; 5.6; 7.14; 8.2; 9.5).[20] Hosea's condemnations of the priests themselves are direct, numerous, and specific. They are a band of robbers (6.9) and nothing better than idolatrous priests (10.5, *kĕmārîm*). They have failed in teaching torah (8.12). The confessional laments they lead (cf. Joel 1.13; 2.17) are parodied as worse than ineffective (6.1–3). The triple address of

19. I owe this insight to Seow, who connects the charge of folly made against Hosea with his 'association with the...''woman of harlotry''' (1982: 221).

20. Even attacks ostensibly directed against the cult of Baal probably refer to practices carried out as part of Yahwistic religion (Albertz 1994: I, 143–75).

5.1 makes it clear that Hosea's priestly opponents were part of the power structure, not marginal or heterodox priests.

Hosea 4.4–10 records an extensive and direct attack on the priesthood, although there are many problems in interpretation.[21] The priest has misled the people and failed in regard to knowledge and torah (4.4, 6). Priests eat the people's sin, apparently a reference to their consumption of sin and guilt offerings (4.8).[22] A curse against three generations (involving mother and sons, vv. 5–6) is reminiscent of Amos' threat against Amaziah's family purity (Amos 7.17).

Hosea condemns the priesthood as part of a wider assault on the religious apostasy of the whole nation ('like people, like priest', Hos. 4.9). The language of committing 'harlotry' empowers his attack on cultic malpractice and the people's faithlessness in general. This language of harlotry is generalized and metaphorical in 4.10, 12; 5.3–4; 9.1. Similar motifs are present in the sexuality implicit in the wild ass comparison of 8.9 and in the reference to corruption as at Gibeah in 9.9 (understanding this as a reference to Judg. 19–20). In 4.11–12 'promiscuity' and 'harlotry' relate to illicit worship practices and forsaking Yahweh. In contrast, 4.13–14 uses harlotry language to refer actual sex acts associated in a tangential way to worship. The men's religious practice and sexual behavior lead to similar behavior on the part of their dependent women, a source of public shame for the men.

4.2 *Sex, Marriage and Ritual Impurity*

Hosea's marriage attacked the priests through the motif of ritual impurity. Hosea utilizes the language of ritual impurity to enhance his condemnation of the nation's apostasy (5.3; 6.10 *ṭāmē*; 9.10 *šiqqûs*). He threatens ritual impurity in exile (9.3) and that the sacrifices themselves would become the functional equivalent of defiling food (9.4). In a similar way, his association through poetic parallelism of the *qĕdēšâ* woman (a religious specialist of some kind) with commercial prostitution undermines her holiness with an insinuation of sexually produced impurity (4.14).

An important aspect of priestly stereotypical behavior involved living a ritually pure lifestyle, much of which had to do with matters of sex and family life. For example, in order to preserve their holy status, priests were explicitly forbidden to marry a prostitute, a defiled woman, or even a divorcee (Lev. 21.7). If a priest's daughter were to be involved in prostitution, the priest himself would fall into a profane (not holy) state (v. 9). The high priest could not even marry a widow, but only a virgin (vv.

---

21. See the commentaries. Lundbom (1986) contends that these verses are intended for the king. DeRoche (1983) argues that these charges are directed at the people.

22. Understanding 'sin' as a sin offering (Lev. 6.19 [E 26]; 7.7; 10.17).

13–15). Ezekiel 44.22 exhibits a similar concern for the marital arrange-
ments of priests, and Neh. 13.29 attacks a scion of the high priestly family
for defiling the priesthood by marrying a foreign woman. Although our
evidence is limited to what was demanded of Judahite priests, it is likely
that expectations were similar in the north. Thus, Amos undermines
Amaziah's priestly identity with a threat that his wife would become a city
prostitute (Amos 7.17). More generally, the tight association of sexual
behavior and ritual impurity is demonstrated by the common use of the
verb 'defile' as a synonym for improper intercourse (Gen. 34.5, defiling the
woman; Lev. 18.24, defiling the man).

As a striking prophetic act, Hosea married a promiscuous woman,
someone who would have been impure with regard to marriage for one of
his priestly opponents. Together Hosea and Gomer produced 'promiscuous children'. Hosea's public and shame-inducing act of sexual involvement with ritual impurity pointed to the transgressions of the priesthood
and the nation. As a prophetic act with a causative effect, it also implicitly
threatened the purity of the priests' family life, thus undercutting their
claims of status and authority as religious leaders. Hosea's marriage thus
imitated the very behavior for which he criticized the male population of
Israel and directed a mocking, destabilizing attack on the priesthood's
commitment to a life of ritual purity.

Hosea's notorious prophetic act was probably an important factor in his
being labeled as a fool and a lunatic (Hos. 9.7). It also may be taken as a
paradigmatic example of the collision of stereotypical role behaviors
considered appropriate for different sorts of religious specialists – marriage
purity for the priest and outrageous prophetic action on the part of the
prophet – as each struggled to achieve and maintain authority and
recognition in the public arena.

BIBLIOGRAPHY

Abma, R.
 1999 *Bonds of Love: Methodic Studies of Prophetic Texts with Marriage
     Imagery* (SSN, 40; Assen: Van Gorcum).
Albertz, Rainer
 1994 *A History of Israelite Religion in the Old Testament Period* (2 vols.;
     Louisville: Westminster John Knox).
Amsler, Samuel
 1980 'Les prophètes et la communication par les actes', in Rainer Albertz
     (ed.), *Werden und Wirken des Alten Testament* (Göttingen:
     Vandenhoeck & Ruprecht): 194–201.
Bird, Phyllis
 1989 '"To Play the Harlot": An Inquiry into an Old Testament

Metaphor', in Peggy L. Day (ed.), *Gender and Difference in Ancient Israel* (Minneapolis: Fortress): 75–94.

Bitter, Stefan
  1975   *Die Ehe des Propheten Hosea: Eine auslesungsgeschichtliche Untersuchung* (GTA, 3; Göttingen: Vandenhoeck & Ruprecht).
DeRoche, Michael
  1983   'Structure, Rhetoric, and Meaning in Hosea iv 4–10', *VT* 33: 185–198.
Dijkstra, Meindert
  1995   'Is Balaam Also among the Prophets?' *JBL* 114: 43–64.
Fohrer, Georg
  1953   *Die symbolischen Handlungen der Propheten* (Zurich: Zwingli-Verlag).
Grabbe, Lester L.
  1995   *Priests, Prophets, Diviners, Sages: A Socio-Historical Study of Religious Specialists in Ancient Israel* (Valley Forge, PA: Trinity Press International).
  2000   'Ancient Near Eastern Prophecy from an Anthropological Perspective', in Martti Nissinen (ed.), *Prophecy in its Ancient Near Eastern Context* (SBLSymS, 13; Atlanta: Society of Biblical Literature): 13–32.
Hornsby, Teresa J.
  1999   '"Israel Has Become a Worthless Thing": Re-Reading Gomer in Hosea 1–3', *JSOT* 82: 115–28.
Huffmon, Herbert B.
  2000   'A Company of Prophets: Mari, Assyria, Israel', in Martti Nissinen (ed.), *Prophecy in its Ancient Near Eastern Context* (SBLSymS, 13; Atlanta: Society of Biblical Literature): 47–70.
Jepsen, A.
  1960   'Die Nebiah in Jes 8 6', *ZAW* 72: 267–68.
Leith, Mary J. W.
  1989   'Verse and Reverse: The Transformation of the Woman, Israel, in Hosea 1–3', in P. L. Day (ed.), *Gender and Difference in Ancient Israel* (Minneapolis: Fortress Press): 95–108.
Long, Burke O.
  1981   'Social Dimensions of Prophetic Conflict', *Semeia* 21: 31–43 (repr. in Robert P. Gordon [ed.], *The Place Is Too Small for Us: The Israelite Prophets in Recent Scholarship* [SBTS, 5; Winona Lake, IN: Eisenbrauns, 1995]: 308–31).
Lundbom, Jack R.
  1986   'Contentious Priests and Contentious People in Hosea iv 1–10', *VT* 36: 52–70.
Michaelsen, Peter
  1989   'Ecstasy and Possession in Ancient Israel: A Review of Some Recent Contributions', *SJOT* 2: 28–54;
Müller, Hans-Peter
  1969   'Die Hebraïsche Wurzel שׁיח', *VT* 19: 361–71

Nelson, Richard D
    1993   *Raising up a Faithful Priest* (Louisville: Westminster John Knox).
Nissinen, Martti
    2000   'The Socioreligious Role of the Neo-Assyrian Prophets', in Martti
                Nissinen (ed.), *Prophecy in its Ancient Near Eastern Context*
                (SBLSymS, 13; Atlanta: Society of Biblical Literature): 89–114.
Overholt, Thomas W.
    1982   'Seeing Is Believing: The Social Setting of Prophetic Acts of Power',
                JSOT 23: 3–31 (repr. in D. J. Chalcraft [ed.], *Social-Scientific Old
                Testament Criticism* [Biblical Seminar, 47; Sheffield: Sheffield
                Academic Press, 1997]: 314–40).
    1986   *Prophecy in Cross-Cultural Perspective: A Sourcebook for Biblical
                Researchers* (SBLSBS, 17; Atlanta: Scholars Press).
    1989   *Channels of Prophecy: The Social Dynamics of Prophetic Activity*
                (Minneapolis: Fortress).
    1990   'Prophecy in History: The Social Reality of Intermediation', *JSOT*
                48: 3–29 (repr. in Philip R. Davies [ed.], *The Prophets* [Biblical
                Seminar, 42; Sheffield: Sheffield Academic Press, 1996]: 61–84).
Parker, Simon B.
    1978   'Possession Trance and Prophecy in Pre-Exilic Israel', *VT* 28: 271–
                85 (repr. in D. E. Orton [ed.], *Prophecy in the Hebrew Bible* [Brill
                Readers in Biblical Studies, 5; Leiden: Brill, 2000]: 124–38).
Parpola, Simo
    1997   *Assyrian Prophecies* (SAA, 9; Helsinki: Helsinki University Press).
Petersen, David L.
    1981   *The Roles of Israel's Prophets* (JSOTSup, 17; Sheffield: JSOT
                Press).
Sellers, O. R.
    1925   'Hosea's Motives', *AJSL* 41: 243–47.
Seow, Choon L.
    1982   'Hosea 14:10 and the Foolish People Motif', *CBQ* 44 (1982): 212–
                24.
Sherwood, Yvonne M.
    1996   *The Prostitute and the Prophet: Hosea's Marriage in Literary-
                theoretical Perspective* (JSOTSup, 212; Sheffield: Sheffield Aca-
                demic Press).
Snyman, Gerrie
    1993   'Social Reality and Religious Language in the Marriage Metaphor
                in Hosea 1–3', *OTE* 6: 90–112.
Stacey, W. David
    1990   *Prophetic Drama in the Old Testament* (London: Epworth).
Törnkvist, Rut
    1998   *The Use and Abuse of Female Sexual Imagery in the Book of Hosea*
                (Acta Universitatis Upsaliensis; A. Women in Religion, 7; Uppsala:
                University Library).

Uffenheimer, Benjamin
    1988   'Prophecy, Ecstasy and Sympathy', in J. A. Emerton (ed.), *Congress Volume: Jerusalem, 1986* (VTSup, 40; Leiden: Brill): 257–69.

van der Toorn, Karel
    2000   'Mesopotamian Prophecy between Immanence and Transcendence', in Martti Nissinen (ed.), *Prophecy in its Ancient Near Eastern Context* (SBLSymS, 13; Atlanta: Society of Biblical Literature): 71–87.

Vogels, Walter
    1984   'Diachronic and Synchronic Studies of Hosea 1–3', *BZ* 28: 94–98.

Wacker, Marie-Theres
    1996   *Figurationen des Weiblichen im Hosea-Buch* (HBS, 8; Freiburg: Herder).

Wilson, Robert R.
    1979   'Prophecy and Ecstacy: A Re-examination', *JBL* 98: 321–37.

    1980   *Prophecy and Society in Ancient Israel* (Philadelphia: Fortress).

WHAT WAS THE IMAGE OF JEALOUSY IN EZEKIEL 8?

Margaret S. Odell

In Ezek. 8, Yahweh takes Ezekiel on a tour of the Jerusalem temple and shows him a series of abominations. The image of jealousy stands near the altar (8.5–6), 70 elders of the house of Israel pray to their idols (8.7–13), women weep at the northern gate (8.14–15), and 25 men bow to the sun (8.16–18). One issue concerns the extent to which Ezek. 8 may be regarded as a reliable account of late sixth-century cult practices, especially since it is presumed that the the idolatries resemble the sins of Manasseh's time, which the Josianic reforms had eradicated (Torrey 1930; Greenberg 1970: xi–xxxv; Fishbane 1984: 134–35; Duguid 1994: 65–68). Even if it is clear that the deity regards these practices as abominations, the nature of the abominations remains a matter of some dispute. Because past efforts to describe a coherent ritual have not met with critical acceptance (e.g. Gaster 1941: 289–97; May 1937: 309–21), it has become customary to regard the scenes as a collage of the idolatries of the house of Israel (see, e.g., Ackerman 1992; Allen 1994: 138–41; Blenkinsopp 1990: 53–54; Block 1997: 283–300; Greenberg 1983: 201–02; Zimmerli 1979: 237–38).

Although these critical judgments have the advantage of scholarly caution, they have had the unintended consequence not only of divorcing the individual scenes in ch. 8 from one another, but also of isolating the entire chapter from its larger literary context, with the result that no interpretation of any particular episode adequately reflects any of Ezekiel's larger themes. Despite previous failures to find coherence in the temple vision, the premise of this essay is that the image of jealousy cannot be adequately interpreted in isolation from ch. 8 or, for that matter, from the book as a whole.

That the chapter can and should be read as an account of a coherent ritual is, in fact, implied in the deity's announcement of judgment in 8.17–18. Although the abominations constitute a major theme of this chapter, Yahweh does not condemn Judah's idols so much as its prayers: 'though they cry with a loud voice in my ears, I will not listen to them' (8.18b). The declaration of judgment suggests that Ezekiel has witnessed a well-established ritual of Yahwistic petition and prayer, which the deity rejects on both ritual and ethical grounds (8.17). I therefore interpret the scenes in the chapter as succeeding stages of a national ritual of complaint. The purpose of the complaint is to implore the return of the deity, whose absence has brought on national distress. Within the framework of this ritual, the image of jealousy signifies devotion to Yahweh and is the justification for the appeal of the elders of the house of Israel. The purpose of this essay is to argue that the image of jealousy functioned as a type of votive statue whose abomination consisted in its use as a substitutionary offering.[1]

1. *The Statue*

One must dispense first with the recently emerging consensus that the image of jealousy is an idol, possibly of the goddess Asherah, which provokes Yahweh's jealousy. Eichrodt put forward this position in his commentary (Eichrodt 1970: 122), and more recent proposals reflect an interest in retrieving elements of popular religion that have been suppressed by the biblical writers (Dohmen 1984: 265; Schroer 1987: 41; Koch 1988: 111–112; Ackerman 1992: 40–41, n. 14; Dijkstra 1996: 91–92; Lutzky 1996: 124).

There are good reasons to question this emerging line of interpretation. H. Lutzky, for example, argues that the logic of the expression 'image of X' requires that the image embody or express the characteristics of X, and not emotional reactions to it (Lutzky 1996: 122). Although one may reject her conclusion, which leaves us with a statue of Asherah after all, Lutzky has at least opened up the question of what the phrase means. If it is an 'image of jealousy', it is reasonable to ask how it embodies or expresses the characteristics of *qin'â*.

Second, the lines of evidence yield only an uncertain equation of the image of jealousy with Asherah. The term that is used here in Ezekiel, *semel*, is used only three times elsewhere in the Hebrew Bible, in contexts that suggest that the noun was not necessarily associated with the goddess (Deut. 4.16; 2 Chron. 33.7, 15). In Deut. 4.16, for example, the term is employed in the prohibition of images of Yahweh. The one context in which *semel* may refer to a representation of Asherah is 2 Chron. 33.7, which preserves 2 Kgs 21.7–8 with only a few variations, among them the substitution of the phrase *pesel hassemel* for *pesel ha'ăšērâ* in 2 Kgs 21.7 (Japhet 1993: 1007). Although this parallel in 2 Kings leads to the inference that the *semel* in 2 Chronicles is an idol of Asherah (McKay 1973: 22), the second use of *semel* in that context supports a different conclusion. As in Ezek. 8, which differentiates between the *semel* and the other idols of the

---

1. I am grateful to Richard D. Weis for help with text-critical matters and to Paul Joyce, K. Lawson Younger, Jr, and John F. Kutsko, for their helpful critiques of an earlier draft of this essay. Their suggestions have helped me to sharpen the argument; any remaining errors are, of course, my own.

house of Israel, this latter reference differentiates between the *semel* and other cult images by referring to them separately as the 'foreign gods and the *semel*' (2 Chron. 33.15). One suspects that this is a distinction that makes a difference, and that the Chronicler's substitution of *pesel hassemel* for the Deuteronomist's *pesel ha'ăšērâ* presents a less polemically distorted account of cult practices from the time of Manasseh. In any case, the use of *semel* elsewehere in the Hebrew Bible does not necessitate the conclusion that it refers to a statue of Asherah in Ezek. 8.3, 5.

Evidence within Ezekiel makes the identification of the *semel* in 8.3, 5 with Asherah even more unlikely. Nowhere does Ezekiel condemn the people for the worship of Asherah. Admittedly, his polemic against the *gillûlîm and šiqqûṣîm* obscures any specific references to gods and goddesses. But the gist of Ezekiel's polemic leads one to suspect rival male deities and powers, as Yahweh's wife Jerusalem prostitutes herself to her implicitly male lovers. Even when women are depicted at worship as in 8.15, where they 'weep the Tammuz', they do not venerate a goddess.

Finally, Ezek. 8.3–5 suggests that the image of jealousy is not an idol. Unlike the other sections of the chapter, where people are engaged in specific rites, no one is depicted venerating the image of jealousy. When Ezekiel sees it, the deity does ask him whether he sees what they are doing (8.6); however, the context can as easily imply that the image of jealousy represents the cultic act and is not itself the object of veneration. Furthermore, since this is the one of the few instances in which Ezekiel refrains from using his preferred terms *gillûlîm* and *šiqqûṣîm*, dungballs and worthless things, to refer to cult images (Kutsko 2000: 28–42), its offense evidently consists of something other than idolatry, if idolatry is construed as the veneration of cult images representing rival deities.

If *semel* does not refer to an image of a divine being, one other possibility exists, since the term was also used of representations of human beings (Hoftijzer and Jongeling 1995: 792; cf. McKay 1973: 22–23, 92–93; Greenberg 1983: 168). Outside of the Bible, cognates of the word appear only in Phoenician and Punic inscriptions, where it refers to anthropomorphic statues of both human beings (e.g. 'this is my own image', *KAI* 3,2; cf. 40,3) and deities (*KAI* 12,3; 26 C IV 13ff; 33).

Although the use of *semel* to refer to statues of human beings is well known, the contexts in which the term appears in the Bible has led to the assumption that it was appropriated solely as a reference to statues of divine beings. In addition, critical efforts to establish the probability that *semel* could be used to denote an idol has obscured one other important question, that of the function of such statues. To use Christoph Dohmen's distinction, the emphasis has been on the essence of *semel*s, and not their function (Dohmen 1984: 263–66). Against this prevailing critical concern, it is worth noting that in a great many instances, *semel*s functioned as votive statues. As such, they not only signified the devotee's faithfulness to the god, they also invoked divine blessings for the recipient (*KAI* 33, 40, 41, 43).

That the statue in Ezek. 8.3 functioned as a type of votive statue is indicated by its designation as *semel haqqin'â hammaqneh*. Although *qin'â*, or zeal, appears more frequently as a characteristic trait of Yahweh, the term is also used, if rarely, of human beings. In the Baal-Peor incident at Shittim, Phinehas averts God's zeal, which has broken out in the form of a plague, by running his spear through an Israelite and his Moabite lover. Phinehas' reward is God's covenant of peace and the promise of perpetual priesthood (Num. 25.10–13). Elijah proclaims that he has been very zealous for Yahweh even as his enemies seek to slay him (1 Kgs 19.14). In the face of this opposition, Yahweh appoints Elijah to set events in motion that will result in further bloodshed as Israel is cleansed of its idolatry (1 Kgs 19.15–17). Jehu slaughters all of the sons of Ahab – and, not incidentally, claims the throne (1 Kgs 9.10). In all of these accounts, the human display of zeal is not an ordinary act of piety, but an expression of extreme devotion to the deity in times of Israelite apostasy.

The second term in 8.3, *hammaqneh*, expresses the intended outcome of the human display of zeal. Although *hammaqneh* is widely translated 'provokes to jealousy', as in NRSV, this translation rests on the tenuous assumption that the verbal form is a variant spelling (i.e. *qnh*) of the root *qn'*, to be jealous (GKC §75 qq). However, such an argument is uncompelling when both roots appear together, as in MT Ezek. 8.3. Moreover, since no other such spelling of *qn'* is attested, the term should be translated as a hiphil participle of *qnh*, to create. As such, the epithet *hammaqneh* reflects ancient traditions that associate creative activity with Yahweh, whose central act of salvation is to beget or acquire the people of Israel (Exod. 15.16; Deut. 32.6; Pss. 78.54, 139.13; cf. Gen. 4.1, 14.19 and 22). The Hiphil form suggests that the *semel* itself did not embody this creative function; rather, through its symbolic expression of human zeal, it invoked Yahweh to act in accordance with these ancient attributes (cf. Waltke and O'Connor 1990: §27.1e; §27.5).

To sum up: If evidence within Ezekiel makes it unlikely that the *semel haqqin'â hammaqneh* was regarded as an idol, the Phoenician usage leads us to consider the possibility that it functioned as a kind of votive statue. The *semel*'s designation as an expression of zeal that invokes divine blessings corroborates this suggestion. As a votive statue, the *semel* need not have been considered a violation either of the prohibition against the worship of other gods or of the construction of idols. Although it came to be regarded as an illicit aspect of temple worship, as suggested by 2 Chron. 33.7, 15, it would be erroneous to assume that its offense consisted of the veneration of cult images representing rival deities.

2. *The Abomination*

One of the difficulties in determining the nature of the abomination of the image of zeal is that so little is said about it. Ezekiel refers to it as if it were a well-known element of the cultic furnishings of the temple, and the parallel references in 2 Chron. 33 add little to our understanding. The matter is further complicated by Ezekiel's pungent polemic, which outside of ch. 8 tends to erase any distinction between cult statues by referring them as *gillûlîm and šiqqûṣîm*, dungballs and worthless things. Fortunately, a handful of more specific references to cult statues can be found scattered throughout the book (16.17; 20.31–32; 23.38–39; 43.7, 9). Although these references are just as ambiguous as the mention of the image of jealousy in 8.3, 5, taken together they suggest a connection with the practice of child sacrifice.

The clearest reference to cult statues is in Ezekiel's vision of the newly built temple (Ezek. 43.7–10). Although this text is not usually discussed in connection with Ezek. 8, a number of clues suggest that it is to be read as its counterpart. As is well known, 43.1–3 explicitly links this vision to that of ch. 8. More particularly, both 43.7–10 and 8.5–6 revolve around themes of drawing near and distancing: what the people had done in 8.3–5 to draw near to the deity had prompted the deity's departure, while in 43.7–10 the deity's return requires a reversal of those earlier conditions. Furthermore, the offense in both visions consists of the presence of cult statues. In ch. 8, the statue in question had been the image of zeal, while in 43.7–9, the offensive objects are *pigrê malkêhem*, rendered in NRSV as 'corpses of their kings':

> The house of Israel shall no more defile my holy name, neither they nor their kings, by their whoring and by the corpses of their kings at their death (*pigrê malkêhem bamôtam*). When they placed their threshold by my threshold and their doorposts beside my doorposts, with only a wall between me and them, they were defiling my holy name by their abominations that they committed; therefore I have consumed them in my anger. Now let them put away their idolatry (*zᵉnûtam*) and the corpses of their kings (*pigrê malkêhem*) far from me, and I will reside among them forever (43.7–10).

A closer analysis of this phrase suggests that the latter are better understood as statues commemorating offerings to the deity.

Elsewhere in the Hebrew Bible, *peger* more routinely refers to corpses. When that meaning is inferred here, Ezek. 43.7–10 appears to describe the existence of royal tombs that have defiled the temple. However, since no archaeological or other evidence bears out this interpretation (Zimmerli 1983: 417; Block 1998: 584–85), other explanations have been sought. Walther Zimmerli follows the argument of David Neiman, which hinged on the parallel use of two Ugaritic terms, *skn* and *pgr*, in dedicatory inscriptions (Neiman 1948: 55–60; cf. Zimmerli 1983: 417). Demonstrating that *skn* and *pgr* referred to monuments, Neiman interpreted *peger* in Ezek. 43.7, 9 and Lev. 26.30 to refer to royal funerary monuments.

One difficulty with Neiman's argument is that the Ugaritic inscriptions do not refer to monuments of human beings or, for that matter, to funerary monuments, but rather to monuments commemorating offerings (e.g. *pgr [š] w-alp*, Gordon 1955: 69, 2, 3; Aisleitner 1963: 2189). In line with this usage of *pgr* in the Ugaritic inscriptions, the expression *pgr mlk* may therefore designate the type of offering that is commemorated by the statues. If that is the case, then the lexeme *mlk* points us in the direction of a handful of difficult biblical texts which refer to offerings *lmlk*, the precise interpretation of which remains a matter of ongoing debate (Heider 1985; Day 1989).

The starting point for modern discussions of *mlk* offerings is Otto Eissfeldt's 1935 study, *Molk als Opferbegriff im Punischen und Hebräischen und das Ende das Gottes Molock* (1935). Although it had been customary to interpret biblical references either as a title ('king') or as the proper name of a deity ('Molek'), Eissfeldt argued that it was a technical sacrificial term. He then applied this finding to the biblical references and argued that the term was best understood to refer to a type of child sacrifice which had been a legitimate part of the Yahwistic cult until the time of the Josianic reforms.

As George Heider has pointed out in his masterful review of the history of research, Eissfeldt's argument has remained the focal point of all subsequent discussions of these difficult texts. Recent works either defend Eissfeldt's thesis (Gibson 1982: 74–75) or adduce new extrabiblical evidence in order to defend the traditional rendering of Molek as the name of a deity (Heider 1985; Day 1989). Despite the continuing disagreement over Eissfeldt's interpretation of the biblical references to *mlk*, however, at least some of his critics concede that he correctly concluded that the Phoenician inscriptions employ *mlk* as a technical sacrificial term (Heider 1985: 185–88; Day 1989: 6–8). Day has further qualified Eissfeldt's findings by suggesting that *mlk* simply means 'offering' (cf. *KAI* 99); other terms like *'dm, 'mr*, and *b'l* specify whether it is an offering of a human being, an animal, or an offering in place of a child, respectively (Day 1989: 6–8). In the ensuing discussion, I follow Day's caution and construe *mlk*-offerings as child sacrifices only when the context demands such a reading.

Although Ezek. 43.7–9 has not been adduced as evidence one way or the other in the *molk*-Molek debate, it bears closer scrutiny as a parallel to the practice of setting up monuments in commemoration of offerings. With respect to monuments commemorating *mlk*-offerings, dedicatory inscriptions reflect two distinct patterns. In one pattern, the inscription identifies the recipient, the donor, and the type of offering, as follows:

> To the Lord, Baal-Hamon, a vow which Adonbaal Son of Abdeshmun
> vowed, an offering of a man (*mlk 'dm*), his own son, his son in perfect
> condition. He heard his voice, he blessed him. (*KAI* 107; translation by
> Day 1989: 5)

In this pattern, the monument is not self-referenced; if anything, it serves
only as a kind of gift tag indicating the nature and purpose of the
transaction.

In a handful of other inscriptions, however, a monument is designated as
nsb mlk (i.e. stele *mlk*), and the subject of the inscription is the monument
itself (*KAI* 62, A, B; cf. Heider 1985: 182–84). Since the same semantic
configuration is present in the phrase *pgr mlk*, I suggest that *malkêhem* be
revocalized *molkêhem* and construed as a reference to a *molk*-sacrifice,
which both the kings and the house of Israel commemorate with their
pᵉgarîm. Such a reading would be consistent with the Ugaritic parallels in
which the phrase *pgr N* indicates that the monument commemorates an
offering.

Indeed, it can be argued that these monuments served as the offerings
themselves. Two of the earliest inscriptions, which on paleographical
grounds have been dated to the seventh century, contain the phrase *nsb
mlk b'l* (*KAI* 61 A, B; Gibson 1982: 73). Although the final word in the
phrase, *b'l*, remains a crux, Day accepts the reading 'in place of a child' as
the most plausible (Day 1989: 6). Day understood the phrase to refer to a
substitute sacrifice; however, the inscription designates the stele *as* the
substitution:

> A stele of an offering in place of a child, which Arsh set up to Baal
> [Hamon], Lord, because he heard his voice. May he be blessed. (*KAI*
> 61A)

In contrast to the above inscription, which describes the offering (i.e. his
own son, in perfect condition), this inscription says nothing about an
offering, but instead focuses on the act of setting up the monument. As
Eissfeldt had suggested, these early inscriptions imply that it was the act of
setting up the monument, and not the sacrifice, that was the focus of
concern (Eissfeldt 1935: 28).

These Pheoenician inscriptions suggest that the *pigrê molkîm* in 43.7, 9
do not commemorate the offerings, but rather serve as the offerings
themselves. According to the logic of votive statues, such monuments
should have served as perpetual reminders of the devotion of Yahweh's
people. Instead, they became perpetual reminders of their apostasy.

The *semel*'s various locations in the temple suggest that it bears
comparison with the *pᵉgarîm*. Like the *pigrê molkîm*, whose *bamôt* or
pedestals (contra NRSV: 'at their death') are placed near the thresholds of
Yahweh's house, the *semel* has its own *môšab* in the doorway of the temple

(8.3). That it also functions as an offering is suggested by the change in its location from v. 3 to v. 5. The apparent contradiction between 8.3 and 5 in the description of the location of the image – in the doorway where Ezekiel stands or north of that position, at the altar – has long been a crux in the interpretation of this passage. Emendations to resolve this contradiction are based on the presupposition that the image of jealousy is a fixed object, and that vv. 3 and 5 describe the same location (Frevel 1991: 296 n.25).

Another possibility, however, is that the *semel* has been moved. Even though the seat of the image of zeal is in the doorway, that is not where Ezekiel sees it. And it is not the image, but its location that provokes Yahweh's question: 'Mortal, do you see what they are doing, the great abominations that they are committing here, so as to drive themselves far from my sanctuary?' (Contra NRSV, 'to drive me far from my sanctuary'; Greenberg 1983: 168–69; Wong 2001: 396–400).

Ezekiel 20.30–32 supports the suggestion that the monuments had become the focal point of the Judean cult. In keeping with its rebellion in the wilderness, Israel defies Yahweh's statutes and ordinances once it enters the land. Israel's defiance is not depicted as a straight-out rebellion but rather as a perversion of the divine decree. The declaration in v. 26, 'I defiled them (*tm'*) through their very gifts, in the offering (*h'byr*) all that opens the womb', is chiastically echoed in v. 31: 'in your lifting up of your gifts, in your passing (*h'byr*) your sons through the fire, you defiled yourselves (*tm'*) with all your *gillûlîm* to this very day'. The close syntactical and verbal correspondence of these two verses suggests that the problem is not that Israel did not fulfill the commandment; indeed, v. 31 exactly mirrors the requirement described in v. 26. Rather, Israel's gifts were compromised by its *gillûlîm*. Israel is not condemned because it sacrifices its children *to* its idols but rather because the offerings occur in conjunction with the making of cult statues, which are here condemned as *gillûlîm*. One may therefore suggest that the phrase *lekol gillûlêkem* indicates the manner in which Israel fulfilled its obligations – not with the required sacrifices but with monuments that served as substitutions.

Although it remains a matter of some debate whether v. 32 belongs with what precedes or follows it, it may shed further light on the manner in which monuments came to be regarded as idolatrous. Having condemned Israel for its failure to fulfill Yahweh's statutes and ordinances, Ezekiel declares that Israel will never be like the nations, who 'minister to wood and stone'. The verb employed here, *śrt*, has the basic meaning of service and is used to refer not only to the priestly duties at the altar, but also to the care of sacred objects and vessels. The creation and maintenance of any statues, whether of human beings or of deities, would have involved this service, and the ambiguity of the term allows for the condemnation of any such monuments which detract from the true service of Yahweh.

Ezekiel 16.17–22 more fully describes the service of cult statues. Jerusalem is accused of melting down the gold and silver that Yahweh had given her in order to fashion for herself *ṣalmê zakar*, usually interpreted as 'male images'. Some commentators interpret the image as a phallic symbol representing some unknown deity, but the elaborate adornment in human garments and other indications of the care and feeding of these images suggests that they were anthropomorphic statues (16.18). That this was a statue of a human being and not of a god in human form is suggested by the fact that the one other use of *ṣelem* in Ezekiel explicitly refers to representations of human beings (23.14). Furthermore, the finery with which the statues are clothed suggests human beings of high status. Given Ezekiel's condemnation of Judah's kings elsewhere in the book, one is tempted to suggest that these are royal statues.

What angers Yahweh is that Jerusalem devotes herself to these statues, but fails to remember (*zkr*, 16.21) what Yahweh had done for her in the wilderness. The condemnation of the care and feeding of these statues implies that they had become deified. The profusion of sacrificial language, as well as the very explicit description of Jerusalem giving her children over to these images to eat, clearly portrays the images as the recipients of the gifts, and not simply commemorations of them. Although Heider has interpreted this account to support his interpretation of the Molek cult as a cult of the dead, to whom offerings are given (Heider 1985: 365–75), another explanation is that this language represents the culmination of theological reflection on the nature of the cult images: any image that becomes the focus of ritual activity is by definition a rival of Yahweh and therefore an idol. This polemic reaches its fullest development in Ezek. 23.38–39, which incorporates many of the themes and motifs found in 16.17–21.

Of the references in Ezekiel to cult statues, three of the five are explicitly associated with the practice of child sacrifice (16.17–21; 20.30–32; 23.38–39). However, only two of these references explicitly describe the sacrifice of children to the statues (Ezek. 16.17–21; 23.38–39), while the remaining references imply a connection with sacrifice but do not explicitly refer to sacrificial victims (8.3, 5; 20.31–32; 43.7, 9). The logic of the law of the firstborn may explain how these diverse references to cult statues and related offerings may be understood.

3. *The Substitution*

Reading the law of the firstborn in Exod. 22.29–30 as an unambiguous declaration that all firstborn males, both animal and human, shall be 'given' to Yahweh in sacrifice, Jon Levenson asks why there is not more widespread biblical evidence for the actual sacrifice of children. His answer is drawn in part from his understanding of the function of ancient Near Eastern law codes, which stipulate theological principles in the form of apodictic laws. For example, the provision for the jubilee year articulates a principle that guided the life of the community even if the law was never actually observed. The same logic obtains for the law of the first-born: the first-born belongs to Yahweh, who may or may not demand that the child be sacrificed. But if God should require the child, as in the case of Isaac in Gen. 22, the child is to be willingly offered up. Dismissing many contemporary readings of Gen. 22 which present it as an etiology rejecting child sacrifice, Levenson argues that the narrative reinscribes the principle that the beloved son belongs to Yahweh. The deity's response in Gen. 22.16–19 authorizes neither a substitution nor a redemption for the child, but rather rewards Abraham for his willingness to give up his dearest son, the son through whom the promise was to be fulfilled (22.16–19). The story of Abraham's binding of Isaac, the report of Mesha's sacrifice in 1 Kgs 3.26–28, and the rhetorical questions of Mic. 6.6–8 all reflect this logic: the human willingness to give up that which is dearest ensures divine blessing, if not also the divine release of the child from this obligation (Levenson 1993: 3–17).

The same demand is inherent in the 'no-good laws' of Ezek. 20.25–26; indeed, the entire point of the the law is the recognition of Yahweh's claim on all Israel:

> I defiled them through their very gifts, in their offering up all their first-born, in order that I might horrify them, so that they might know that I am the Lord. (20.26)

While it cannot be denied that Ezekiel's formulation of the law makes it into an instrument of judgment, the demand that Israel give up its firstborn to Yahweh is unequivocal. In this respect, Ezek. 20.26 and Exod. 22.28–29 are radically different from pentateuchal legislation that makes provisions for substitutions and redemptions.

That this law has never been fulfilled is the burden of Ezekiel's accusation in the references to child sacrifice in 20.30–32, 16.17–22, and 23.38–39. But the precise nature of Judah's failure to fulfill this requirement may be more clearly reflected in the practices that are alluded to in Ezek. 8 and 43: acting in the spirit, but not the letter of the law, the Judean cult erected effigies of its offerings but did not make the offerings themselves. I have argued above that the *pgr mlk* of ch. 43 can be so construed; I now turn to consider whether the *semel* of ch. 8 may also be interpreted as a substitute offering.

Phoenician evidence of the construction of *semel*s corroborates this understanding of *semel*s as substitute offerings. Unlike monuments that are found in cemeteries in conjunction with the bones of animals and young children, *semel*s – absent sacrificial remains – are usually found in or near temples. In an excavation of the temple of Eshmoun in Sidon, eleven such statues of infants have been found (Dunand 1965: 105–09). These skillfully carved statues portray infants at the age of about eighteen months to two years, though the faces bear a dignity and repose more typical of adult, even royal, figures. At one time, the statues had been displayed just north of the temple on plinths, some of which bore carefully engraved dedicatory inscriptions. One such inscription (ca. 400 BCE), refers to itself as a *semel* of an heir to the Sidonian throne; Gibson conjectures that the occasion for setting up the statue was the recovery of the prince from an illness (Gibson 1982: 114–15). If Gibson is correct, then implicit in this offering of a *semel* is the conviction that the prince belonged to the god, who could have taken him through illness. But since the son was spared, the king gave the god a *semel*, a simulation, of the child instead.

When we examine the dynamics of the ritual in Ezek. 8 in light of the principle of child sacrifice, the image of zeal can be construed as a substitute offering to the deity during a time of great crisis. The crisis is implicit in the actions of the 70 elders, who are quoted as accusing Yahweh of abandoning the land. Because such protests of divine abandonment are entirely possible within the framework of Yahwistic petition and complaint (cf. Pss. 22.2; 38.22; 71.12), one need not read their complaint as the justification for idolatry. Rather, it becomes the basis for all subsequent actions in the chapter, as the entire house of Israel entreats the deity to return.

Accordingly, the next scene discloses women weeping 'the Tammuz' (8.14–15) at the northern gate. Whether this location bears any correspondence to the location of *semel*s in the temple of Eshmoun cannot be determined, although it is tempting to see a connection. NRSV and many commentators construe the women's act as a veneration of the dying and rising vegetation deity Tammuz. Block has, however, argued that the women sing a lament that has distant associations with the myth of this dying and rising god but which has been syncretistically incorporated into the Jerusalem cult (Block 1997: 294–96).

If the women do not weep for a dying god, it may be that they weep for a dying child, and the reference to the Tammuz may indicate the kind of child that is mourned. Levenson has argued that child sacrifice was not widely practiced in Judah but was, rather, restricted to the sacrifice of the 'beloved son', a term that he associates with the royal heir. As evidence for his suggestion, he notes that the only explicit references to child sacrifice in the Hebrew Bible all involve royal heirs (e.g. sons of Ahaz, 2 Kgs 16.3; Manasseh, 2 Kgs 21.6; and Mesha, 2 Kgs 3.27; Levenson 1993: 26–27). The unusual reference to a song called 'the Tammuz' may further corroborate Levenson's suggestion, especially if such a song had become syncretistically linked with Jerusalemite royal theology. If the women were mourning the death of an heir to the throne, then they may indeed have believed that they were mourning the death of a Tammuz, a 'son of God' (cf. 2 Sam. 7.14; Ps. 2.7), whose life would be given back again.

The final scene, 8.16–17, in which the deity brings Ezekiel back to where he had begun, depicts the anticipated result of the ritual. Unlike the first scene, in which the court was completely devoid of anything except the image of jealousy, there are now 25 men between the vestibule and the altar. The scene is reminiscent of a national lament described in the book of Joel (Joel 2.17). Far from being an act of rejecting Yahweh, the prostration toward the east reflects the associations between Yahweh and the sun that appeared with increasing frequency during the monarchy (Smith 1990: 29–39). The act of awaiting the appearance of the sun is the climax of the ritual, which had begun with the elders' entreaties in their darkened room and which will end in the morning, when Yahweh's appearing is as 'sure as the dawn' (Hos. 6.3, see also Pss. 44.4b; 80.2b, 4, 8, 20; 89.16; 90.14; 123.1–2; 130.5–6).

From beginning to end, the ritual is an expression of confidence in Yahweh's faithfulness to Israel – and misplaced confidence in Israel's faithfulness to Yahweh, as it enacts its devotion by way of the image of zeal, which takes the place of the 'Tammuz' as it is offered on the altar, perhaps even passed through the fire as a *molk*-offering. In the very act of fulfilling the statutes of giving its firstborn to Yahweh, the house of Israel proliferates its monuments. And, because these monuments constitute an evasion of Yahweh's demand for real devotion, they have become *šiqqûṣîm*, worthless things. The use of a monument to express submission to the will of God thus becomes the parade example of Jerusalem's rejection of Yahweh's statutes and ordinances (11.12). Despite its name, the likeness of zeal is no substitute for the thing itself and has in fact supplanted what the deity really wants, the hearts and minds of the house of Israel.

Behind Ezekiel's polemic, one detects a rich vocabulary for cult statues which goes well beyond our usual understanding of idolatry as the veneration of cult images of rival deities. Since the image of zeal turns out not to be idolatry in the ordinary sense of the word, Ezekiel's iconoclasm also turns out to be concerned with something considerably more complex than the eradication of rival deities. If the image of zeal is a representation of human devotion, then the the use of such monuments constitutes a form of self-deification. Ezekiel's condemnation of the practice as an abomination is therefore at least as concerned with spiritual transformation as it is with cultic reform. In this respect it is worth noting that while child sacrifice is no longer demanded in the era of the reconstructed Israel, neither is Yahweh satisfied with tokens of devotion or half-hearted measures. The judgment will not be complete until hearts of stone are replaced with hearts of flesh (11.19) and the whole house of Israel, cleansed and replanted on Yahweh's holy mountain, become themselves the 'pleasing odor' of sacrificial devotion (20.41).

BIBLIOGRAPHY

Ackerman, Susan
1992   *Under Every Green Tree: Popular Religion in Sixth-Century Judah* (HSM, 46; Atlanta, GA: Scholars Press).
Aisleitner, Joseph
1963   *Wörterbuch der ugaritischen Sprach* (Berlin: Akademie-Verlag).
Allen, Leslie H.
1994   *Ezekiel 1–19* (WBC; Dallas, TX: Word).
Blenkinsopp, Joseph.
1990   *Ezekiel* (Interpretation: Louisville, KY: John Knox).
Block, Daniel
1997   *The Book of Ezekiel: Chapters 1–24* (NICOT; Grand Rapids, MI: Eerdmans).
1998   *The Book of Ezekiel: Chapters 25–48* (NICOT; Grand Rapics, MI: Eerdmans).
Day, John
1989   *Molech: A God of Human Sacrifice in the Old Testament* (University of Cambridge Oriental Publications, 41; Cambridge: Cambridge University Press).
Dijkstra, Meindert
1996   'Goddesses, Gods, Men and Women in Ezekiel 8', in Bob Becking and M. Dijkstra (eds.), *On Reading Prophetic Texts: Gender-Specific and Related Studies in Memory of Fokkelien van Dijk-Hemmes* (Leiden: Brill): 83–114.
Dohmen, Christoph
1984   'Heisst סמל "Bild, Statue"?', *ZAW* 96: 263–66.
Donner, H., and W. Röllig
1966   *Kanaanäische und Aramäische Inschriften* (3 vols.; Wiesbaden: Otto Harrassowitz).
Duguid, Iain
1994   *Ezekiel and the Leaders of Israel* (VTSup, 56; Leiden: Brill).
Dunand, M.
1965   'Nouvelles Inscriptions Phéniciennes du Temple d'Echmoun à Bostan Ech-Cheikh, prés Sidon', *Bulletin du Musâee de Beyrouth* 18: 105–09.
Eichrodt, Walther
1970   *Ezekiel* (trans. Cosslett Quin; OTL; Philadelphia: Westminster).
Eissfeldt, Otto
1935   *Molk als Opferbegriff im Punischen und Hebräischen und das Ende das Gottes Molock* (Beiträge zur Religionsgeschichte des Altertums, 3; Halle: Niemeyer).

Fishbane, Michael
    1984   'Sin and Judgment in the Prophecies of Ezekiel', *Int* 38: 138–50.
Frevel, Christian
    1991   'Die Elimination der Göttin aus dem Weltbild des Chronisten',
            ZAW 103: 263–71.
Gaster, T. H.
    1941   'Ezekiel and the Mysteries', *JBL* 60: 289–310.
Gibson, J. C. L.
    1982   *Textbook of Syrian Semitic Inscriptions*. III. *Phoenician Inscriptions,
            Including Inscriptions in the Mixed Dialect of Arslan Tash* (Oxford:
            Clarendon).
Gordon, Cyrus H.
    1955   *Ugaritic Manual* (Rome: Pontifical Biblical Institute).
Greenberg, Moshe
    1970   'Prolegomenon', in Charles Cutler Torrey, *Pseudo-Ezekiel and the
            Original Prophecy* (New York: KTAV Publishing House)
    1983   *Ezekiel 1—20: A New Translation with Introduction and Commen-
            tary* (AB, 22; New York: Doubleday).
Heider, George C.
    1985   *Cult of Molek: A Reassessment* (JSOTS, 43; Sheffield: JSOT Press).
Hoftijzer, J., and K. Jongeling
    1995   *Dictionary of the North-West Semitic Inscriptions* (HdO; Leiden:
            Brill).
Japhet, Sara
    1993   *1–2 Chronicles: A Commentary* (OTL; Louisville, KY: Westmin-
            ster/John Knox Press).
Koch, Klaus
    1988   'Aschera als Himmelskönigen in Jerusalem', *Ugarit-Forschungen*,
            20: 111–112.
Kutsko, John F.
    2000   *Between Heaven and Earth: Divine Presence and Absence in the
            Book of Ezekiel* (Biblical and Judaic Studies from the University of
            California at San Diego, 7; Winona Lake, IN: Eisenbrauns).
Levenson, Jon D.
    1993   *Death and Resurrection of the Beloved Son: The Transformation of
            Child Sacrifice in Judaism and Christianity* (New Haven: Yale
            University Press).
Lutzky, H. C.
    1996   'On the "Image of Jealousy" (Ezekiel viii 3, 5)', *VT* 46: 121–25.
McKay, John W.
    1973   *Religion in Judah under the Assyrians, 732–698 B.C.* (SBT, 2nd
            Series; London: SCM Press).
May, H. G.
    1937   'The Departure of the Glory of Yahweh', *JBL* 56: 309–21.
Neiman, David
    1948   '*PGR*: A Canaanite Cult-Object in the Old Testament', *JBL* 67: 55–
            60.

Schroer, Sylvia
    1987   *In Israel gab es Bilder: Nachrichten von darstellenden Kunst im Alten
                Testament* (OBO, 74; Fribourg & Göttingen).
Smith, Mark
    1990   'The Near Eastern Background of Solar Language for Yahweh',
                JBL 109: 29–39.
Torrey, Charles Cutler
    1970   *Pseudo-Ezekiel and the Original Prophecy* (New York: KTAV).
    [1930]
Waltke, Bruce K., and M. O'Connor
    1971   *An Introduction to Biblical Hebrew Syntax* (Winona Lake, IN:
                Eisenbrauns).
Wong, Ka Leung
    2001   'A Note on Ezekiel viii 6', *VT* 51: 396–400.
Zimmerli, Walther
    1979   *Ezekiel 1: A Commentary on the Book of the Prophet Ezekiel
                Chapters 1–24* (Trans. R. E. Clements; Hermeneia; Philadelpia:
                Fortress).
    1983   *Ezekiel 2: A Commentary on the Book of the Prophet Ezekiel
                Chapters 25–48* (Trans. J. D. Martin; Hermeneia; Philadelphia:
                Fortress).

Corrine Patton

When the subject of priesthood comes up, Jeremiah is not usually the first book to come to mind. If we were discussing the conflict between true and false prophecy, then Jeremiah would be the natural place to look. But the casual reader may be hard-pressed to articulate Jeremiah's attitude toward the priesthood. Even many serious readers of the book, if we count authors of monographs and commentaries of Jeremiah to be 'serious readers', have little to say about the topic. Most note that the condemnation of priests is part of the book's inclusive condemnation of Judah's leadership. A few people remark on Jeremiah's priestly origin that is mentioned in the superscription. Yet, few have taken this social identification as a hermeneutical lens through which to filter the book. Excluding analyses of the Temple Sermon, two general trends can be detected in the interpretation of texts that refer to ritual matters (priests, sacrifice, sacred space, Sabbath). One strategy is to simply ignore them (Bright 1965; Bogaert 1981; Clements 1988). The other more common approach is to 'dismiss' them by deeming them late additions to the text at odds with the book's central messages (McKane 1986). Is this just another example of liberal Protestant bias? Or are there rhetorical reasons why the reader of Jeremiah ignores priesthood as a major concern of the text?

While I suspect that a general lack of contemporary concern for ritual matters in ancient Israel may contribute to the problem, this essay will focus on the latter question. To put a finer point on it: how does the rhetoric of the book convey ideologies of priesthood? Are texts within Jeremiah that advocate limitations placed on the efficacy of sacrifice (6.20; 7.22) and temple (7.1–15) an appropriate interpretive lens through which to read texts that are either ambivalent or positive in their assessment of temple ritual? This study presumes the existence of redactional layers within the text, but seeks to explore the reading of the final form of the text as the product of the dialogue of these layers.[1] As such, I presume that the MT of Jeremiah is the end-product of various authors.[2] While differing

---

1. This approach follows the lead of Willis (1985); O'Connor (1988); Diamond (1993); Biddle (1996); and. Stulman (1998).
2. Redactional analyses of Jeremiah abound, since the text's 'messiness' requires some explanation. I do not intend to review this scholarship here. For some of the most influential reconstructions of the text's final form, see Duhm (1901); Mowinckel (1914); Bright (1965);

ideologies remain in the final text, the final redactor has manipulated and contextualized the meaning of these ideologies by adding to and framing earlier material. As a result, while a close reading of Jeremiah may uncover conflicting ideologies, the text's final form projects a more unified assessment of the priesthood.

Just the Facts, Ma'am

Although priesthood may be a minor theme in the book, the fact is, the root כהן appears more often in the book of Jeremiah (40 times including the two references in the oracles against the nations), than it does in either the whole book of Isaiah (7 times) or Ezekiel (25 times) combined. The word appears in a wide variety of contexts, and in various strata of the book. The priests are the subjects of oracles of condemnation. Priests, both as a group and as named individuals, are among the audience in many narrative settings. The root כהן is used as a title or descriptor of several individuals (Jeremiah, Passhur, Zephaniah, Seraiah, and Jehoiada).[3] Salvation oracles contain a few references to priests. Even the oracles against the nations specifically mention the priests of other nations. Simply at the level of lexical frequency, the priesthood was a subject of concern for the book.

The book also exhibits interest in ritual cult. References to sacrifices, ritual space and even ritual time can be found throughout the book. For example, the book queries the efficacy of animal sacrifice (6.20 and 11.15),

Nicholson (1970); Thiel (1973); Carroll (1981; 1986); McKane (1986); Holladay (1986 and 1989); and Seitz (1989a). More recent studies of redaction can be found in Stulman (1998) and Ferry (1999).

More limited studies of smaller sections of the book or of possible Deuteronomistic redaction can be found in various essays in Perdue and Kovacs (1984); López (1987); Clements (1990 and 1993); Smith (1990); Dutcher-Walls (1991); Albertz (1992: 382–87); Person (1993); and Römer (2000). For recent critiques of 'pan-Deuteronomism', see the essays in de Pury *et al.* (2000), as well as Schearing and McKenzie (1999).

While the existence and date of each redactional layer are debated, Jeremiah remains 'lumpy'. While I appreciate Carroll's general skepticism over 'making sense' of the layers as well as McKane's recognition of a continuous accretion of material, I do agree with those who see certain clusters of redactional material. Some chapters, such as 1–6 and 30–31, seem to presume a pre-587 audience. Some sound Deuteronominstic, even granting the differences in vocabulary and ideology. Large sections within chs. 34–45 differ again in style, content and ideology from other parts of the book; their treatment of Jeremiah as a literary figure resonates as later reflection on the prophet. However, even if one wants to reject the language of redaction completely, the fact remains that material in chs. 1–6 is literarily distinct (genre, style, characterization) from material in 34–45. My argument is not concerned with dating individual oracles, but with examining the ways that the 'lumpiness' of the text contributes to the various meanings within the material.

3. For a study of the names in Jeremiah, see Glatt-Gilad (2000).

the need for proper observation of the Sabbath (17.19–27), and the nature of Yahweh's presence in the temple (7.1–15). Even oracles of restoration mention a ritual cleansing of the nation, and the re-establishment of sacrificial cult and a sacrificing priesthood (chs. 17 and 33).

To be sure, Jeremiah's struggles over prophetic legitimation are far more prominent in the book; the focus on priesthood in this study does not seek to deny this. Prophetic legitimation probably lies behind Jeremiah's call, his confessions, as well as the narratives that depict blatant rivalry among competing prophetic claims.[4] More importantly, while the superscription announces that Jeremiah is a priest, the book presents him as a prophet. The book's concern with priesthood takes place within this more overarching concern with true prophecy.

Oracles condemning Israelite priests can be found in Jer. 1.18–19; 2.8; 2.26; 4.9–10; 5.30–31; 6.13–15; 8.1–3; 8.10; 13.13–14; 14.18; 18.18;[5] 23.11; 23.33–34; 31.14; 32.31–32 and 34.18–19.[6] Out of these 15 occurrences, 6 are imbedded in chs. 1–6, the material generally deemed part of the earliest layer of the text (Sweeney 1999). Thirteen are in chs. 1–25, redactionally the first half of the book (Carroll 1986; O'Connor 1989; Stulman 1998). Condemnation of priests is part of the agenda of the first section of the book.

Within these oracles, not once are they condemned on their own. In 13 of the cases, prophets are also condemned;[7] eleven of these oracles place the condemnations of priests and prophets right next to each other.[8] The oracles against the priests are clearly not part of a unique antagonism between priests and prophets. In fact, the common combination of these two social groups, what Olyan (2000: 4–5) would call a dyad of totality, suggests that they are condemned as representatives of a socially

---

4. O'Connor (1988: 85–92) cites research on this topic. In addition, see Overholt (1970); Laberge (1980); Carroll (1981:158–87); Auld (1984); and Berquist (1989).

5. This verse is a bit out of the ordinary, because it quotes the people who say that Jeremiah has condemned the priests. However, within the narrative flow of the book, the quote occurs after he has delivered 10 oracles against priests, so the reader takes the chorus here at its word.

6. At least three (2.8, 2.26 and probably 5.30–31) seem to address the northern priesthood, although what this means to a post-722 audience is unclear.

7. The only exceptions are 1.18 (which condemns kings, officials [שרים], priests and the people of the land), and 34.18–19 (which includes priests with officials of Judah, officials of Jerusalem, eunuchs and people of the land). This latter verse is odd in many respects. It contains the only mention of eunuchs in the book, and seems to refer to the covenant with Abraham, rather than the Sinai covenant. These considerations lead me to believe this is a post-exilic text concerned with the covenant of land possession, and the social position of eunuchs in restored Yehud (see Isa. 56.4–5; note also the prominence of eunuchs as a social class in Esther).

8. The only place where they are separated is in 2.8 and 18.18 (the quote from the people).

established religious leadership, whom Jeremiah holds responsible for the nation's fall. This conclusion is supported by the fact that, outside of longer narratives describing prophetic conflict,[9] prophets receive additional condemnation only 4 times (5.13; 14.13–15; 23.9–40 and 29.8), two of which (chs. 14 and 23) have oracles against the priests imbedded within them.

Priests also appear within the narrative material as opponents to Jeremiah. In this material, priests and prophets are more distinct. Priests oppose Jeremiah in chs. 19–21, 26–29 and 37. Within the final form of the book, this opposition crops up after Jeremiah's attacks on the priests, beginning with the people's summary of Jeremiah's message in 18.18. Is this arrangement of the material a later redactor's attempt to add the reaction of the priesthood to Jeremiah's message, or is it a narrative strategy to depict the opposition to Jeremiah as merited? It can be read both ways.

In addition, references to a priestly audience are mentioned when the context warrants it.[10] Some of the oracles directly address cultic matters; for instance, ch. 27 focuses on the return of the temple vessels. Sometimes priests are present because the oracle is delivered in the temple (19.14–20.2; 26.2; 28.5) or some other cultic area (19.1–3). The content of most of these latter oracles, however, is not cultic irregularity or even idolatry; most often the oracle concerns Judah's policy toward Babylon. While ch. 19 begins as an oracle against child sacrifice, the punishment is exile to Babylon. In ch. 21, Jeremiah asserts that, since Yahweh is leading the Babylonian army, the only proper response is surrender. In chs. 27, 28, and 29 Jeremiah repeatedly informs the priests, both within Jerusalem and among the exiles in Babylon, that the exile will last a long time. This material depicts the priests as major opponents to Jeremiah's pro-Babylonian stance. Chapter 37 reinforces this conclusion: it depicts Zedekiah sending at least one priest to Jeremiah to intercede to God on behalf of the city. The occasion? Egypt's attack on Babylonia's siege (37.7). This narrative material implies that the priesthood during 597–587 was a pro-Egyptian faction, who had some effect on Zedekiah's policies.

What are the rhetorical functions of the antagonism between Jeremiah and the priests (he condemns them; they oppose him)? On the one hand, it focuses attention on the failure of the Judean leadership to address the international crisis effectively. On the other hand, it focuses on the particular failure of the religious leadership (priests and prophets). But it may also communicate something about the text's view of the ideal functions of both priests and

---

9. For example, the conflict with Hananiah in chs. 26–28

10. Stulman (1998: 39) has noted a similar phenomenon in 3.1–4.4, where 'priestly language' promotes the condemnation of cultic abuse.

prophets. In order to explore this question further, it is essential to allow the text itself to define these two social groups.

What's It All About, Jerry?

How do the authors of Jeremiah conceive of the social location and function of priesthood, especially in distinction from prophecy? Certainly the text at all of its layers presumes that there is a group (כהנים) distinct from other social groups, such as prophets, scribes, and officials (Long 1981). By this I mean that, while an individual may be both a priest and a prophet, the author presumes that talking about 'priests' and 'prophets' connotes two different social groups.

In oracles that condemn priests and prophets for not doing their jobs, the division of labor is consistent with what is seen in Ezekiel, as well as other biblical texts. Priests are in charge of some kind of instruction related to the תורה (18.18),[11] and determining or seeking divine presence (2.8).[12] In addition, priests might have some kind of control over prophetic activity (5.30–31).[13] In this material, they are not depicted as ritual specialists. Prophets, on the other hand, are supposed to deliver a divine message, neither speaking on their own, nor distorting a divine message, nor delivering a message from the 'wrong' deity (5.13, 31; 14.13–15; 18.18; 23.9–40 and 29.8). In other words, they are intermediaries (Wilson 1980; Overholt 1989). For the authors of Jeremiah, both priests and prophets are supposed to be 'knowledgeable' (4.9–10; 14.18; 23.34 and 37) and unpolluted (23.11).[14]

The descriptions of priests in both narrative settings and in oracles of restoration add to the composite picture. The oracles of restoration address their sacrificial responsibilities, depicting them as ritual specialists. Jeremiah 33.17–22 contains a 're'-affirmation of an eternal covenant with the levitical priesthood. Here priestly duties are wholly sacrificial.[15] 'As for

---

11.   The texts do not specify what this תורה consists in. I am not comfortable simply equating it with the Deuteronomistic law code.

12.   Studies of the Temple Sermon, in particular, focus on the book's assertions about God's presence (see below). I am leaving aside the statement in 6.14 that 'they' were irresponsible in declaring שלום, since the text does not make clear if 'they' are the priests and prophets or everyone 'from the least to the greatest' (NRSV). While I suspect the declaration of שלום would come from priests and prophets, the text itself is ambiguous.

13.   This verse is ambiguous. See the discussion in Carroll (1986: 190). At the least, the verse shows a concern with the relationship between priesthood and prophecy.

14.   Priests and prophets are also supposed to be people of integrity, and exclusive followers of Yahweh, but these criteria are also applied to either the whole community or all leaders; they do not help us distinguish the specific responsibilities of priests and prophets.

15.   Brueggeman (1991: 99–101) asserts that this text elevates priests over the king.

the Levites, the priests, I will not cut off having one of them before me, that is, from bringing up the whole burnt offering עלה, offering incense קטר, offering grain מנחה or performing a ritual slaughter זבח every day' (33.18).[16] Although it is easy to dismiss this text as a later addition,[17] the text raises the question of the attitude toward sacrifice and temple ritual imbedded in the book of Jeremiah.[18] Can we simply assume that the earlier layers of the text are hostile toward or not concerned with sacrificial ritual, or that they subsume the efficacy of ritual to ethical norms? Since sacrifice in ch. 33 is attached to priests, the attitude of earlier layers of the text toward sacrifice impacts the way the reader assesses the role and status of priesthood in the rest of the book. Therefore, texts about sacrifice add to our assessment of the relationship between priesthood and prophecy. Do texts dealing with sacrifice reflect the view that prophetic mediation is a 'better' way to bridge the human-divine gap than sacrifice?

Although most texts in Jeremiah which describe priestly activity ignore sacrifice, the book as a whole does not. References to sacrifices and offerings occur throughout the book, in every redactional layer. While these texts do not focus on the priests' role in sacrifice, perhaps reflecting a time period when ritual slaughter was not an exclusively priestly prerogative, some interesting consistencies do appear. First, not a single reference to rituals performed to gods other than Yahweh contains a reference to animal sacrifice. The most common assertion is that these gods are offered incense לבונה or קטר, drink offerings נסך, and/or grain offerings מנחה.[19] Two texts mention whole burnt offerings to other gods, but in both cases the reference is to child sacrifice (19.5 and 32.35), a practice the book of Jeremiah consistently claims is not part of the worship of Yahweh.

Neither the priests nor the people are condemned for failing to perform sacrifices to Yahweh, however. The people bring their sacrifices to the temple, even in the one case where they bring grain and incense offerings to Mizpah, for the 'house of Yahweh' (41.5; Blenkinsopp 1998: 27–30). Sacrifice is important in two other restoration texts as well. Jeremiah 33.11

---

16. Translations are my own, unless otherwise noted.

17. On dating chs. 30–33, see Carroll (1981: 198–225). On the attitude toward the temple reflected in chs. 29–33, see Stulman (1998: 78–83).

18. I will not try to reconstruct the history of Israelite priesthood. I accept the view that this text parallels Deuteronomy's view of the Levites. On the history of the Levites, see O'Brien (1990); Nurmela (1998); and Schaper (2000).

19. 7.9, 18; 11.12, 13, 17; 18.15; 19.4, 13; 32.29; 44.3, 5, 8, 15, 17, 18, 19, 21, 23, 25; and 48.35. Chapter 44 is an indictment of Jews living in Egypt; every time the Queen of Heaven is mentioned, they are accused of offering both incense and drink offerings (vv. 17, 18, 19 and 25). Jeremiah 48.35 depicts the Moabites offering incense to their gods.

promises that in the restoration thank offerings and obedience to Sabbath rituals will result in the restoration of whole burnt offerings, ritual slaughter, grain offerings, incense offerings and thank offerings in the 'house of Yahweh' (17.26; O'Connor 1988: 142–43).

There is no hint that the priests serving at the temple in Jerusalem were considered illegitimate. This means that the text does not depict the priesthood as illegitimate. Nor does the text have any overt reference to rivalry among priestly groups comparable to Num. 16 or Ezek. 44, whether we conceive of these as Zadokites vs. Levites, country priests vs. urban elite, or Shiloh/Mushite priests vs. Jerusalem/Zadokite priests. If Jeremiah came to Jerusalem as a Mushite priest with the hope of usurping control of the temple, the book has hidden his animosity well.

The book's attitude toward the efficacy of sacrifice is more ambiguous. While most texts presume that sacrifice is a good thing, three texts (Jer. 6.20, 7.22 and 11.15) explicitly critique sacrifice. Jeremiah 6.20 asserts that incense, whole burnt offerings and ritual slaughter are not pleasing to God, while 11.15 states that animal sacrifices are not sufficient to avert the impending punishment. The context of 6.20 asserts that sacrifices are meaningless without attention to God's 'words' דברים and 'instruction' תורה. Jeremiah 11.15 implies that sacrifice is ineffective if the participants continue in their pre-meditated evil מזמה. The verses do not preclude ritual atonement and/or ritual purification; in other words, institutionalized ritual is not categorically condemned.

Jeremiah 7.22, on the other hand, states that neither whole burnt offerings nor ritual slaughter were commanded of the people in the wilderness.[20] Embedded in Deuteronomistic-like texts, the focus of 7.21–26 is on the centrality of obedience, especially to the messages of the prophets. While it may be part of a late layer of the text (Leene 2001), the rhetorical result is that, though the book contains numerous references to the good of sacrifice, Jer. 7.21–26 shapes how the reader of the final form of the book interprets the importance of sacrifice for Jeremiah. It implies that sacrifices would be efficacious only if commanded by a prophet. As part of an ideology that reflects on social groups within Israel, the effect of 7.21–26 is to subordinate priestly prerogative to prophetic pronouncement.

Does the whole book of Jeremiah reflect a similar subordination? Once again, there are multiple answers. Some texts assert the priesthood's control of prophets. While Jer. 5.31 may be ambiguous, later additions clarify a priest's right to arrest prophets. Priests are condemned for not controlling prophetic activity (Renkema 1997). In the narratives, we see

20. Jeremiah 11.15 may also contain a reference to the ineffectiveness of sacrifice; the text is rather corrupt, however. See, for instance, Carroll (1986: 272); Holladay (1986: 354–56); and McKane (1986: 247–49).

Jeremiah arrested by priests (chs. 20 and 26), and Zephaniah scolded for
not doing so more quickly (29.26–28). Eventually Jeremiah is barred,
presumably by the priests, from entry into the temple (36.5).[21] Therefore,
priests had *de jure* control over prophetic activity.

But what the Lord giveth, the Lord taketh away: if Jeremiah condemns
priests for not controlling prophets correctly, Passhur is portrayed
negatively for exerting this control. Jeremiah as prophet is elevated over
the power of the priesthood. On the one hand, I could conclude that the
texts do not question a priest's right to control prophetic activity; instead,
they are about these particular priests' ability or discernment in doing so.
On the other hand, I could also assert that the text has a hidden agenda: to
demonstrate how unworkable this system is. These texts seem to
demonstrate the ineffectiveness of both prophecy and priesthood,
especially compared to the person of Jeremiah.[22]

In summary, references to priests and ritual can be found throughout the
book,[23] although they are found less frequently in chs. 34–45. Within these
references, priests are closely associated with controlling access to and
activity within the temple. They also seek God and instruct. Restoration
texts associate them explicitly with sacrifice, although other material
asserts that ritual irregularity defiles those things that the priests control
(the temple, God's name). Politically these priests are depicted as
collaborators with the government against Babylon. Sociologically they
are coupled with prophets, who also appear to be cultic functionaries
(prophets prophecy in the temple at the discretion of the priests; the two
groups function in the oracles as a designation of the entire cult).

Is That All There Is?

I could play it safe at this point, and conclude here by stating, 'Jeremiah's
condemnation of the priesthood is part of his larger program to condemn

21. We will discuss this text in more detail below.
22. Carroll (1995) has highlighted several points in the book where such inconsistencies
cannot be explained away.
23. Ritual categories are used throughout the book. Idolatry, as the text defines it
(Ackerman 1992), is an abomination that defiles טמא the idolaters (2.23), their houses (19.13),
the land (2.7; 3.1–2; 3.9; 16.18), the temple (7.30; 32.34), and God's name (34.16). Prophets
and priests should not be 'profane' חנף. 'Setting apart' or 'sanctification' קדש is used in two
capacities: as a preparatory ritual (soldiers preparing for war [6.4; 22.7; 51.27, 28]; God's
preparation of the guilty [12.3]), and as a description for various persons and objects (2.3;
11.15; 17.2, 22–27; 23.9; 25.30; 31.40 and 50.29). Most important, Jeremiah is himself 'set
aside' or 'sanctified' in his call narrative (1.5). Carroll (1986: 95–96) notes that this may be a
reflection of his priestly status, although Courturier (1990: 270) associates it with his prophetic
ministry.

all Judean leadership'. I could even venture a bit and state, 'Prophets are particularly singled out in this condemnation because of the rhetorical need to establish Jeremiah as a true prophet. Condemnations of priests serve this larger goal.' Other evidence within the book supports these conclusions. What follows is more speculative, an activity of what David Penchansky (2003) calls 'imagination'.[24]

What I have done to this point is to look at the content of the oracles and redactional material in order to explore the socio-historical context for the passages. However, a larger issue remains. Ideology within prophetic books is communicated not just through the oracles themselves, but also through the characterization, the 'persona', to use Polk's (1984) term, of those within the text. We learn at least as much about how the authors conceived of priests by their representation of them as we do through what the prophet says about them.

The book of Jeremiah is an excellent place to explore this question, since the person of Jeremiah is such a prominent element in the text. Ellis (1992: 453) expresses a 'classic' approach to the book: 'With the exception perhaps of Jesus and St. Paul, we know more about Jeremiah as an individual than about any other person in the whole history of Israel.' Bright (1965), Holladay (1986), and others have taken this abundance of personal material in the book as an indication that we can get back to the historical Jeremiah through the book. More recent scholarship rejects this idea, recognizing that the presentation of the prophet is a literary projection.[25] Therefore, we can explore the ideology of priesthood in the book by looking at the presentation of both the priests who oppose Jeremiah and Jeremiah himself (Patton 2000: 701–10).

In the narrative materials, the priests embody that classic anthropological characterization of a priest: conservative, associated with the hierarchical power, opposed to innovative ideas, ruled by tradition. For example, in Jer. 26, tradition prevails over the priests' plan to execute Jeremiah. When priests act, they often do so at the behest of the king (21.1–2; 37.3). When they are addressed or condemned, they are associated with elite groups (kings, princes, elders; Long 1981).

---

24. By this he means the unavoidable process of filling in gaps in our evidence. For the use of imagination in biblical theology, see the essays in Jones and Buckley (1998).

25. The interpretation of the function of the portrayal of Jeremiah has been mixed. For instance, in the same volume of *Interpretation*, Holladay (1983: 146–59) sees this material as reliable biographical information, while Brueggeman (1983: 135–45) considers it more of a 'portrait'. Jobling (1978) explores various options. McConville (1993: 61–78) considers Jeremiah to be a symbol for both Yahweh and Israel, Smith (1990: 43–64) as a representative of God, and Stulman as both innocent sufferers (1998: 63–69) and of the book itself (1998: 158–65).

What is central to the reader's assessment of the priests is their opposition to Jeremiah (O'Connor 1988 and 1989). Narrative strategies in the book render Jeremiah a sympathetic character; the effect can be seen on contemporary readers who empathize with the 'suffering prophet'. The romantic attachment of some scholars to the historical Jeremiah demonstrates the ancient authors' effectiveness in creating a sympathetic character. Furthermore, Jeremiah is depicted as authoritative and reliable, both through his interactions with Yahweh and through the prophecy-fulfillment schema of the book.[26] Priestly opposition to Jeremiah leads to their characterization as stubborn, blind to God's purposes, and actively evil.

While the characterization of priests presents an unambiguous source for the authors' ideology, less ambiguous is the portrayal of Jeremiah. That Jeremiah is the antithesis of the specific priests within the book is clear. To what social group Jeremiah belongs may be less certain. Clearly, Jeremiah is a prophet, in particular a prophet as defined by Deuteronomistic texts. Seitz (1989b) has highlighted the degree to which he is a 'prophet like Moses', and, like Moses, Jeremiah's status is elevated by his acquisition of ever-widening social roles. Just as Moses acts as prophet, priest, and king, so does Jeremiah act as a prophet, priest and wise man. This ideology of accretion is seen most clearly in the superscription, which designates Jeremiah a priest (1.1).

Commentaries have varied in how they interpret and utilize this notice.[27] For some, it is simply a late addition that is 'foreign' to the text itself. Nothing in the historical or earliest layers of the text indicates Jeremiah was a priest; therefore, this notice is unhelpful in recreating or interpreting the prophet. Others note the designation, without question, but then do not utilize it in exploring how the prophet is portrayed in the rest of the book.[28] Others see this as an important piece of evidence in the search for the historical Jeremiah, but these scholars often fall short of asking how it functions rhetorically.[29] In contrast, Hill (1999: 25) notes that the superscription presents Jeremiah as a 'unifying factor' in the book, the lens through which the book is read. Yet, since his focus is on the symbolic

---

26. For example, in Jer. 28.16, Jeremiah predicts Hananiah's death, which is fulfilled in the following verse. The book as a whole ends with the description of Jerusalm's defeat by Babylon, as predicted by Jeremiah. See, further, O'Connor (1988: 130–31) and McKane (1996: clxxi–clxxii).

27. This verse is rarely explored outside of commentaries. Studies focusing on ch. 1 usually begin with v. 4. For example, van der Toorn (1989) suggests that the almond tree in the first chapter was a stylized version of Aaron's staff which Jeremiah saw while serving in the temple, but he does not spend much time discussing 1.1.

28. See Miller (2001).

29. See, for instance, Bright (1965: lxxxvi–lxxxix) and Carroll (1986: 90–92).

function of Babylon, he does not explore Jeremiah's status as priest (Hill 1999: 23–36).

What were the redactors hoping to achieve with this notation? That question nags me. While it may simply be an historical fact, why was this particular fact repeated in such a prominent position? Although the date of the addition of the superscription is debatable,[30] it most probably serves a rhetorical, rather than an historical function. It sets the stage for the oracles that follow. Although brief, it provides the reader with vital information this author believes the readers need to keep in mind as they read/hear the book.[31] For Jeremiah, someone wants the reader to think of him as a 'priest from Anathoth'.

The classic location to explore Jeremiah's relationship to the temple is in his Temple Sermon, especially the version preserved in ch. 7.[32] While it is clear that Jeremiah objects to the people's confidence in the temple, it is debatable why he does so. Do his critiques stem from his social location as a peripheral prophet (Wilson 1980), priest of Anathoth (Bright 1965), central prophet with access to the temple (Long 1981), or priest with access to the temple (Reventlow 1963)? One way to read the function of the superscription is to see it as a redactor's attempt to clarify this question. Without the superscription, we would not read Jeremiah's oracle as the expression of a competing priestly group. Yet, with 1.1, his negative attitude toward the temple has at least some motivation, some context. References to Anathoth in 11.21–23; 29.27 and 32.7–9 may have also added impetus to the conclusion by the author of 1.1 that Jeremiah speaks, not just as a prophet, but also as a priest from Anathoth.

If Jeremiah 1.1 and the texts referring to Anathoth date from an exilic or early post-exilic period, are they also meant to trigger the associations with priests in Anathoth that contemporary canonical readers make? Is it assumed that the audience has the books of Kings at hand? Is ch. 7 'fraught with the background' (Auerbach 1953: 12) of Solomon's expulsion of Abiathar? Is Jeremiah 'Abiathar Re-Dux'? Of course, the questions are unanswerable; all that can be said is that such imagining adds something that 'makes sense' to a modern reader, even if it is deemed historically improbable.

---

30. It probably pre-dates the split between the traditions that led to the LXX and MT texts.

31. I may be putting too much emphasis on contemporary, western modes of reading. However, recent work on 'reading' the final forms of such collections as the book of the Twelve and the Psalms indicate that some fruit can be gained by this stance.

32. There are numerous studies of chs. 7 and 26, especially of their redactional relationship. See, for example, Nicholson (1970: 68–79); Wilcoxen (1977: 151–66); Laberge (1980); Carroll (1981: 84–106); Holt (1986); Brueggeman (1991: 5–13); Hardmeier (1991) and Smelik (1992). See also O'Connor (1988: 125–27 and Kraus (1991).

The reprise of the Temple Sermon in ch. 26 focuses on the reaction to this oracle, a reaction depicted as a confrontation among social groups.[33] If ch. 7 can be read as a priestly outsider's critique of the national shrine, Jeremiah's solitary voice in 26 and his salvation by scribes distance him from any group, especially the Jerusalemite priests (Carroll 1981: 91–106). Chapters 27–29 which further distance him from the other cult functionaries, the prophets, prepare the reader for the reference to his banishment from the temple in ch. 36.

The focus on Jeremiah's social location in ch. 7, and throughout the book, brings to the fore the contemporary impasse about the definition of the terms, priest and prophet. While ch. 7 clearly marks Jeremiah's speech as prophetic, questions remain. What is the sociological significance that so many prophetic oracles are set within the temple precincts? Why are some oracles associated with ritual actions? Why are priests and prophets grouped together? These are problems for contemporary readers that extend beyond the book of Jeremiah,[34] and even beyond Israel.[35] As will be shown below, the evidence in the book of Jeremiah undercuts the attempt to reconstruct an imagined conflict between priesthood and prophecy in the pre-monarchic or even exilic period.[36]

Jeremiah is depicted as a cultic functionary, that is as someone who works within the social sphere of an institutionalized cult, such as the temple.[37] In the most serious attempt to read Jeremiah as a cultic functionary, Reventlow (1963) begins with form-critical assumptions about individual laments.[38] Central to his argument is the role played by Jeremiah's laments. He argues that, just as the singer of individual laments was a cultic functionary who represented the community before God, so too Jeremiah's laments do not tell us anything about the historical prophet, but instead express the laments of the community. Reventlow's study, unconvincing on numerous grounds, suffers from his assumptions about the *Sitz im Leben* of individual laments, and about the applicability of this *Sitz im Leben* for the laments within Jeremiah.

---

33. Further studies on ch. 26 can be found in O'Connor (1989) and Stulman (1998: 63–69).

34. See the contributions by Zevit and Grabbe in this volume.

35. See Fleming's essay. On Jeremiah within the context of ancient Near Eastern prophecy, see Barstad (2002), as well as the literature he cites there.

36. This does not deny that individual priests and prophets may be in conflict; each group can accuse the other of not doing its job, corrupting their office, or acting in a wicked fashion. However, there is little evidence that either group felt the other group's function was illegitimate, subordinate, or even static.

37. At this juncture I do not wish to define these functions as either priestly or prophetic, since our definition of these terms do not seem to match ancient usage adequately.

38. See also Johnson (1962).

The laments in Jeremiah do not present themselves as pieces performed within a ritual context. O'Connor, who categorically rejects a cultic setting for the laments, shows the ways in which they are connected to prose sermons within the final form of the book. The catalyst of the laments is the failure of Judah to obey God's word revealed through the prophet Jeremiah. Yet, when the laments are read through the lens of Jeremiah's cultic function, it becomes clear that two of them address cultic issues.

Chapter 12 is framed by an oracle against the people of Anathoth, who had sought to silence him ('You will not prophesy in the name of Yahweh, or else[39] you will die by our hand' [11.21]). Read in the context of 1.1, this seems to be an example of Jeremiah's own priestly group attempting to exert control over him. This frame provides a setting for the subsequent lament. This lament focuses on the prosperity of the wicked, even if they are found among 'your own brothers and your father's house' (12.6). In the context of 11.21–23, this is read as an accusation against the Anathoth priesthood. While 11.21–23 may be a later addition to the text, it would be one that pushes the interpretation of an ambiguous lament in a particular direction.[40]

The lament in 17.14–18 is framed on both sides by cultic references: the praise of God's throne (Metzger 1991), and the regulations of the Sabbath. Jeremiah 17.12–13 in its present context seems to interrupt the flow between the reason for Jeremiah's complaint in 17.1–11, and the lament proper in 17.14–18. Therefore, many commentators simply state that vv. 12–13 are a late addition, as if that explains their present context (Holladay 1986: 500; McKane 1986: 404 and O'Connor 1988: 46–48). Similarly, the Sabbath regulations (17.19–27) do not seem to address concerns extant in the rest of the book of Jeremiah, let alone in the lament of 17.14–18.[41]

But, does the praise of Yahweh's throne serve a rhetorical function in the book? First, the verses mirror issues in the material that surrounds it. On the one hand, vv. 5–6 describe the wicked as those who trust in humanity (as opposed to God [17.13]), whose punishment will be desert-like dryness (as

39.   Reading with the LXX.

40.   O'Connor calls this an example of 'midrashic' expansion intended to highlight the crimes of the people (1988: 56–57 and 112–113). Bogaert (1991) uses the term 'relecture', while Carroll uses the term 'intertexuality' (1999). However, I also think it serves to highlight Jeremiah's troubled entanglement with cultic groups: he is a priest and prophet with a right to speak, but he is incrementally removed from the very institution where he should be located. A parallel example is found in ch. 18, where the complaint against Jeremiah's enemies is introduced (perhaps secondarily) by the accusation that Jeremiah has attacked all of Judah's leaders, including the priests. It is unclear to me, however, what is at stake in designating 11.21–23 and 18.18 as secondary? Why is this important? Does it help us read the lamentations better if they are read as free-floating entities apart from their rhetorical context?

41.   Many commentators remark how odd 17.19–27 are in light of Jeremiah's supposed rejection of the efficacy of temple ritual. See, for example, Couturier (1990: 281). It is probable that these verses are among the last additions to the MT, since they are absent from the LXX.

opposed to living water [17.13]). On the other side, verses 12–13 introduce the lament itself in which Jeremiah, who knows the fate of the unrepentant, prays to God for healing. The placement of the regulations on Sabbath that follow the lament now read as the word that Jeremiah's foes requested in v. 15. It is a kind of priestly תורה, although the term is absent here. Sabbath is explicitly linked to God's 'house', since the blessings of Sabbath result in cultic sacrifice in the temple (17.26).

The chapter as a whole moves in parallel blocks. The people sin and are dried out just as those who forsake God's throne distance themselves from living water. Jeremiah, the cultic functionary, prays for God's healing and God tells him to instruct the community (like a priest) on proper Sabbath observation and its blessings: the restoration of cultic ritual in the 'house of Yahweh'. Priestly concerns are at the very heart of this chapter, concerns made more evident if we think of Jeremiah, not as an outsider opponent to proper ritual, but as an insider who critiques a cult gone bad.

O'Connor (1988: 142–43) notes that the Sabbath regulations in ch. 17 'bookend' the concerns of ch. 7. Jeremiah 17.12–13 is a further counter-point to the earlier chapter. In ch. 17, the community is called on to 'trust' in Yahweh, while ch. 7 says they should not 'trust' in the temple. If the people are improperly trusting in 'human' effort (17.5) and they are castigated for trusting in the temple (7.4), does Jeremiah view the temple as a human production? Or is the text about the effects of that presence? The lament suggests that it is the latter; the issue is not whether God is in the temple, but rather what that presence means for the community. Does it mean blessing or curse, disease or healing?

Jeremiah's cultic setting is also demonstrated by the passages in which God directs him not to intercede on behalf of the people (7.16; 11.14 and 14.11). In ch. 11, God's injunction is followed by a description of the people's actions when petitioning the prophet to intercede on their behalf: the people are offering בשׂר קדשׁ. Here intercession is paralleled with sacrifice. Similarly, in Jer. 14.12–13 the people offer burnt offerings, and grain offerings. In Jer. 7.16, set within the temple precincts (7.2), the people's rituals directed toward other gods lead Yahweh to order a halt on intercession. Jeremiah 7, 11, and 14 seem to presume a temple setting for intercession.[42]

In spite of Bright's objection that the prophets 'emphatically did not speak as paid personnel of the cult' (1965: xxii),[43] the book of Jeremiah itself explicitly designates a cultic setting for many of Jeremiah's

42. Does this mean intercession is a priestly or a prophetic activity? I would imagine that it is a function assigned to someone called a 'prophet' נביא at least some of whom do this act within the temple in the context of animal sacrifice.
43. See the equally strong statement from Blenkinsopp that it is 'beyond reasonable doubt that cultic prophets formed part of the temple staff during the pre-exilic period' (1977: 134).

prophecies.[44] Jeremiah prophesies at the temple (28.1; 24.1), the temple gate (ch. 7), the temple courtyard (19.14; ch. 26), the 'third' entrance to the temple (38.14) and in a room above the doorkeeper's room (ch. 35). When he is restricted from the temple, Baruch goes to a room in a gate in the upper courtyard to read his oracle. Jeremiah prophesies in front of priests in 19.1, 27.16, and 28.1. When Zedekiah sends to Jeremiah for an oracle, he sends a priest (21.1–2 and 37.3). Jeremiah's prosecution occurs within the temple (26.10–11),[45] and his confrontation with Hananiah takes place before the priests, within the temple (28.1);[46] as a result of judgments against him, he is placed in stocks within the temple (20.2) and banned from the temple (36.5), actions supported by the letter from Shemaiah in 29.26. Are the authors of these texts making up locations for Jeremiah's activities based on their own knowledge of where prophets worked? Or are the repeated occurrences of Jeremiah speaking in the temple an indication that they saw Jeremiah as a voice stemming from within the central religious institution of the nation? Does his physical location signal confrontation or collusion?

The final reading of the text indicates that the answer is 'both'. In Jer. 1–33, the location of Jeremiah and other prophets within the temple suggest that they had an officially recognized function there. In this layer of the text, the struggles between Jeremiah and Jerusalem priests are a struggle between religious functionaries of the temple. Jeremiah's characterization suggests that the authors do not challenge the symbiotic structure of the relationship between priests and prophets; what is wicked is not the institution of priesthood, but the moral quality of these particular individuals at this particular time. This conclusion makes the reading of the restoration of the priesthood in ch. 33 less surprising. The envisioned restoration may limit priestly function to sacrificial duties, but it does not eliminate priesthood altogether.

Later redactors further the divide between priests and Jeremiah. In the legends of Jeremiah (chs. 34–45),[47] Jeremiah is not just arrested; he is

---

44. See also Carroll (1986: 90).

45. While it is clear that some biblical texts, most explicitly Deut. 17.8–13 give priests judicial powers, it is not clear when priests judge and when judgment is left to royal or 'secular' courts. The problem is evident in Mesopotamian texts as well; although priests judge certain cases and temple names include a building associated with justice in larger temple precincts, the precise distinction between royal and cultic justice remains obscure. I would expect that priests judge cases involving vows sworn before a deity, issues of cultic impurity (such as medical situations that render a person unclean), and any case involving the transgression of cultic regulations. If so, the authors of Jeremiah (and, as others have noted, other prophets such as Amos) seem to assume that prophesying falsely is a cultic violation.

46. On the temple theology in Jer. 28, see Schriener (1987).

47. I am following Carroll's lead of reading chs. 30–33 as a unit in the final form of the text, even though the individual oracles were probably written at different times (1981: 198–225).

completely barred from the temple (Jer. 36). When it comes to Jeremiah's relationship to the temple and the temple priesthood, the reader of the final form of the book reads the book through the lens of the heightened antagonism between these characters in the later additions to the book.[48] The narrative of ch. 36 places Jeremiah completely outside of the temple. There is no symbiosis, only opposition. Jeremiah is a voice from outside the temple institution predicting (correctly for the readers of the later addition) the fall of this very institution (Stulman: 1995). By separating Jeremiah from the temple space, the collapse of the temple in no way implicates the prophet. Instead he sits, like Jonah, as an outsider who witnesses the sin and punishment of a wicked city.[49] Here we have another example of later *midrash* (O'Connor 1988: 112–13). The authors of 34–45 have picked up on the tension in Jeremiah's characterization, and have shaped Jeremiah's character by driving a wedge between the two functions.[50]

As an outsider, Jeremiah is further divorced from the priestly office. He is in no way portrayed as a cultic functionary, neither as priest nor as temple prophet. Various conclusions about the redactional layers can be drawn from this evidence. On the one hand, it seems likely that the superscription is part of an earlier collection of material, the layer that portrays Jeremiah's work within the temple. The final chapters silence this designation by placing Jeremiah outside of the temple. Perhaps these later chapters wish the reader to reject the efficacy of priesthood in favor of the efficacy of the prophet; if so, they could represent a kind of 'classic' rivalry between prophets and priests (Petersen 1991; Blenkinsopp 1998).

On the other hand, if chs. 34–45 address a restoration audience experiencing the rivalry among priestly groups for control over the Second Temple, and if the identification of Jeremiah as a priest is important for this layer, then chs. 34–45 depict Jeremiah as a righteous priest banned from temple service by wicked priests in collusion with the government. Perhaps this layer represents a group whose priests combined elements of pre-exilic priesthood and prophecy. Perhaps it was a group who wanted to re-institute official prophets back into the temple function and perhaps the 'Aaronids' rejected a place for prophecy within the cult of the Second Temple. While my historian's imagination likes this idea, I have to admit evidence for these conclusions is scanty.

48. This follows Stulman's treatment of ch. 26 (1998: 63–69).

49. Carroll notes that Jeremiah's banishment also serves to elevate the scribe Baruch (1981: 151–52); for more on this, see below.

50. Both Boadt (1999: 339–49) and Carroll (1995) note that the historical layers within the text make it more 'messy', not less.

Look, Ma, No Priest

The problem with imagining an historical setting for material is that it can cut against the rhetorical force of the book that transcends the historical setting. In other words, in the continued life of the text, I do not think rivalry among priestly groups continues to have much force. Instead, I do think that the majority of readers of Jeremiah are correct to see this book, not as asserting a group's power, but in creating an ideology of written prophecy.

As Nicholson (1970) and others (O'Connor 1989; Carroll 1993 and 1996; Stulman 1998: 100–108 and Römer 2000) have pointed out, Jeremiah increasingly interacts with scribes as the book progresses. The scribal family of Shaphan pops up at key moments in the text, often to rescue Jeremiah. Similarly, the book credits the scribe Baruch with preserving Jeremiah's words. The second part of the book depicts the writing of Jeremiah's oracles (25.13; 30.2; 36.4, 28; 45.1 and 51.60; it may be implied in 39.15–18). Although writing is a common element in ancient Near Eastern prophecy,[51] Niditch (1996) points out that written down oracles function in a milieu where writing itself was seen as efficacious.[52] Just as historical books, for instance, refer to earlier writings as authoritative, so too does the act of writing prophecies participate in their 'effectiveness'.[53] The written oracle lives on, in a sense, beyond the individual prophet's spatial and temporal limitations.

Studies of the book of Ezekiel note the literary character of this book. Presumably, the social changes that happened with the exile were an impetus to literary productions. Jeremiah 34–45 can be read as an exploration of the interplay between oral word and written record. At first glance, written texts last longer and are more efficacious than either priestly action or prophetic revelation (McConville 1993: 86–89). Carroll (1996) has shown the anxiety over 'permanence' revealed in these texts: is the scroll less stable because it can be burned? Or is it more stable because it can be infinitely re-produced? Is the text a concrete, unchangeable object or is it infinitely revisable (O'Connor 1989: 625–27)? Is the text self-evident, or is it in need of an authoritative interpreter, such as priest or prophet? These ambiguities remain in the text, as if the author floats the questions without landing on any answers.

The authority of the written word informs the reading of Jer. 31.33, which envisions restoration as a covenant written upon the people's hearts. Here

---

51. Writing is an essential element in prophetic letters and execration texts, for example. On letter writing as a form of prophecy, see Dijkstra (1983).

52. On writing and textual authority as a precursor to canonization, see Blenkinsopp (1986); Peckham (1993); Clements (1996) and Davies (1998).

53. This does not mean that the authority of a written text meant it was unchangeable or to be preserved *verbatim*.

the substance of the covenant is the תורה, that is, the teaching, which is usually 'taught' by the priests.[54] In fact, 31.34 says that, as a result of this writing, each and every person, from the least to the greatest, will 'know' God. In fact, no one will have to 'teach' למד anymore. Is this a world without priests then? Chapter 33 addresses this question: the emphasis on sacrifice there assures the reader that the perfect world will not be without its priests; they will simply have for adjustment in their job description.

Yet, while the priests might still remain, Jeremiah disappears. First, like Tom Riddle in the second Harry Potter book, he disappears as his scroll takes on a life of its own (Brueggeman 1999: 367).[55] This is only one in a long list of ways that the book implodes. In Jer. 43.5–6 Jeremiah himself exits stage left, as he is forcibly taken off to Egypt. If Jeremiah, as the righteous victim, represents the true remnant of the nation, then the book depicts the complete undoing of the nation of Israel: they are once more in bondage in Egypt.[56] Weinfeld (1976) notes a number of 'antitheses' in the book of Jeremiah.[57] The book speaks of the ark, but the ark is no longer there. It mentions the covenant, but the covenant has been replaced by an internal disposition. Moses is gone, replaced for a while by Jeremiah, who himself is led by the people back into slavery (Holladay 1984 and Seitz 1989b). What is left? A scroll that can be burned, thrown into a river, or changed by later scribes, foreign nations that do not deserve their own exalted state, and at the last, a Jerusalem lying in ruins, its temple destroyed, its cultic treasures carted off to Babylon.[58] The land is empty for this book's audience: Jeremiah is gone.[59]

These observations affect the ideology of priesthood. On the one hand, writing limits priestly function: no longer must they instruct (תורה is internal), but they still must sacrifice. The vision asserts that while an internal 'written' תורה should replace the priest within the temple, and all the people should 'know' God, some type of mediation is still necessary. In other words, the text still struggles with a fundamental theological issue:

54.   Although it is tempting to equate this תורה with the Deuteronomistic law, all we know from the text is that it is contrasted with the covenant made in the wilderness.

55.   See also Brueggemann (1999: 367).

56.   Read in this light, ch. 34's discourse on slavery also mirrors this same sinful journey: from slavery to freedom and back to slavery.

57.   Domeris (1999) calls this the book's 'anti-language'.

58.   There is a fair amount of discussion about the book's provenance: Babylonian exiles, Palestinian remnant, or Egyptian refugees. Each suggestion collapses since each group comes under its own condemnation. The fact that the book unravels all of Israel's institutions and its history means that no single entity remains as a positive force in the book. I do think that the scribal groups who wrote and transmitted this material have left a heavy imprint, but where they are located is difficult to conclude.

59.   On the 'myth of the empty land', see, among others Klein (1979); Seitz (1985); Smith (1989); Barstad (1996) and the essays in Grabbe (ed.) (1998).

the question of revelation and mediation. Anthropological studies recognize both prophets and priests as 'mediators', that is to say they both bridge the gap between the human community and divine realm and thus function as vehicles for divine revelation. Using a modern definition of the terms, they do so in distinct ways: the prophet communicates with the divine realm, while the priest mediates the *sancta* attached to the divine realm.[60] The book of Jeremiah maintains these two distinct avenues of mediation, but the book's final chapters highlight a third vehicle for God's revelation: writing. Writing does so, not just for the historical community who heard Jeremiah, but also for future communities who perceive of themselves in continuity with the historical audience.

The book ends with the fulfillment of Jeremiah's prophecies: Jerusalem falls in the closing scene of the book. But if the description of the fall of the city in ch. 52 depicts a prophet's success, then Jeremiah's complaints over having to mediate that message make horrible sense. While some people read ch. 52 as hopeful, since it implies that God's promises for restoration will also come to pass, the arrangement of the book leaves a nagging question. If the main function of Jer. 52 is to show that Jeremiah's oracles are fulfilled, why do the preceding chapters contain accounts of the prophet after his job is complete? If the preceding chapters, especially 26–45, explore the problem of mediation, then what message does the final chapter communicate?

Chapter 52 highlights the ultimate tragic irony that the authors face: it vindicates Jeremiah as a true prophet, while at the same time it shows how ineffective all forms of human mediation were in preventing disaster. The authors know that Jeremiah's prophecies were ineffective. Chapter 52 depicts this ultimate failure of the prophet to either convince the people to change their ways or to intercede on their behalf to God. Even the mention of Jehoiakin at the end is slim comfort, since this king eats a royal feast every day, while his city lies in ruins and the true Israel has disappeared back into Egypt. The fact that the death of the nation in ch. 52 follows the notice in 51.64 that, 'These are the words of Jeremiah so far', implies that Jeremiah, as either person or scroll, does not have the final word.[61] The

---

60. I realize that there are many definitions for the two offices. What I offer here is my own, based on wide readings on sociological approaches to cult, ritual and personnel. See, for example, Weber (1952); Cody (1969, 1973); Sabourin (1973); Gammie (1989); Beard and North (eds.) (1990); Gorman (1991); Jenson (1992); Bell (1992, 1997; Matthews and Benjamin (1993); Blenkinsopp (1995); McNutt (1999); Olyan (2000) and Millar (2001). By 'manipulation of *sancta*' I include purity regulations that protect the community, parceling out divine holiness in ways that benefit but do not destroy the community, and providing opportunities for the blessings of holiness (especially fertility broadly construed) to function.

61. Holladay suggests that the death of the nation replaces the death of the Jeremiah (1989: 444).

final chapter deconstructs Jeremiah's words: the scroll unrolls itself like a roll of tissue paper in a child's destructive act of play. The scroll's final chapter laughs at its own ideology: nothing stops God: not prophet, not scribe, not scroll. The text's self-destruction is more effective than Jehoiakim's fire.

Although the book of Jeremiah asserts the authority and 'endurability' of textual revelation over both priestly mediation and prophetic pronouncement, the book ends with death, devastation, and an uncertain future. Jeremiah, whether acting as priest, prophet, or text, fails to mediate. He fails to convince the people to change policy and behavior, and he fails to intercede for the people. Chapter 52 undercuts the authority ascribed to Jeremiah in 1.1 as both priest and prophet. In light of the book's anxiety over efficacious mediation, the authors seem to stop just short of voicing the real question that is on their mind: was it Jeremiah who failed, or was it God? Did Jeremiah fail to instruct the תורה, to communicate true prophetic revelations, or to insure that these words would have an authoritative life in a text? The problem isn't just that Jeremiah is absent from the chapter. The real question is, where is God as the temple vessels are being carted off, the people are being executed, and the remnant is being exiled? Has God disappeared with Jeremiah?

Jeremiah and Johnny Appleseed

The final form of the text turns Jeremiah into a legend. He does not die; he simply disappears off the stage. But the portrayal of this legend communicates; it serves the book's final rhetorical functions by layering earlier texts with later authoritative (or manipulative) additions. The text of Jeremiah replaces the oracular Jeremiah, who was concerned with condemning priests as part of a general condemnation of the leaders of Judah, first with the sermonic Jeremiah, a siphon for struggles among priestly groups or between prophets and priests, then with the legendary Jeremiah, whose authority is defeated by the authority of the text. Jeremiah vanishes; text remains.

Yet, this replacement is incomplete. The rhetorical effect of the multiple layers is that various ideologies remain (text cannot silence) and the crucial theological issue remains unresolved: where is God authoritatively accessed? Is it in special, historical moments of prophetic revelation (the person of Jeremiah), in cultic settings where God's holy presence is mediated by ritual specialists (the social and religious functions that Jeremiah represents), or in texts preserved and controlled by some group(s) who 'win(s)' in historical struggles (the book of Jeremiah as a rhetorical ideology)? If all three have failed to save the nation, then perhaps the problem is not with human mediation *per se*, but ultimately with God. At the end of the book, God and nation, priest and prophet disappear. All that is left is a ruined temple site, and a feasting king without nation, priest or prophet.

BIBLIOGRAPHY

Ackerman, S.
  1992   *Under Every Green Tree: Popular Religion in Sixth Century Judah*
            (HSM, 46; Atlanta: Scholars Press).
Albertz, R.
  1992   *A History of Israelite Religion in the Old Testament Period.* II. *From
            the Exile to the Maccabees* (OTL; Louisville: Westminster John
            Knox).
Auerbach, E.
  1953   *Mimesis: The Representation of Reality in Western Literature*
            (Princeton: Princeton University Press).
Auld, A. G.
  1984   'Prophets and Prophecy in Jeremiah and Kings', *ZAW* 96: 66–82.
Barstad, H. M.
  1996   *The Myth of the Empty Land: A Study in the History and
            Archaeology of Judah during the 'Exilic' Period* (Oslo: Scandinavian
            University Press).
  2002   'Prophecy in the Book of Jeremiah and the Historical Prophet', in
            A. G. Hunter and P. R. Davies (eds.), *Sense and Sensitivity: Essays
            on Reading the Bible in Memory of Robert Carroll* (JSOTSup, 348;
            Sheffield: Sheffield Academic Press): 87–100.
Barton, J.
  1986   *Oracles of God: Perceptions of Ancient Prophecy in Israel after the
            Exile* (New York/Oxford: Oxford University Press).
Beard, M., and J. A. North (eds.)
  1990   *Pagan Priests: Religion and Power in the Ancient World* (Ithaca:
            Cornell University Press).
Bell, C.
  1992   *Ritual Theory, Ritual Practice* (New York/Oxford: Oxford Uni-
            versity Press).
  1997   *Ritual: Perspectives and Dimensions* (New York/Oxford: Oxford
            University Press).
Berquist, J. L.
  1989   'Prophetic Legitimation in Jeremiah', *VT* 39: 129–39.
Biddle, M. E.
  1996   *Polyphony and Symphony in Prophetic Literature: Rereading
            Jeremiah 7–20* (Studies in Old Testament Interpretation, 2; Macon,
            GA: Mercer University Press).
Blenkinsopp, J.
  1977   *Prophecy and Canon: A Contribution to the Study of Jewish Origins*
            (University of Notre Dame Center for the Study of Judaism and

Christianity in Antiquity, 3; Notre Dame/London: University of Notre Dame Press).

1995   *Sage, Priest, Prophet: Religious and Intellectual Leadership in Ancient Israel* (Library of Ancient Israel: Louisville: Westminster John Knox).

1998   'The Judaean Priesthood during the Neo-Babylonian and Achaemenid Periods: A Hypothetical Reconstruction', *CBQ* 60: 25–43.

Boadt, L.

1999   'The Book of Jeremiah and the Power of Historical Rectiation', in A. R. P. Diamond, *et. al.* (eds.), *Troubling Jeremiah* (JSOTSup, 260; Sheffield: Sheffield Academic Press): 339–49.

Bogaert, P.-M.

1991   '*Urtext,* texte court et relecture Jerémie xxiii 14–26 TM et ses préparations', in J. A. Emerton (ed.), *Congress Volume: Leuven 1989* (VTSup, 43; Leiden: Brill): 236–47.

Bogaert, P.-M. (ed.)

1981   *Le livre de Jérémie: Le prophète et son milieu les oracles et leur transmission* (ETL, 54; Leuven: Peeters/Leuven University Press).

Bright, J.

1965   *Jeremiah: A New Translation with Introduction and Commentary* (AB, 21; New York: Doubleday).

Brueggeman, W.

1983   'The Book of Jeremiah: Portrait of the Prophet', *Int* 37: 130–45.

1988   *To Pluck Up, to Tear Down: A Commentary on the Book of Jeremiah 1–25* (International Theological Commentary; Grand Rapids: Eerdmans).

1991   *To Build, to Plant: Jeremiah 26–52* (International Theological Commentary; Grand Rapids: Eerdmans).

1999   'The "Baruch Connection": Reflection on Jeremiah 43:1–7', in Diamond *et al.* (eds.): 367.

Carroll, R. P.

1981   *From Chaos to Covenant: Prophecy in the Book of Jeremiah* (New York: Crossroad).

1986   *Jeremiah: A Commentary* (OTL; Philadelphia: Fortress).

1993   'Inscribing the Covenant: Writing and the Written in Jeremiah', in A. G. Auld (ed.), *Understanding Poets and Prophets: Essays in Honour of George Wishart Anderson* (JSOTSup, 152; Sheffield: Sheffield Academic Press): 61–76.

1995   'Synchronic Deconstructions of Jeremiah: Diachrony to the Rescue?', in J. C. de Moor (ed.), *Synchronic or Diachronic? A Debate on Method in Old Testament Exegesis* (OTS, 34; Leiden: Brill): 39–51.

1996   'Manuscripts Don't Burn—Inscribing the Prophetic Tradition: Reflections on Jeremiah 36', in M. Augustin and K.-D. Schunk (eds.), *'Dort ziehen Schiffe dahin...': Collected Communications to the XIVth Congress of the International Organization for the Study of the Old Testament, Paris 1992* (Beiträge zur Erforschung des

Alten Testaments und des antiken Judentums, 28; Frankfurt am Main: Peter Lang): 31–42.

1999   'The Book of J: Intertextuality and Ideological Criticism', in A. R. P. Diamond, *et al.* (eds.), *Troubling Jeremiah* (JSOTSup, 260; Sheffield: Sheffield Academic Press): 220–43.

1990   'The Prophet and His Editors', in D. J. A. Clines, S. E. Fowl, and S. E. Porter (eds.), *The Bible in Three Dimensions: Essays in Celebration of Forty Years of Biblical Studies in the University of Sheffield* (JSOTSup, 87; Sheffield: JSOT Press): 210–20.

Clements, R. E.

1992   *Jeremiah* (Interpretation; Atlanta: John Knox).

1993   'Jeremiah 1–25 and the Deuteronomistic History', in A. G. Auld (ed.), *Understanding Poets and Prophets: Essays in Honour of George Wishart Anderson* (JSOTSup, 152; Sheffield: Sheffield Academic Press): 93–113.

1996   *Old Testament Prophecy: From Oracles to Canon* (Louisville: Westminster John Knox).

Cody, A.

1969   *A History of Old Testament Priesthood* (AnBib, 35; Rome: Pontifical Biblical Institute).

1973   'Priesthood in the Old Testament', in G. Bernini (ed.), *Priesthood and Prophecy in Christianity and Other Religions* (Studia Missionalia, 22; Rome: Gregorian University Press): 309–29.

Couturier, G. P.

1990   'Jeremiah' in R. E. Brown, *et al.* (eds.), *The New Jerome Biblical Commentary* (Englewood Cliffs, NJ: Prentice Hall): 265–97.

Davies, P. R.

1998   *Scribes and Schools: The Canonization of the Hebrew Scriptures* (Library of Ancient Israel; Louisville: Westminster John Knox).

Diamond, A. R. P.

1993   'Portraying Prophecy: Of Doublets, Variants and Analogies in the Narrative Representation of Jeremiah's Oracles – Reconstructing the Hermeneutics of Prophecy', *JSOT* 57: 99–119.

Diamond, A. R. P., K. M. O'Connor, and L. Stulman (eds.)

1999   *Troubling Jeremiah* (JSOTSup, 260; Sheffield: Sheffield Academic Press).

Dijkstra, M.

1983   'Prophecy by Letter (Jeremiah xxix 24–32)', *VT* 33: 319–22.

Domeris, W.

1999   'When Metaphor Becomes Myth: A Socio-Linguistic Reading of Jeremiah', in A. R. P. Diamond, *et al.* (eds.), *Troubling Jeremiah* (JSOTSup, 260; Sheffield: Sheffield Academic Press): 244–62.

Duhm, B.

1901   *Das Buch Jeremia* (Kurzer Hand-commentar zum Alten Testament, 11; Tübingen/Leipzig: J. C. B. Mohr [P. Siebeck]).

The Priests in the Prophets

Dutcher-Walls, P.
    1991   'The Social Location of the Deuteronomists: A Sociological Study
                of Factional Politics in Late Pre-Exilic Judah', *JSOT* 52: 77–94.
Ellis, P. F.
    1992   'Jeremiah', in *The Collegeville Bible Commentary: Old Testament*
                (Collegeville: Liturgical Press): 453–80.
Ferry, J.
    1999   *Illusions et salut dans le prédication prophétique de Jérémie* (BZAW,
                269; Berlin/New York: de Gruyter).
Gammie, J. G.
    1989   *Holiness in Israel* (Overtures to Biblical Theology; Minneapolis:
                Fortress).
Glatt-Gilad, D. A.
    2000   'The Personal Names in Jeremiah as a Source for the History of the
                Period', *Hebrew Studies* 41: 31–45.
Gorman, F. H.
    1991   *Ideology of Ritual: Space, Time and Status in the Priestly Theology*
                (JSOTSup, 91; Sheffield: Sheffield Academic Press).
Grabbe, L. L.
    1995   *Priests, Prophets, Diviners, Sages: A Socio-historical Study of
                Religious Specialists in Ancient Israel* (Valley Forge, PA: Trinity).
Grabbe, L. L. (ed.)
    1998   *Leading Captivity Captive: 'The Exile' as History and Ideology*
                (JSOTSup, 278; Sheffield: Sheffield Academic Press).
Hardmeier, C.
    1991   'Die Propheten Micha und Jesaja im Spiegel von Jeremia xxvi und 2
                Regum xviii-xx: Zur Prophetie-Rezeption in der nach-joschija-
                nischen Zeit', in J. A. Emerton (ed.), *Congress Volume: Leuven,
                1989* (VTSup, 43: Leiden: Brill): 172–89.
Hill, J.
    1999   *Friend or Foe? The Figure of Babylon in the Book of Jeremiah MT*
                (BibInt, 40; Leiden: Brill).
Holladay, W. L.
    1983   'The Years of Jeremiah's Preaching', *Int* 37: 146–59.

    1984   'The Background of Jeremiah's Self-Understanding: Moses,
                Samuel, and Psalm 22," in L. G. Perdue and B. W. Kovacs
                (eds.), *A Prophet to the Nations: Essays in Jeremiah Studies*
                (Winona Lake: Eisenbrauns): 313–24.

    1986,   *Jeremiah: A Commentary on the Book of the Prophet Jeremiah* (2
    1989   vols.; Hermeneia; Philadelphia: Fortress).
Holt, E. K.
    1986   'Jeremiah's Temple Sermon and the Deuteronomists: An Investiga-
                tion of the Redactional Relationship between Jeremiah 7 and 26',
                JSOT 36: 73–87.

Jenson, P. P.
1992   *Graded Holiness: A Key to the Priestly Conception of the World* (JSOTSup, 106; Sheffield: Sheffield Academic Press).

Jobling, D. K.
1978   'The Quest of the Historical Jeremiah: Hermeneutical Implications of Recent Literature', *USQR* 34: 3–12.

Johnson, A. R.
1962   *The Cultic Prophet in Ancient Israel* (Cardiff: University of Wales Press).

Jones, L. G. and J. J. Buckley (eds.)
1998   *Theology and Scriptural Imagination* (Directions in Modern Theology; Oxford: Basil Blackwell).

Klein, R. W.
1979   *Israel in Exile: A Theological Interpretation* (Overtures to Biblical Theology; Philadelphia: Fortress).

Kraus, H.-J.
1991   'Tora der Gerichtigkeit', in D. R. Daniel, *et al.* (eds.), *Ernten was man sät: Festschrift für Klaus Koch zu seinem 65. Geburtstag* (Neukirchen: Neukirchener Verlag): 265–72.

Laberge, L.
1980   'Le drame de la fidélité chez Jérémie', *Église et Théologie* 11: 9–31.

Leene, H.
2001   'Blowing the Same Shofar: An Intertextual Comparison of Representations of the Prophetic Role in Jeremiah and Ezekiel', in J. C. de Moor (ed.), *The Elusive Prophet: The Prophet as a Historical Person, Literary Character and Anonymous Artist* (OTS, 45; Leiden: Brill): 175–98.

Long, B. O.
1981   'Social Dimensions of Prophetic Activity', *Semeia* 21: 31–53.

López, F. G.
1987   'Construction et destruction de Jérusalem: Histoire et prophétie dans les cadres rédactionnels des livres des Rois', *RB* 94: 222–32.

Matthews, V. H. and D. C. Benjamin
1993   *Social World of Ancient Israel: 1200–587 BCE* (Peabody: Hendrickson).

McConville, J. G.
1993   *Judgment and Promise: An Interpretation of the Book of Jeremiah* (Leicester, England: Apollos; Winona Lake: Eisenbrauns).

McKane, W.
1986,   *A Critical and Exegetical Commentary on Jeremiah* (2 vols.; ICC;
1989   Edinburgh: T & T Clark).

McNutt, P. M.
1999   *Reconstructing the Society of Ancient Israel* (Library of Ancient Israel; Louisville: Westminster John Knox).

Metzger, M.
1991   '"Thron der Herrlichkeit": Ein Beitrag zur Interpretation von Jeremia 17, 12f', in R. Liwak and S. Wagner (eds.), *Prophetie und*

geschichtliche Wirklichkeit im alten Israel: Festchrift für Siegried Herrmann zum 65. Geburtstag (Stuttgart: Kohlhammer): 237–62.

Millar, W. R.
2001   *Priesthood in Ancient Israel* (Understanding Biblical Themes; St. Louis: Chalice).

Miller, P. D.
2001   'The Book of Jeremiah: Introduction, Commentary, and Reflections', in L. E. Keck, *et al.* (eds), *The New Interpreter's Bible*, VI (Nashville: Abingdon): 553–926.

Mowinckel, S. O. P.
1914   *Zur Komposition des Buches Jeremiah* (Kristiania: Jacob Dybad).

Nelson, R. D.
1993   *Raising Up a Faithful Priest: Community and Priesthood in Biblical Theology* (Louisville; Westminster John Knox).

Nicholson, E. W.
1970   *Preaching to the Exiles: A Study of the Prose Tradition in the Book of Jeremiah* (New York: Schocken).

Niditch, S.
1996   *Oral World and Written Word: Ancient Israelite Literature* (Library of Ancient Israel; Louisville: Westminster John Knox).

Nurmela, R.
1998   *The Levites: Their Emergence as a Second-Class Priesthood* (South Florida Studies in the History of Judaism, 193; Atlanta: Scholars Press).

O'Brien, J. M.
1990   *Priest and Levite in Malachi* (SBLDS, 121; Atlanta: Scholars Press).

O'Connor, K. M.
1988   *The Confessions of Jeremiah: Their Interpretation and Role in Chapters 1–25* (SBLDS, 94; Atlanta: Scholars Press).
1989   '"Do Not Trim a Word": The Contributions of Chapter 26 to the Book of Jeremiah', *CBQ* 51 (1989) 617–30.

Olyan, S. M.
2000   *Rites and Rank: Hierarchy in Biblical Representations of Cult* (Princeton: Princeton University Press).

Overholt, T. W.
1970   *The Threat of Falsehood: A Study in the Theology of the Book of Jeremiah* (SBT, 16; London: SCM).
1989   *Channels of Prophecy: The Social Dynamics of Prophetic Activity* (Minneapolis: Fortress).

Patton, C.
2000   'Priest, Prophet and Exile: Ezekiel as a Literary Construct', in *Society of Biblical Literature: 2000 Seminar Papers* (SBLSP, 39; Atlanta: Society of Biblical Literature): 700–27.

Peckham, B.
1993   *History and Prophecy: The Development of Late Judean Literary Traditions* (Anchor Bible Reference Library; New York: Doubleday).

Penchansky, D.
2003   'The Israelite Intelligentsia', unpublished paper read at the AAR/
        SBL Upper Midwest Regional Meeting.

Perdue, L. G. and B. W. Kovacs (eds.)
1984   *A Prophet to the Nations: Essays in Jeremiah Studies* (Winona
        Lake: Eisenbrauns).

Person, R. F.
1993   *Second Zechariah and the Deuteronomic School* (JSOTSup, 16;
        Sheffield: JSOT Press).

Petersen, D. L.
1991   'The Temple in Persian Period Prophetic Texts', *BTB* 21: 88–96.

Polk, T.
1984   *The Prophetic Persona: Jeremiah and the Language of the Self*
        (JSOTSup, 32; Sheffield: JSOT Press).

Pury, A. de., T. Römer, and J.-D. Macchi, (eds.)
2000   *Israel Constructs its History: Deuteronomistic Historiography in
        Recent Research* (JSOTSup, 306; Sheffield: Sheffield Academic
        Press).

Renkema, J.
1997   'A Note on Jeremiah xxviii 5', *VT* 47: 253–55.

Reventlow, H. G.
1963   *Liturgie und prophetisches Ich bei Jeremia* (Gütersloh: Gütersloher
        Verlagshaus/Gerd Mohn).

Römer, T.
2000   'Is There a Deuteronomistic Redaction in the Book of Jeremiah?' in
        A. de Pury, *et al.* (eds.), *Israel Constructs Its History: Deuter-
        onomistic Historiography in Recent Research* (JSOTSup, 306;
        Sheffield: Sheffield Academic Press): 399–421.

Sabourin, L.
1973   *Priesthood: A Comparative Study* (Studies in the History of
        Religions, 25; Leiden: Brill).

Schaper, J.
2000   *Priester und Leviten im achämenidischen Juda: Studien zur Kult- und
        Sozialgeschichte Israels in persischer Zeit* (Forschungen zum Alten
        Testament, 31; Tübingen: Mohr/Siebeck).

Schearing, L. S. and S. L. McKenzie (eds.)
1999   *Those Elusive Deuteronomists: The Phenomenon of Pan-Deuterono-
        mism* (JSOTSup, 268; Sheffield: Sheffield Academic Press).

Schreiner, J.
1987   'Tempeltheologie im Streit der Propheten: Zu Jer 27 und 28', *BZ*
        31: 1–14.

Seitz, C. R.
1993   'The Crisis of Interpretation over the Meaning and Purpose of the
        Exile: A Redactional Study of Jeremiah xxi-xliii', *VT* 35: 78–97.

1989a   *Theology in Conflict: Reactions to the Exile in the Book of Jeremiah*
        (BZAW, 176; Berlin/New York: de Gruyter).

1989b   'The Prophet Moses and the Canonical Shape of Jeremiah', *ZAW*
                   101: 3–27.
Smelik, K. A. D.
     1992   'Hidden Messages in the Ark Narrative', in *Converting the Past:
                   Studies in Ancient Israelite and Moabite Historiography* (OTS, 28;
                   Leiden: Brill): 35–58.
Smith, D. L.
     1989   *Religion of the Landless: The Social Context of the Babylonian Exile*
                   (Bloomington, IN: Meyer-Stone).
Smith, M. S.
     1990   *The Laments of Jeremiah and their Contexts: A Literary and
                   Redactional Study of Jeremiah 11–20* (SBLMS, 42; Atlanta:
                   Scholars Press).
Stulman, L.
     1995   'Insiders and Outsiders in the Book of Jeremiah: Shifts in Symbolic
                   Arrangements', *JSOT* 66: 65–85.
     1998   *Order amid Chaos: Jeremiah as Symbolic Tapestry* (The Biblical
                   Seminar, 57; Sheffield: Sheffield Academic Press).
Sweeney, M. A.
     1999   'Structure and Redaction in Jeremiah 2–6', in A. R. P. Diamond, *et
                   al.* (eds.), *Troubling Jeremiah* (JSOTSup, 260; Sheffield: Sheffield
                   Academic Press): 200–218.
Thiel, W.
     1973   *Die Deuteronomistische Redaktion von Jeremia 1–25* (WMANT, 41;
                   Neukirchen: Neukirchener Verlag).
Toorn, K. van der
     1989   'Did Jeremiah See Aaron's Staff?', *JSOT* 43: 83–94.
Weber, M.
     1952   [1920] *Ancient Judaism* (New York: Free Press).
Weinfeld, M.
     1976   'Jeremiah and the Spiritual Metamorphosis of Israel', *ZAW* 88:17–
                   56.
Wilcoxen, J. A.
     1977   'The Political Background of Jeremiah's Temple Sermon', in A. L.
                   Merrill and T. W. Overholt (eds.), *Scripture in History and
                   Theology: Essays in Honor of J. Coert Rylaarsdam* (Pittsburgh
                   Theological Monograph Series, 17; Pittsburgh: Pickwick): 151–66.
Willis, J. T.
     1985   'Dialogue between Prophet and Audience as a Rhetorical Device in
                   the Book of Jeremiah', *JSOT* 33: 63–82.
Wilson, R. R.
     1980   *Prophecy and Society in Ancient Israel* (Philadelphia: Fortress).

THE PRIESTS IN THE BOOK OF MALACHI AND THEIR OPPONENTS

Joachim Schaper

In this paper I shall attempt to tackle the problem of the identity of the priests described in the book of Malachi and of that of their opponents, namely that of the writer/s and redactor/s of the book and their allies. Since the book of Malachi gives us no obvious hints of its time and place of origin, it is very difficult to make use of it in any reconstruction of the history of the Judean priesthood. This is why I did not rely on it when I wrote my account of the history of the priests and Levites in the Persian period.[1] However, there are mentions of 'priests' and of 'Levi' in Malachi. The denunciation of what is perceived as the priests' wrongdoings takes up much room in that book and seems to have been one of the main concerns of its author/s and redactor/s. It is therefore worthy of consideration even if it does not aid historical reconstruction in any straightforward way. However, there may be some clues as to the book's background that may aid us in our quest for understanding Judean religion in the Persian period.

Let us first have a closer look at the book's structure. It is characterized by six *Diskussionsworte* (I. 1.2–5; II. 1.6–2.9; III. 2.10–16; IV. 2.17–3.5; V. 3.6–12; VI. 3.13–21 [3.22–24: Additions])[2] which are likely to be of literary origin.[3] As is most clearly obvious from Mal. 1.2–5, each unit is composed of four parts – I. *Feststellung* (declaration), II. *Einrede/Widerspruch der Adressaten* (response/objection by the addressees), III. *Entfaltung der Feststellung* (unfolding of the declaration), IV. *Folgerung(en)* (conclusion[s]) – half the declarations are proceeded by theological introductions (1.6abα; 2.10a; 3.6), and significant departures from the usual pattern in units II, III, and IV may indicate later hands.[4]

In locating the book of Malachi in space and time, it may be helpful to pay attention to Mal. 1.4–5, which concludes the denunciation of Edom stating (v. 5):

ועיניכם תראינה ואתם תאמרו יגדל יהוה מעל לגבול ישראל

---

1. Cf. Schaper (2000: 24)
2. Most commentators agree on this demarcation of the units; cf., for example, Meinhold (2000ff.: 3) and Hill (1998: xxxvi).
3. Cf. Utzschneider (1989: *passim*) on written 'prophecy' in Mal. 1.6–2.9.
4. According to the analysis provided by Meinhold (1992: 7 and 2000ff.: 24–29).

'Your own eyes shall see this, and you shall say, "Great is the LORD beyond the borders of Israel!"'[5]

Some exegetes[6] translate מעל לגבול ישראל as '*over* the territory of Israel', which leads to the interpretation of God's action as restricted to the territory of Israel. This, however, goes against the grain of the preceding verses (2–4) that depict God as active against and present in Edom; cf. v. 4: 'If Edom says, "We are shattered but we will rebuild the ruins," the LORD of hosts says: "They may build, but I will tear down, until they are called the wicked country, the people with whom the LORD is angry forever."'

Clearly, God's action is considered to affect Edom *and its territory*. He is thus thought of as being powerful beyond the borders of Israel, which Wellhausen saw clearly when he translated the passage in question as 'Jahve ist gross über Israels Grenze hinaus'.[7] This concept indicates a post-exilic date for the book. The same is indicated by the use of the term פחה in 1.8 where it says about offering inappropriate sacrificial animals:

הקריבהו נא לפחתך הירצך או הישא פניך אמר יהוה צבאות

'Try presenting that to your *governor*; will he be pleased with you or show you favor? says the LORD of hosts.'[8]

In the Hebrew Bible, פחה refers exclusively to the governors of the Achaemenid period.

All we have, however, are the most general hints about the book's date. If it indeed originated in the Persian era, when *precisely* did that happen? There are some further clues: the Jerusalem temple has been restored (1.10; 3.1, 10) and YHWH has shown his favour towards Israel by devastating Israel's old enemy, Edom. Because of the first-mentioned fact, the *terminus post quem* for the book must be the year 515 BCE when the temple was rededicated. The *terminus ante quem* is the conclusion of the mission of Ezra, which in my view[9] – informed by the classic arguments of Van Hoonacker[10] – must be dated to the year 398 BCE. The *terminus ante quem* becomes obvious from the observation that Malachi demands the dissolution of mixed marriages (Mal. 2.12), a practice which was abolished for good by Ezra.

Narrowing down the period of origin any further presents difficulties. In the whole book there is no reference whatsoever to precise events or situations that might help us to date the book as a whole or any of its

---

5. All biblical references in English are taken from the *New Revised Standard Version* (Anglicized Edition).
6. Cf., for example, Meinhold (2000ff.: 21).
7. Wellhausen (1963: 52).
8. Emphasis added by the present author.
9. Cf. Schaper (2000: 226–268)
10. First promoted by Van Hoonacker (1890).

individual oracles. However, B. Glazier-McDonald thinks that 'A date shortly before Nehemiah's arrival suits Malachi with regard to the content of its message (i.e., 470–450 B.C.). Further to narrow down these limits is precarious because Malachi offers no reference points for concrete dating. Nevertheless, the poor economic circumstances to which both Malachi and Nehemiah attest appear to have become prevalent during the reign of Artaxerxes I (465–25 B.C.). As a result, it is likely that Malachi was active some time after 460 BCE'[11]

This leaves us with a date between 460 and 398 BCE. We have to keep in mind, however, that, strictly speaking, there is no *conclusive* evidence whatsoever even for the time span just delineated. It does not help that the description of the behaviour of the 'sons of Levi' castigated in what is the most important passage for the purposes of the present paper, viz. Mal. 1.6–2.9, is too unspecific to serve as the basis for a precise dating.

Let us now have a closer look at the structure and history of Mal. 1.6–2.9. In its present form, it consists of three sub-units: 1.6–10; 1.11–14; 2.1–9.[12] Given the basic structure of the *Diskussionsworte* sketched by A. Meinhold,[13] however, it is possible to reconstruct an original layer underlying the present shape of Mal. 1.6–2.9. It varies only slightly from the basic structure visible in Unit I (Mal. 1.2–5),[14] and Meinhold posits that that original layer consisted of 1.6–8a; 2.1, 9a. These verses were much amplified by later hands. Meinhold rightly stresses, though, that the unit resulting from those additions, viz. Mal. 1.6–2.9, must be understood as thematically coherent and was intended to be read as a whole.[15] For the purposes of the present article, I am going to do exactly that. I am interested in the final text of Unit II. That text originated within the time span indicated above, viz. 460–398 BCE (and *predates* the additions of the final redaction of the book of Malachi). My conclusions concerning the identity of the Levitical priests and their adversaries will thus apply to that period.

Whom does Mal. 1.6–2.9 address? We read in 1.6: 'And if I am a master, where is the respect due to me? says the LORD of hosts to you, O priests, who despise my name.' Indeed, Mal. 1.6–2.9 addresses the priests exclusively. Their wrongdoings are enumerated. They are called כֹּהֲנִים, 'priests' in 1.6 and 2.1. In 2.7 there is a general reference to the office of

---

11. This is the position taken by Glazier-McDonald (1987: 17).
12. Following Meinhold (2000ff.: 74).
13. Cf. above, p. 1.
14. Cf. the analysis of Mal. 1.6–8a; 2.1, 9a provided by Meinhold (2000ff.: 77): '0. Vorspruch', 'I[1] Feststellung (allgemein)', 'II[1] Einrede/Widerspruch der Adressaten (allgemein)', 'I[2] Feststellung (konkret)', 'II[2] Einrede/Widerspruch der Adressaten (konkret)', 'III Entfaltung der Feststellungen', 'IV Folgerungen'.
15. Cf. Meinhold (2000ff.: 73–76, 87).

priest: 'For the lips of a priest should guard knowledge, and people should seek instruction from his mouth, for he is the messenger of the LORD of hosts.' The priests are reminded of the covenant of Levi (for Levi, cf. Mal. 2.4, 8; 3.3). God, addressing the priests (cf. 2.1), says: 'Know, then, that I have sent this command to you, so that my covenant with Levi (אֶת־לֵוִי בְּרִיתִי) may hold, says the LORD of hosts' (2.4). Thus in the original layer (Mal. 1.6–8a; 2.1, 9) of Unit II (Mal. 1.6–2.9) the priests are addressed but are not reminded of the covenant of Levi, nor are they called 'sons of Levi' or the like. The covenant with Levi/of Levi (אֶת־לֵוִי בְּרִיתִי v. 4b; בְּרִית הַלֵּוִי v. 8 [*hapax legomenon*]) is, in later additions, introduced as the 'benchmark' for assessing the behaviour of the priests. Levi is extolled as an image of virtue (2.6–7): 'True instruction was in his mouth, and no wrong was found on his lips. He walked with me in integrity and uprightness, and he turned many from iniquity. For the lips of a priest should guard knowledge, and people should seek instruction from his mouth, for he is the messenger of the LORD of hosts.'

The latter verse is yet another indication that the priests are the ones with whom God concluded the covenant that, in Mal. 2.4, had been referred to as בְּרִיתִי אֶת־לֵוִי 'my covenant *with* Levi'. This is made abundantly clear in 2.8 which blames the present-day priests for corrupting (שׁחת) the 'covenant *of* Levi' (בְּרִית הַלֵּוִי). In a different discourse, an eschatological perspective is held out to the priests and, by extension, to the whole of Judah when it says about the Lord of Hosts: 'For he is like a refiner's fire and like fullers' soap; he will sit as a refiner and purifier of silver, and he will purify the descendants of Levi and refine them like gold and silver, until they present offerings to the LORD in righteousness'(3.2b-3).

From all the passages addressing the priests or referring to them and the ones that mention the covenant with Levi or the sons of Levi it becomes obvious – if they are read in context! – that it is the priests who are viewed as the members of the covenant with Levi and that the כֹּהֲנִים must be identical with the בְּנֵי־לֵוִי. Wellhausen took that for granted when he commented בְּרִיתִי אֶת־לֵוִי in Mal. 2.4 saying that 'the priests are here still called sons of Levi, not sons of Aaron; in spite of Ezek. 44'.[16] J. M. O'Brien, in her study on the priests and Levites in Malachi, demonstrated that Wellhausen was right.[17] I have just adduced further arguments in favour of identifying the 'priests' and the 'sons of Levi'. And there is yet

---

16. Wellhausen (1897: 206) writes: 'Wie im Deuteronomium werden auch hier die Priester noch Söhne Levis genannt, nicht Söhne Aharons; trotz Ezech. 44.'

17. Cf. O'Brien (1990: 27–48) and her conclusion (1990: 144) that the terms כהן, בְּנֵי־לֵוִי and לֵוִי 'are treated as equivalent in the book. Contrary to the position of Hanson, the book demonstrates no evidence of acrimony between the groups described by these terms. All of these groups are described as exercising the same functions, those of sacrifice and of teaching.'

another observation that supports this identification, namely, the use of נגשׁ
hiph. in Mal. 3.3.[18] Its original meaning is 'to draw near', 'to approach',
but it was soon employed in cultic language to signify the drawing near of
the priests to the altar (in the qal) and their bringing near of sacrifices (in
the niph. and, more rarely, in the hiph.). In exilic and post-exilic texts, it is
often used to denote, *pars pro toto*, the priestly service, as in Exod. 19.22:
'Even the priests who approach the LORD (הַכֹּהֲנִים הַנִּגָּשִׁים אֶל־יְהֹוָה) must
consecrate themselves or the LORD will break out against them.'

נגשׁ also occurs in Ezek. 44.13: 'They shall not come near to me
(וְלֹא־יִגְּשׁוּ אֵלַי), to serve me as priest, nor come near any of my sacred
offerings (וְגֶשֶׁת עַל־כָּל־קָדָשַׁי), the things that are most sacred.' Interestingly,
the Levites – and that means, in Ezekiel, the second-rank cultic
functionaries – are excluded from drawing near and serving as priests.
נגשׁ is thus a privilege of the priests. In Lev. 2.8 (נגשׁ hiph.) it is the task of
the priests to bring near the sacrifice: 'You shall bring to the LORD the
grain offering that is prepared in any of these ways; and when it is
presented to the priest, he shall take it (וְהִגִּישָׁהּ) to the altar.'

Lev. 8.14 (נגשׁ hiph.) provides another example of that usage with
reference to the חַטָּאת sacrifice; in Exod. 32.6 נגשׁ hiph. is used in the context
of the שְׁלָמִים sacrifice.

Such is the background of the use of נגשׁ in Malachi. It adds further
weight to our thesis that the בְּנֵי־לֵוִי in Malachi are priests, not Levites in the
sense of Ezekiel and the Priestly Writing.

There is another hint that the author(s) of Malachi, in spite of not
making use of it, must have been aware of the distinction between priests
and Levites, namely, the terminology used in Mal. 3.8 where mention is
made both of the מַעֲשֵׂר and the תְּרוּמָה:[19] according to Num. 18.20–32, the
Levites collect the people's tithe and receive a תְּרוּמָה; cf. also the use of the
terms in Neh. 10.38. The author/s and redactor/s of Malachi seem to have
been aware of and to have affirmed this rule, which is yet another
indication that the people behind the book of Malachi knew and supported
at least parts of the legislation of the Priestly Writing but did not take over
its concept of priesthood and the terminology used to formulate it. This
also becomes obvious from the fact that a term denoting the priesthood
that is very prominent elsewhere in exilic and post-exilic Judaean literature
is conspicuously absent from the book of Malachi, namely the term

---

18. It makes sense to adduce 3.3–4 in order to understand 1.6–2.9 since, as Rudolph
(1976: 280) writes with reference to 3.3–4: 'Sachlich gehören die Verse also in den dortigen
Zusammenhang [i.e. 1.6–2.9], sind aber dann wohl bei einer anderen Gelegenheit gesprochen.'

19. Cf. Meinhold (1992: 9): 'Die Differenzierung zwischen Zehnt und Hebe geht auf
priesterliches Denken zurück, das zwischen Leviten und Priestern unterscheidet (Num 18,20–
32; vgl. Neh 10,38f).'

בְּנֵי אַהֲרֹן 'sons of Aaron'. This raises questions concerning the position of Malachi and the priesthood the book refers to.

As J. M. O'Brien puts it, 'Malachi's lack of explicit references to the sons of Aaron and its mention of a "covenant with Levi" (2:4), a "covenant of Levi" (2:8) and the "sons of Levi" (3:8), along with what many consider to be the Deuteronomic character of the book, raise the questions of whether the author knows the Priestly Code and whether he or she uses the terms "sons of Levi" and "priests" synonymously. Four major positions are taken on these issues.'[20] O'Brien further states that 'The large majority of those discussing Malachi contend that in the book the terms are equivalent and, therefore, that Malachi reflects a point in the history of the priesthood prior to the enactment of the reforms of the Priestly Code.'[21] It is obvious from what we have said earlier that we cannot accept this view.

The second position can be described thus: 'Many...have suggested that while Malachi relies heavily on Deuteronomy its description of the tithe in ch. 3 resembles more that of the Priestly legislation than that of the Deuteronomic Code. This observation has led some scholars to propose that Malachi reflects the transition from D to P.'[22] We shall see soon why this position, too, is not convincing.

A third position is taken by, amongst others, Y. Kaufmann and B. Glazier-McDonald who are convinced that Malachi is aware of P and yet treats בְּנֵי־לֵוִי 'sons of Levi' and כֹּהֲנִים 'priests' as synonymous. B. Glazier-McDonald, arguing on the basis of A. Cody's and J. Pedersen's work, 'contends', in the words of J. M. O'Brien, 'that in this period the entire priesthood was subsumed under the genealogy of Levi. In this way, the identity of the terms "priest" and "Levite" rests not on a Deuteronomic notion that all members of the tribe may be priests but rather on the post-exilic notion that the "sons of Aaron" also were "sons of Levi".'[23] We shall return to this problem in due course.

Finally, there is another view, held most prominently by P. D. Hanson, stating that the terms בְּנֵי־לֵוִי and כֹּהֲנִים are actually 'in bitter tension; while the book reflects P's distinction between priest and Levite, it does not support P's agenda'.[24] We shall discuss this view, too.

So far, our investigation of the view of the priesthood in the book of Malachi has led us to the conclusion that the book's author/s and redactor/s do not distinguish between priests and Levites, that is, between first-rate and second-rate cultic functionaries. Furthermore, the classification of the priests as "sons of Levi" betrays a certain proximity towards

20. O'Brien (1990: 24).
21. O'Brien (1990: 24).
22. O'Brien (1990: 24).
23. O'Brien (1990: 25), summarizing Glazier-McDonald (1987: 76–77).
24. O'Brien (1990: 25), summing up Hanson (1986: 253–290).

Deuteronomic and Deuteronomistic thinking, as Wellhausen quite rightly pointed out.[25] We cannot follow Wellhausen, however, when he states that the people behind the book of Malachi were not aware of the Priestly Writing.[26] Rather, their use of נגש seems to me to indicate· that they were acquainted with the portrayals of the priesthood, more precisely: of the priests and the Levites, in Ezekiel and P. However, they do not differentiate between two distinct classes of cultic personnel, as do Ezekiel and P. The בְּנֵי־לֵוִי – and presumably this means: *all* the בְּנֵי־לֵוִי – are, according to Malachi, priests. This is indeed identical with the view proposed by Deut. 18.1–8. But it is a Deuteronomic/Deuteronomistic view of the priesthood upheld *not in ignorance* of Ezekiel and P, *but in the face of* Ezekiel and P, since the book of Malachi was composed a good while after the relevant passages in Ezekiel and the priestly *Grundschrift* were formulated.

This result on the whole coincides with P. D. Hanson's *general* statement that in 'sharp contrast to the division between priests and Levites that had developed under the leadership of the Zadokites, that is reflected in the Priestly Writing and Ezekiel 44, Malachi's "covenant with Levi" recognizes no such distinction. It reflects instead the earlier ideal expressed in Deuteronomy 18:1–8.'[27]

Kaufmann's and Glazier-McDonald's suggestion that the 'identity of the terms "priest" and "Levite" rests not on a Deuteronomic notion but rather on the post-exilic notion that the "sons of Aaron" also were "sons of Levi"'[28] is interesting, but not entirely convincing. Glazier-McDonald states that 'in post-exilic times the entire priesthood was subsumed under one genealogy with Levi as its first ancestor, the priests proper being sons of Aaron, "the Levite" *par excellence*, cf. Exod 4:14–16. The Zadokites traced their lineage through Eleazar, the son of Aaron (1 Chr 5:27f, 24:1f), and Aaronic priests of the house of Abiathar traced their descent through Ithamar, another of Aaron's sons. Thus, "levite" became a generic name, and the "sons of Aaron" who belonged, in toto, to the tribe of Levi could surely be called, in that sense, levites or levitical priests.'[29]

They could be – but they were not ... Of course, Glazier-McDonald is right in drawing our attention to the fact that P and, following it, Chronicles establish a genealogy of the supposed tribe of Levi that incorporates both Zadokites and Aaronites. Both the Zadokites and the Aaronites, however, are classed as priests, as opposed to the other

---

25. Cf. Wellhausen (1963: 206, 207).
26. Wellhausen (1963: 209–210) locates Malachi in a transitional phase ('Übergangsstufe') from D to P.
27. Hanson (1986: 282–283).
28. O'Brien (1990: 25) thus appropriately summarizes their views.
29. Glazier-McDonald (1987: 77).

members of the supposed tribe of Levi. The latter are called Levites (1 Chron. 6.33: וַאֲחֵיהֶם הַלְוִיִם; that is, the 'brothers' of the priests) and 'were appointed for all the service of the tabernacle of the house of God. But [!] Aaron and his sons made offerings on the altar of burnt-offering and on the altar of incense, during all the work of the most holy place' (1 Chron. 6.33–34). Thus, Chronicles differentiates between 'Levites' who are equal and 'Levites' who are 'more equal' than others. In the genealogies of P, this is even more obvious.[30]

Our passage in Malachi, however, *does not differentiate at all* between separate classes or groups within the priesthood. It is thus clear that the view of the priesthood proposed in Mal. 1.6–2.9 comes closest to that of Deut. 18.1–8. In *this* respect Hanson is right. Also, the thesis claiming 'that Malachi reflects the transition from D to P'[31] is much too simplistic. Malachi proposes some views, like that of the priesthood, that are reminiscent of Deuteronomy and others, like its concept of sacrificial practices, which remind us of P. In other respects, Malachi is at variance with P, but also with Deuteronomy. It thus seems that its authors were highly independent in their views. For the moment suffice it to say that Hanson is right when he states that Malachi's view of the priesthood is close to that of Deut. 18.1–8.

In analogy with 'the opposition group to which Isaiah 56–66 bears witness'[32] and with the group responsible for Zech. 10–11, Hanson reconstructs a '"Malachi" group'.[33] 'In the case of the material in Isaiah 56–66, disenfranchised Levitical elements making common cause with disciples of Second Isaiah were likely behind the attack on the Zadokite leadership. It is not impossible that the combination of cultic concerns and apocalyptic themes in Malachi hints at a similar coalition of prophetic and priestly elements active some fifty years later.'[34]

Hanson thus seems to imply that Levites were involved in a coalition against the leading priestly caste whom he considers to have been Zadokite. Why, then, one is tempted to ask, should Levites have referred to the priests – to whom, according to Hanson's theory, they were bitterly opposed – by means of the honorific name of Levi? Also, it is obvious from the text that criticism is levelled against the priests because of their current abuses but that they are promised a restoration to their former splendour and righteousness. Furthermore, it seems well nigh impossible that Levites

---

30. Cf. Schaper (2000: 26–42).
31. O'Brien (1990: 24), referring to Wellhausen (1963), Mitchell, Smith and Bewer (1912) and others.
32. Hanson (1986: 282).
33. Hanson (1986: 283).
34. Hanson (1986: 281).

should have opposed priests, assigned to them the title 'sons of Levi' and *not* have indicated that they, the Levites, also had a right to that title.

The strangest thing about the book of Malachi is that it does not give us the slightest indication that Levites, in the sense of second-rank cultic officials, existed at all in the Persian period. And yet they did exist, as is universally attested by all the other relevant sources of the time. I can only conclude that we are therefore confronted, in the book of Malachi, either with the views of outsiders, who were, as far as the temple personnel was concerned, interested only in the priests proper or did not or could not differentiate between priests and Levites, *or* with the views of dissident priests whose desire it was to denounce their ungodly colleagues and simply were not interested in the Levites.

If we now look at the textual evidence again, there are another two important observations to be made. As S. M. Olyan has rightly pointed out, the cultic vocabulary used in Malachi is remarkable. He states that 'Malachi 1 goes farther than any other biblical text concerned with blemished sacrificial animals. Unlike other materials, it associates such animals with impurity…. The verb *g'l*, used here for the blemished sacrifices, is attested as a synonym for the more common verb *tm'* ("to pollute", "to be polluted") beginning in texts of the sixth century and continuing thereafter…. The equivalence of the verbs *g'l* and *tm'* and their derivatives is suggested not only by Mal 1:7–12, but also by texts such as Neh 13:29–30; Lam 4:14–15; and Dan 1:8. The association of blemished sacrificial animals with uncleanness in the polemic of Malachi 1 reflects an ideological position that contrasts with that of texts such as Deuteronomy, the Holiness Source, and the Priestly Writing; it functions as an effective means to underscore the inappropriateness und unacceptability of such sacrifices.'[35]

Thus, Malachi contains a fundamental critique of the sacrificial practices of the time and is highly independent in its views. This coincides with another observation, made by M. Fishbane, who detects, in Mal. 1.6–2.9, 'a remarkable post-exilic example of the aggadic exegesis of Num. 6:23–7', 'a systematic utilization of the language of the Priestly Blessing and a thorough exegetical transformation of it'.[36]

'The prophet', writes Fishbane[37], 'has taken the contents of the Priestly Blessing – delivered by the priests, and with its emphasis on blessing, the sanctity of the divine Name, and such benefactions as protection, favourable countenance, and peace – and inverted them. The priests, the

---

35. Olyan (2000: 105).
36. Fishbane (1985: 332).
37. Fishbane (1985: 332).

prophet contends, have despised the divine name and service; and this has led to a threatened suspension of the divine blessing.'

We thus have a harsher than ever indictment of the sacrificing of blemished animals as well as an indictment of the priesthood that rivals and exceeds any other in the Hebrew Bible, and a very sarcastic one at that (cf. the puns in Mal. 1.9, 12; 1.8, 13; 1.10, 14; 2.2; 1.6, 12; 2.9). Since all this is imparted to the hearers and readers as a divine utterance, we can only confirm Fishbane's conclusion that 'Malachi's speech is revealed to be no less than a divine exegesis of the Priestly Blessing, and a divine mockery of the priests who presume to bless in his name. The sacerdotal language of the Priestly Blessing is thus, by further irony, systematically desecrated and inverted by YHWH himself.'[38] And, even more to the point: 'The deep ironical core of Malachi's speech inheres in its destabilizing liturgical mockery, a mockery which curses the forms and language of order, cosmos, and blessing as entrusted to the priesthood. The *Mischgattung* created by this interweaving of liturgical language with prophetical discourse thoroughly transforms the positive assurances of the former into the negative forecasts of the latter.'[39] At the same time, Mal. 1.6–2.9 embodies some of the highest praises of the priestly office in the whole of the Hebrew Bible; just compare 2.7 and its designation of the priest as the 'messenger of the LORD of hosts'. The book of Malachi is very clear in differentiating between the *office* and its present *incumbents*.

Let us now sum up our results and try to arrive at a conclusion. The priests denounced in the book of Malachi were the Zadokite priests who, led by the high priest, ran the Jerusalem temple in the Persian period[40] (and therefore also during the period in question here, namely, the time from 460–398 BCE). The community of priests together with the high priest were one of the institutions that governed Yehud and thus embodied political as well as religious power.[41] The author/s and redactor/s responsible for the book of Malachi, who were antagonists of those Zadokite priests, are characterized by their staggering proficiency in the exegesis of author-itative religious texts, demonstrated by their re-interpretation of the Priestly Blessing. Such consummate skill could only have been found amongst priests and Levites. We saw that the Levites must be discounted as authors of the book of Malachi. This leaves us with the priests, more precisely: with a group of dissident priests. Other biblical and non-biblical documents give us no direct hint of the existence of such a group during the period in question. In the book of Nehemiah, however, we find

38. Fishbane (1985: 334).
39. Fishbane (1985: 334).
40. Cf. Schaper (2000: 41 and 2002: *passim*) on the identity of the post-exilic Jerusalemite high priesthood.
41. Cf. Schaper (2000: 162–225 and 2002: *passim*)

criticism of the then priesthood, for example in Neh. 13.4–14, which is part of the Nehemiah *Denkschrift*. Not all of the priests were untrustworthy, however, as is obvious from Nehemiah's report that he appointed a priest (called Shelemiah), a scribe and a levite as overseers of the temple treasury and storage rooms. These people are described as נֶאֱמָנִים, 'trustworthy'. The 'trustworthy' priest Shelemiah thus replaces the not so trustworthy priests, that is those that had opposed – and continued to oppose – Nehemiah. All this indicates a rift in the Jerusalem temple priesthood. It seems to have been the case that some priests did not toe the line of the high priest. It is tempting to identify them with the people behind the book of Malachi. I am inclined to think that a small group of dissident priests whose views of central tenets of cultic theory and practice differed, at least in some respects, from those propagated by the major works of Judaean religious literature in the exilic and post-exilic periods, who may be described as traditionalists with exacting standards in their cultic practice and a more or less Deuteronomic view of the priesthood and who opposed current practices of high-ranking temple personnel, are responsible for the harsh criticism of their colleagues gathered in the book of Malachi.

BIBLIOGRAPHY

Cody, A.
  1969   *A History of the Old Testament Priesthood* (Analecta Biblica, 35; Rome: Pontifical Biblical Institute).
Elliger, K.
  1959   *Das Buch der zwölf Kleinen Propheten. II. Die Propheten Nahum, Habakuk, Zephanja, Haggai, Sacharja, Maleachi* (Das Alte Testament Deutsch, 25; Göttingen: Vandenhoeck & Ruprecht).
Fishbane, M.
  1985   *Biblical Interpretation in Ancient Israel* (Oxford: Clarendon Press).
Glazier-McDonald, B.
  1987   *Malachi: The Divine Messenger* (Society of Biblical Literature Dissertation Series, 98; Atlanta, GA: Scholars Press).
Hanson, P. D.
  1986   *The People Called: The Growth of Community in the Bible* (San Francisco: Harper & Row).
Hill, A. E.
  1998   *Malachi: A New Translation with Introduction and Commentary* (The Anchor Bible, 25D; New York: Doubleday).
Hoonacker, A. Van,
  1890   'Néhémie et Esdras, une nouvelle hypothèse sur la chronologie de l'époque de la restauration', *Muséon* 9: 151–184.317–351.389–400.
Kaufmann, Y.
  1977   *The History of the Religion of Israel. IV. From the Babylonian Captivity to the End of Prophecy* (New York: KTAV).

Meinhold, A.
  1992   'Maleachi/Maleachibuch', in *Theologische Realenzyklopädie* 22
             (Berlin and New York: de Gruyter): 6–11.
  2000ff   *Maleachi* (Biblischer Kommentar zum Alten Testament, XIV/8;
             Neukirchen-Vluyn: Neukirchener Verlag).
Mitchell, H. G., J. M. P. Smith and J. A. Bewer
  1912   *A Critical and Exegetical Commentary on Haggai, Zechariah,
             Malachi and Jonah* (International Critical Commentary; Edin-
             burgh: T. & T. Clark; reprint 1999).
O'Brien, J. M.
  1990   *Priest and Levite in Malachi* (Society of Biblical Literature
             Dissertation Series, 121; Atlanta, GA: Scholars Press).
Olyan, S. M.
  2000   *Rites and Rank: Hierarchy in Biblical Representations of Cult*
             (Princeton, NJ: Princeton University Press).
Pedersen, J.
  1973   *Israel: Its Life and Culture* (4 vols.; London: Oxford University
             Press).
Robinson, Th.H., and F. Horst
  1954   *Die Zwölf Kleinen Propheten* (Handbuch zum Alten Testament, I/
             14; Tübingen: J. C. B. Mohr [Paul Siebeck], 2nd edn).
Rudolph, W.
  1976   *Haggai – Sacharja 1–8 – Sacharja 9–14 – Maleachi* (Kommentar
             zum Alten Testament, XIII/4; Gütersloh: Mohn).
Schaper, J.
  2000   *Priester und Leviten im achämenidischen Juda* (Forschungen zum
             Alten Testament, 31; Tübingen: Mohr Siebeck).
  2002   'Numismatik, Epigraphik, alttestamentliche Exegese und die Frage
             nach der politischen Verfassung des achämenidischen Juda',
             Zeitschrift des Deutschen Palästina-Vereins 118: 150–168.
Utzschneider, H.
  1989   *Künder oder Schreiber? Eine These zum Problem der 'Schriftpro-
             phetie' auf Grund von Maleachi 1,6–2,9* (Beiträge zur Erforschung
             des Alten Testaments und des Antiken Judentums, 19; Frankfurt/
             Main and New York: Peter Lang).
Wellhausen, J.
  1963   *Die kleinen Propheten übersetzt und erklärt* (Berlin: de Gruyter; 4th
             edn).

The Prophet versus Priest Antagonism Hypothesis: Its History and Origin

Ziony Zevit

> 'the farmer and the cowboy should be friends'
> –*Oklahoma*, lyrics by Oscar Hammerstein II

It is widely taught that the classical prophets of ancient Israel were individuals concerned primarily with Israel's ethical behavior. Consequently, for them, adherence to the ethical stipulations of the covenant was deemed more important than the punctilious fulfillment of cultic minutiae. To make their point, prophets condemned the cult in YHWH's name. Amos 5.21–24 is regularly cited in this context:

> I hate, I despise your feasts, and I take no delight in you solemn assemblies... Take away from me the noise of your songs; to the melody of your harps I will not listen. But, let justice roll down like waters and righteousness like an ever-flowing stream.

If it be true, as the consensus maintains, that prophets valued ethics over cult, it is clear that they must have given some thought to priests, promoters of that which they felt impeded Israelites from fulfilling their ethical covenant obligations.[1] Following this line of thought, it is

---

1. Textbooks: J. A. Bewer (1962, originally printed in 1922, revised in 1933 and printed eleven times, third revision in 1962): 'Amos emphasized upright conduct as opposed to mere cult, Amos insisted that God's sole requirement was social justice' (1962: 94); H. K. Beebe (1970: 220): 'When one reads Amos 5:21–24 and Isaiah 1:12–20 he finds a bitter criticism of cultic rites and appeal for ethical integrity. These and other passages make the prophets appear opposed to traditional cultic practices in Israel.' Although he doesn't reject the idea that such passages only make the prophets appear as if opposed to traditional cult, he does not dwell on this aspect of their message. J. H. Hayes (1971: 166): 'That Amos attacked and denied the value of the entire Israelite cultic ritual cannot be denied. Whether he would have been opposed to the ritual if it had been accompanied by social justice and fidelity is a matter for discussion but is ultimately unanswerable.' For similar comments about Hosea, cf. p. 173; Isaiah, cf. p. 181; Jeremiah, p. 206. J. Carmody, L. Carmody and R. L. Cohen (1988: 74–5): 'Moses predominates over Aaron which suggests the primacy of prophecy over priesthood.' Somewhat qualified assessments of the relationship between the types are found also. B. W. Anderson draws attention to the conflict between prophet and priest, but argues that prophets could not have been anti-cult since 'every religion must have a cultus – that is, forms in which faith and worship can find expression' (1975: 457). Noting differences between the two types, Anderson points out that the differences do not mean that the two types were incompatible

reasonable to infer that some prophets must have felt animus toward priests, and their hostility should be imprinted in the preserved literature. Though an obvious topic for research, the validity of the basic claims underlying the consensus, or the lack thereof, as is actually the case, has not been submitted to critical review until recently.[2] The following observations are intended as a contribution to the new discourse.

My objectives in this paper are to get rid of sacrificial smoke so as to be able to respond to the following questions:

> (1) How, when and why did the prevailing view of prophet versus priest antagonism – hereafter, the 'antagonism hypothesis' – emerge?
> (2) What was the actual priestly reality against which the prophets are said to have harangued?

My approach, like that of other recent investigators, some of whom are cited below, is historical and literary. It does, however, engage both theological and psychological approaches to the second question because of their influence on the prevailing view.

The Prevalent Image of Israel's Prophets

We know the haranguers, the *nebi'im*, of ancient Israel through two sources: (1) stories about them in the historical books, Judges, Samuel, Kings and Chronicles, and (2) edited collections of their primarily poetic speeches. This distinction by genre is not absolute. Short prophetic speeches are found also in the historical books while the edited collections include some stories. Despite this qualification, the statement retains usefulness as a generalization. It indicates that distinctive literary genres, each emerging from a different *Sitz-im-Leben* with its corresponding *raison d'être*, provide access to the *nebi'im*. Furthermore, although in their final redaction the individual exemplars within each genre were curated by 'final' editors, each possesses its own history of origin, development, and transmission. Considered this way, the Hebrew Bible contains many unique, and partially independent sources of information about *nebi'im*.

(1975: 457–58). G. A. Larue allows that there was tension between priest and prophet but refers to evidence that prophets were also involved with cultic ritual. Furthermore, Larue argues that the connection between cult and morality could have existed in Israel as it is known to have existed outside of Israel; accordingly prophets should not be characterized as anti-cultic (1968: 180–81).

The statements of Anderson and Larue are atypical; the unqualified ones cited at the beginning of the note are more common. They occur regularly in scholarly papers, class lectures, and sermons. They extend from the academy through the classroom to the pew. One question investigated below inquires as to the origin and direction of this movement.

  2. This statement is qualified by Curtiss (1877) mentioned below.

Since there is not much overlap between individual *nebi'im* appearing in the different genres, much fuss is made distinguishing between those mentioned in historical books and those cited in prophetic books. The division according to literary genre has given rise to a qualitative distinction between Elijah and Isaiah types.

Those known from the historical books are described variously as 'primitive', 'ecstatic', 'enthusiastic' or 'pre-classical' while the latter are known as the 'classical', 'canonical', or 'writing' prophets. Since the 'primitive' prophets appear in books whose major focus is on the history of Israel as a reflection of the policies of its leaders, their words are directed mainly to kings and nobles under concrete, historical (or historicized) time-bound circumstances. 'Classical' prophets are known from scrolls edited so that most of their addresses appear directed to the people at large as general pronouncements; consequently the former tend to be discounted in theological discussions and the latter esteemed.[3]

The reasons for this are clear. The former are perceived as people of action; the latter as people of words. The former had things to do in their own days; the latter are understood as having had principled instruction for their own as well as for future generations. While it is certain that the former may have spoken volumes, even as they were actively involved in exciting historical events, their words are no longer extant. The latter certainly spoke, even if most of them didn't do all that much that was interesting. The former tend to be portrayed as excitable, emotional, and drunk from their experience of divine presence. The latter are presented as cerebral, poised and, even when excited or agitated, capable of giving sublime voice to the songs of their souls. They are imagined or thought to be pre-philosophic philosophers. Had they lived today, they would teach ethics and theology in the best seminaries, deliver inspired lectures addressing pressing issues of the moment in the highest moral tones, and they would publish with Fortress Press. The former would be scruffy political activists, working public places by haranguing passers-by.

The Reality of Israel's Prophets

Unfortunately, the claim that classical prophets were primarily bearers of moral and ethical teachings addressing common social concerns does

---

3. Despite their bold stances against powerful figures, the likes of Nathan, Ahijah, and Micaiah are secondary characters in the narratives at best. Elijah and Elisha differ significantly, but only because they are presented in connected strings of anecdotes which enable contemporary readers to construct them as rounded characters. Classical prophets loom large in their books because they are usually the only voice heard. Books containing their speeches rarely provide descriptions of the circumstances precipitating specific remarks.

not bear up under scrutiny. I am able to discern passages expressing such concerns in Isaiah, Jeremiah, Ezekiel, Hosea, Amos, Micah, Habakkuk, Zephaniah and Malachi, but not in Joel, Obadiah, Nahum, Haggai and Zechariah. The total number of verses dedicated to such topics is small. According to my reckoning, based on counts in the masoretic notes printed in BHS, speeches concerned with the misuse of wealth, carousing, drinking, illicit or immoral behavior by authorities, namely the king, prophets and judges; miscreant priests, immoral cities and territories, and all Israelites as immoral totals 553 out of the 4975 verses – excluding Jonah's 48 – comprising the Latter Prophets, that is 11 percent (cf. Zevit 2001: 509).

On the rare occasion when prophets did point out social ills, they rarely proposed ways of mitigating them. Isaiah 58.7, in which the prophet suggests feeding the hungry with 'your bread' and bringing the homeless poor into 'your house', is a most notable exception. Prophets neither proposed to pay judges or market inspectors for their services nor did they advocate the establishment of public or private charities or the breaking up of large estates. They were largely impractical men who thought that drawing attention to faults and threatening punishments for offensive behavior concluded their task (Ginsberg 1979: 16–7). (Not unlike many high-minded people of our own times.)

These observations suggest that contrary to what is commonly taught, *the ethics and morality of Israel's social behavior were not major concerns* of these prophets and consequently, not of particular interest to the collectors of their oracles and editors of books bearing their name.

Allowing for the fact that though we possess written, edited speeches from one group of prophets this does not, in and of itself, warrant construing that there was any difference with regard to worldview and social role between them and their colleagues who left no literary legacy. *Nebi'im* were public scolds. Their major concern, as attested in the extant prophetic books, was to chastise Israel for whatever behaviors violated (1) a particular comprehension of covenant cultic obligations, (2) a concern for what they considered the proper conventions for worshipping YHWH, and (3) chastising those of Israel's enemies who were particularly successful militarily against Israel.

These people were interactively and dynamically involved with fellow Israelites. They did not found cults based on revelations of a new ethic for a society that would replace the one in which they lived, whose practices they castigated. However their subversiveness is understood, nothing in extant texts suggests that it attempted to attack and undermine the Israelite ethos or political elites with the objective of replacing them with those who would support a new order. Hence, the idea that classical prophets considered themselves revolutionary and innovative rather than reactionary and restorative, is historically (and psychologically) problematic. The God of the prophets was not – except, perhaps, in the case of Ezek. 40–48 – a 'solution-God' (Riley, 1988:353–7).[4]

Given the overriding interest of *nebi'im* in Israel's private and public *cultic* behaviors, it was inevitable that priests as a group would fall within purview of their critical gaze and that priests and their activities would become an object of their cogitation and caviling evaluations.[5]

Secondary Origins of the Antagonism Hypothesis

A rather benign expression of the hypothesis is found in the writings of Abraham Kuenen, a Dutch contemporary of Wellhausen, whose publications, regularly translated into English were important during the last quarter of the nineteenth century and can still be read profitably today:

> It is true that some of the prophets of Jahveh were sprung from the priestly tribe of Levi, but this origin did not confer on them their prophetic character. It is even far from unusual for them to address their exhortation and reproaches to the priests, as well as to the people. With regard to the sacrifices and the festivals in honour of Jahveh they have their peculiar ideas, which clearly prove that they have not to live by the altar, and which, moreover, *render very comprehensible a certain antagonism between them and the priests*' (my emphasis cf. Kuenen 1874: 189).

L. L. Grabbe concludes his own analysis of Israelite prophets with the observation that no sociological distinction may be made between pre-classical and classical ones. The distinction commonly asserted emerges on the one hand from failing to consider prophetic books as a whole and not allowing that priests or sages – who, he argues, were not bereft of social

4. Cf. B. T. Riley (1988: 353–57). Riley speaks of 'prophetic religion' as a solution-type of religion that introduces teachings from a solution-God through a charismatic prophet to resolve inequities and problems that emerge in times of severe cultural dissolution. These movements are revolutionary and personality centered.

5. For a general orientation to different conceptions of the types of prophets and prophecy that reigned in Biblical studies from the mid-nineteenth to the mid-twentieth century, cf. Lindblom (1962: 47–65). Lindblom observes a gradual shading from the earlier, primitive type to the later, canonical type, but is clearly more comfortable with the latter. To this list should be added their important role as intercessors on behalf of individuals for personal matters and of the people as a whole in times of trouble, including unpromising military circumstances. Cf. 1 Kgs 22.5–6; Isa. 7–8; Jer. 14.11, 15.1, 21.1–2, 37:3 and see the often overlooked essay of Y. Muffs 'Who Will Stand in the Breach? A Study of Prophetic Intercession' (1992: 9–48; and cf. 2002: 21–7, 56).

R. R. Wilson provides a useful social-anthropological approach to prophecy that uniquely maps form-critical issues on his distinctions between an Ephraimite and Judean tradition (1980: 135–295) and cf. Zevit (2001: 495–503).

concerns – may have influenced the contents of the books. On the other hand, theological judgments about the messages influenced by 'an idealized picture commensurate with what might be acceptable to a nineteenth century Protestant' contributed to the acceptance of the distinction (1995: 117).[6] R. R. Hutton, allowing for the idea's influence in the nineteenth century and the role of Wellhausen as a prime mediator, considers it a legacy from sixteenth–seventeenth-century Reformation thinking that was fascinated with the freedom of the 'word' over against the restrictiveness of the 'law' (1994: 137–38).[7] W. R. Millar pushes beyond Hutton for the origin of the negative image of priests *vis-à-vis* prophets. He proposes that it be sought long before the Enlightenment: 'Perhaps it is because Sadducees and Pharisees are presented in a negative light' (2001: 2–3).

This situating of the origin of the pattern of popular explanation in nineteenth-century theology, even if its origins are to be sought earlier, concords well with an observation that N. K. Gottwald made more than 40 years ago. He suggested that nineteenth-century biblical scholarship created the image of the prophet as a social reformer because Christian Socialism in Britain and the Social Gospel movement in America 'were eager to lay claim to the courageous communal conscience of the Hebrew prophets' (1959: 276). Recently, J. D. Plein augmented this observation, noting that the social reform movements led some to claim that prophets viewed religion and ethics as inseparable and even more, that they viewed ethical conduct as the supreme religious act. As a consequence, individual reformers of that era thought, incorrectly, that sacrificial ritual was a hindrance to ethical religion (2001: 214–5).[8] He observes further that their idea, timebound as it was then, is assumed to be so self-apparent by some recent authors that they do not bother to demonstrate its validity by contemporary standards. In his respected history of Israelite religion, a work characterized by sophisticated attention to social history, R. Albertz asserts that the prophets rejected cultic practices of their time because they covered up 'the social justice and misery in society' (1984: 171).

The nineteenth-century views, acceptable to the (then) new historical-critical study of Israelite religion were buttressed by researchers in the newly-evolved discipline, psychology of religion. G. A. Coe, one of the founding fathers of psychology of religion at the beginning of the twentieth century, employed a mix of anthropological and psychological models to

---

6.   Grabbe, then, shortens the list of prophetic passages condemning improper behaviors by attributing some to redactors.

7.   M. A. Sweeney aligns himself with the opinion of Hutton, suggesting that the historically false understanding, insofar as ancient Israel is concerned, has misled some scholars seeking the origins of apocalyptic in the alleged antagonism (2001: 133–34).

8.   Plein's ambitious book considers the socio-ethical passages in socio-historic and edited literary contexts.

distinguish between three types of religious leaders: shamans, priests and prophets. According to Coe, shamans combine elements of the psychic, clairvoyant and wise man; additionally, they have or claim access to some outside power. Coe considered the prophetic bands in the Bible shamans. He also assigned Joseph Smith and Mary Baker Eddy to this type as well. Their inclusion illustrates clearly that although he worked with an evolutionary typology, he evaluated his data phenomenologically, not historically.

Priests, according to Coe, exist in established institutions, are conservative and see to practices. They take care that traditions are handed down accurately and are ultimately committed to writing. They train men to the idea of law and sacred literature. Coe stated that this type can ultimately give rise to dead formalism, mechanical routine, and lazy revenue for himself. He described his third type, the prophet, as possessing direct contact with the deity rather than gaining access through priestly and ceremonial ritual. Prophets go directly to the source of religious life and set themselves in contrast with priests and priestly systems. The prophet is the mouthpiece of the power conceived as 'ethical will'. To exemplify prophets as a type of religious personality, Coe cited Amos 5.21–23; 8.4–6, famous passages denouncing the cult.

Somewhere along the line, Coe's objective observations and deductions based on anthropological studies available in the early-twentieth century slid into a sort of evolutionary triumphalism modeled on the Bible and normative theology. For readers of his important book who failed to discern this leitmotif in its subtle enunciations, Coe sounded it boldly: 'It was the prophetic, not the priestly element in Judaism that attracted Jesus and formed his character and the basis of his message; and Paul, in spite of his legalistic training...was conquered by it' (Coe 1917: 176–87; citation from p. 184).[9]

W. Houston Clark whose popular book was used widely through the early 1960s, distinguished four religious types: mystics, prophets, priests and intellectuals. Among the prophets, Clark included Moses, Isaiah, Amos, Elijah, Jesus, Paul, Martin Luther, George Fox and Gandhi (1958: 290–3). He characterized them as individuals with a sense of mission as

9. In the quotation, Coe's use of 'Judaism' to refer to what contemporary scholars refer to as 'Israelite religion' reflects his era. The Bible was held to contain an authentic, early form of Judaism before it lapsed into legalistic Rabbinic Judaism. This view, a view that appears quaintly old-fashioned nowadays, remained common in many academic circles until the 1960s when scholars began to work out the implications of the Dead Sea Scrolls for the history of Judaism.

Coe's book helped define what many consider the 'golden age' of the field, from 1880–1930. Other major figures of this period were Henry James, D. Stanley Hall, E. D. Starbuck. These early explorers were generally sympathetic to religion.

God's mouthpiece, concern for rightness of living, and trust in their own intuition to provide individualized expressions of religious truth. Clark distinguished between them as religious liberals and an innate priestly conservatism. Consequently, 'it is the priest who stands in judgment at the heresy trial, while the prophet is the defendant'. The only fault Clark discerned in prophets was that they could become egotistical. Priests, in contrast, could become fussy and dull.

According to him the role of priests was to preserve the values of the past 'chiefly by means of providing for them institutional and ritualistic expression'. Clark's choice of vocabulary to describe this role is telling: 'The priest is the expression of the death urge in the religious life, by which is meant that his function is a conserving and more passive rather than a creative one' (1958: 300–02).

The views expressed by Coe in 1917 represent what B. Beit-Hallahmi describes as the first wave of research in the psychology of religion that persisted through the 1930s. This wave declined in influence because of its obvious inability to separate itself from theology, philosophy of religion, and the influence of dogmatic institutions. One of its later developments was pastoral psychology, a discipline that exists only in theological seminaries.

Coe, Clark and others of the first wave employed the metalanguage of psychology to analyze phenomena that were conceived primarily through normative religious categories (Beit-Hallahmi 1991: 189–90). This enabled psychology of religion to clarify religious phenomena in clinical terminology and contributed an understanding of how the metaphysical influenced psychical processes such as faith, belief and visions. Clark's work of 1958 appears to come from the same tradition but, in its more cautious formulations, reflected a growing tension between academic psychology which started to avoid psychology of religion and 'religious psychology' which attempted to accommodate mid-twentieth century advances in psychology through apologetics (Brown 1987: 1–9).

This circumstance is clarified somewhat by biographical studies of individuals engaged in psychology of religion. These suggest strongly that the religious background of psychologists – even those not working in seminary settings – their attitude towards this background, and the type of knowledge that they possessed all influenced their selection, analysis, and interpretation of data (Beit-Hallahmi 1985: 18–19).[10] Since the 1960s, B. Beit-Hallahmi notes, psychology of religion has broken into three traditions: (1) religious psychology, discussed above, which functions as a type of religious apologetics; (2), psychology of religion, focusing on

---

10. D. Capps describes the psychological elements predisposing boys to be religious, boys who became students of religious psychology (1997: xi-xiii, 205–14).

psychological explanations of religious phenomena; and (3) social-psychology of religion. He states that the few psychologists who deal with the topic are individuals maintaining strong religious commitments or frustrated theological ambitions, and that many are ordained and affiliated with divinity schools (1991: 191–2).

The implications of Beit-Hallahmi's observations are that although the discipline enjoys prestige in certain non-academic circles, and benefits from being associated semantically with general psychology, it is quite unlike that discipline with regard to its methodologies. It is less science than it is the application of a particular philosophical mode of inquiry and explanation employing information and categories drawn from psychology.[11] However, insofar as the early work drew the notion of prophet versus priest antagonism in ancient Israel from a mix of anthropology and theology, its comprehension of the antagonism as general and universal is doubtful. In fact, studies of prophecy in ancient Mesopotamia locate prophets, some of whom were officiating priests, within the temples under the aegis of priests.

Academic psychologists have all but written off psychology of religion because of their low evaluation of the quality of its work and its problematic relationship to ongoing developments in psychology. Consequently, it is rarely treated in introductory psychology texts. In part, this is due to the fact that psychologists working within scientifically based paradigms prefer to study general processes, regardless of content, and do not find anything unique in religious behavior (Beit-Hallahmi 1989: 55–60). In short, whatever corroborative influence psychology of religion may have had in propping up the inevitable naturalness of the antagonism hypothesis may be factored out of contemporary discussion. Its claims were baseless.

One recent monograph, however, maintains the notion of antagonism while explaining it so as to eliminate the notion of its naturalness and inevitability. R. R. Hutton, recognizing fully that prophetic literature contains many negative statements about sacrifice, for example Hos. 8.12–13, Amos 4.4–5, Jer. 6.19–20, and attacks on priests, argues that 'whenever the prophet criticizes the priest, the complaint is not that he is acting just like a priest; rather the objection is that he has *ceased* acting like a priest'. What is at stake, according to Hutton, is that whereas the prophets assume

---

11.   Two exemplars of this methodology that I have found to be both insightful and useful are the following: A. T. Boisen (1936 and often reprinted), a work that applies insights drawn from clinical psychology, personal experience with mental illness, and personal involvement with the mentally ill to prophecy in a successful attempt to distinguish between prophecy and mental illness; D. J. Halperin (1993), an interesting, experimental work applying depth psychology and insights from psychotherapy to clarify literary features and philological problems in a prophetic book. Boisen deals with Ezekiel, Halperin discusses him exclusively.

that torah, justice, and faithfulness are connected to sacrifice, neither priests nor people associate them and consequently miss the ethical element in sacrifice (1994: 161–2).

The main evidence supporting Hutton's argument comes from lines within a few psalms in which these elements appear to be connected, or in which their connection may be inferred: Pss. 40.6; 50.8–15; 51.16–17; 69.30–31. These snippets from texts whose *Sitz-im-Leben* was the central institution of Judah's sacrificial system may have been chanted by a levitical choir even as priests dashed blood on the altar and nodded their heads to the rhythm of the words. They support a priestly understanding of sacrifice, not a prophetic one. Although highly appreciative of his idea as an interpretative stratagem, I am unaware of prophetic passages that support Hutton's interpretation of the prophetic critique explicitly. Were such passages extant, much of the contemporary uncertainty about the relationship between prophet and priest in ancient Israel would dissipate. In any event, even if a prophetic understanding may be read into the snippets of psalmody, it is ambiguous at best. The notion of prophets as loving reprovers of the priests would have to be viewed as an atypical development in the contemporaneous ancient Near East.

T. L. Fenton, viewing the problem from the vantage of one intimately familiar with the ancient Near East, gives strong voice to what students of ancient Near Eastern cultures have long known. He notes that those who believe that prophets considered sacrifice positively only when offered by the righteous and morally pure maintain a scenario that would have been incomprehensible to Israel and its neighbors during the Iron Age. Sacrifice was ubiquitous and deemed a common sense form of proper behavior. Piety and morality were not necessarily linked to sacrifice. He opines that prophets could only have said that the intent behind the offering would have been considered when an Israelite sought divine favor or forgiveness of sins (2001: 134–5).

My own description of the dearth of ethical and moral comments in prophetic literature, presented above, supports Fenton while Hutton's view clearly moves prophets into a sympathetic relationship with priests and cults. Grabbe, who compared Israelite prophecy with other ancient Near Eastern traditions concluded that 'there is no qualitative difference between Old Testament prophets and those known from Mesopotamia' (1995: 117).[12]

Fenton and Hutton, as co-opted above, are supported further by the work of A. R. Johnson. In 1944, Johnson, combining form-critical insights

---

12. See also M. Weinfeld, who cites Akkadian texts demonstrating that 'morality' was also a factor affecting divine judgments in Mesopotamia (1995: 47–49) and A. Malamat (1995: 50–73).

from H. Gunkel, S. Mowinckel and a few other scholars, argued that (1) oracular types of statements in certain psalms, (2) the primary role of Levites as teachers and instructors in cultic norms, (3) the obvious involvement of pre-classical prophets in cultic matters, and (4) the critiques of cult found in the classical prophets indicated that the '*nābī' qua* professional "prophet", was important among the personnel of the cultus – particularly that of the Jerusalem temple' (1962 [1944]: 74–5). After he advanced this proposal, others suggested that Joel, Habakkuk, Haggai, and Zechariah were cult prophets (Gordon 1995: 9–10). R. P. Gordon, who studied this development recently, avers that it marks a shift in the study of prophets by breaking down the notion of an antagonistic opposition between the prophets and the cult (1995: 12). But what of the antagonistic opposition between prophets and priests?

J. Blenkinsopp, a scholar well known for his work on the literature, life, and culture of the exilic and post-exilic periods, wrote a few years ago that 'the Israelite priesthood and its literary productions have not had a good press in Christian Old Testament scholarship since the Enlightenment'. He traced the common contrast between the ethical religion of prophets and priestly concern for detail back to Wellhausen's characterization of P as 'legalistic, restrictive, and servile' and as 'destructive of spontaneity and the religion of the heart' (1995: 66–7). Blenkinsopp himself then went on, without making such harsh judgments, to describe prophets as those called to a mission while priests were those who occupy an office (1995: 116).[13]

W. R. Millar recently published a study intended 'to recover for Protestant Christians the spirituality of the priestly traditions of ancient Israel'. His work investigates different modalities of priestly spirituality as expressed through themes in DtrH and Chronicles and is premised on a notion that priests were keepers of stories as well as sacred traditions. Loosely based on the ideas of F. M. Cross and R. E. Friedman and his distinction between Dtr's statements and the reported speech of characters, his conclusions provide Israel's priests with some 'good press', to use Blenkinsopp's phrase. They are the most rounded and three-dimensional priests that recent scholarship has produced (2001: 27–31).

Before engaging what the *nebi'im* said about *kohanim*, it is worthwhile clarifying succinctly exactly what reality in ancient Israel was conjured up by the word *kohen*, 'priest'. The two most useful sources are different strands within Torah legislation and some narratives in Former Prophets and in Chronicles.

---

13. The 'call' terminology that Blenkinsopp uses in this citation is derived from a theological, not a historical, lexicon.

The Biblical Image of Israel's Priests

According to P, priests were in charge of the Tabernacle sanctuary where they officiated at the outside altar and within the tent. Offerings brought to the sanctuary were presented to them and presumably approved. Subsequently, blood of slaughtered animals was presented to them and they took the blood to the altar for appropriate sprinklings and pourings. The actual slaughtering, skinning and butchering of animals was the responsibility of individual Israelite offerants, whether or not they actually did the work or had it done on their behalf. This is explicit in the wording of Lev. 1.5–9, 11–13; 3.2–5, 8–11, 13–16. Variations in the procedure occur when the beneficiaries of the ritual are individual priests or the congregation as a whole (Lev. 4.4–11, 14–21). Bird offerings constitute the only exception to this procedure. Living birds were dispatched by priests at the altar (Lev. 1.15; 5.8). Most likely, this was because the amount of recoverable blood was so small that it was deemed best that priests control the whole ritual after presentation.

Within P, the altar under total control of the *kohanim*, was a platform where prescribed animal fats, organs, and selected parts could be burnt; a pinch from vegetable gift offerings, the *minḥāh*, burnt; and the blood of some sacrificial animals manipulated. Blood from *'ōlāh*, *zebaḥ* and *'āšām* offerings was thrown against its sides (Lev. 1.5, 11; 3.2, 8, 13; 7.2). Blood from the *ḥaṭṭa't*, purification/expiation, offerings, was daubed on its horns and poured out on its base, the *yĕsôd* (Lev 4.25, 30, 34; 8.15; 9.9). So far as P was concerned, all such blood manipulations fell in the province of *kohanim*.

The altar law of Exod. 20.24–26 indicates that outside of P, there were those who thought otherwise: An altar of earth you will make for me, and you will offer on it *'ōlôteykā*, your burnt offerings, and *šĕlāmeykā*, your well-being offerings, and your flock animals and your herd animals" (v. 24). The law here presupposes that Israelites themselves executed all elements of the ritual without benefit of clergy. This would have included the throwing of blood against the sides of the altar. Indeed, Lev. 17.1–6, again a P text, recognizes that Israelites maintained such views, and reckons any individual slaughtering outside of the camp without presenting sacrificial blood to a priest at the Tabernacle as one who spilled blood. Allowing that the Exodus law grants broader license than that of Leviticus, it is interesting to observe what it does not include in its formulation. It excludes from consideration the *ḥaṭṭa't*, purification/expiation offering that necessitated both altar horns and an altar base.

At a minimal level, *kohanim* may have been considered absolutely necessary only for the blood manipulations of *ḥaṭṭa't* offerings that could be performed solely on altars with four horns on which sacrificial blood was daubed. This was the purification/expiation offering par excellence (cf.

Dennis 2002: 111–12). It purified individuals from the miasmic blemish of impurity (1) incurred naturally through infection or contact with people infected by certain diseases, contact with corpses, and a range of natural bodily and genital discharges (cf. Lev. 11–18; Num. 19), (2) brought into existence by misconduct in sexual, cultic, or homicidal matters (cf. Lev. 18.24–30, 19.31; Num. 35.33–34); and (3) brought into existence in circumstances involving testimony in court proceedings (cf. Lev. 5.2, 4). The last two categories involve what contemporary people may prefer to label 'moral transgressions'. Completion of the ritual indicated not only that the offerant was ritually pure, but also that the shrine itself had been cleansed of any pollution that he or she may have caused. Purified, the offerant could then enter the presence of the deity within the temenos to present other offerings, to observe public offerings, to participate in festivities, or simply to take pleasure from being in the shrine. Apparently, if people felt no desire to be within the temenos, they performed their own sacrifices wherever they wished without presenting a *ḥaṭṭā't*. The upshot of this analysis is that *kohanim were specialists whose expertise was not always considered necessary*.

According to the extant form of a narrative at the end of Judges, an Ephraimite named Micaihu established a 'house of God/gods' in which there was an *ephod* and *teraphim* – an image (?) and figurines – and installed one of his sons as *kohen* (Judg. 17.5). Sometime later he invited an itinerant Levite from Judah to accept his appointment as personal *'āb* and *kohen* 'advisor'(?) and priest, a full-time 'cultician'. Agreeing, the Levite returned with Micah to his homestead where he was installed as *kohen*, most likely replacing the son (Judg. 17.9–12). The use of *kohen* in this story indicates that it could refer to an individual dedicated to a particular task, like a sword-bearer or woodcutter or shepherd, even if the individual had no particular genealogy or source of arcane knowledge. The requisite knowledge could possibly be gained through oral instruction or by observing others. In any event, when the opportunity arose, Micaihu preferred the services of a Levite whom he assumed could do a more competent job. Later, Danite tribesmen migrating northward raided the house of God/gods carrying off its contents and coerced the same Levite to join and serve the tribe in the same capacities as he had served the Ephraimite, as advisor and full-time cultician (Judg. 18.17–31). Throughout Judg. 17–18, the Levite was never required to determine the contents of the cult in which he officiated, only to render service at the cult established by others.

Just as Micaihu's son had served as *kohen*, so too did David's sons according to the list of his officials in 2 Sam. 8.16–18. Two others are listed in the same capacity, Zadoq, an individual of uncertain lineage, and Ahimelek son of Abiathar, descended from a family of Levites that had served as priests for many generations (2 Sam. 8.17; cf. 1Sam 21.1, 22.11,

19–20). Abiathar himself, who served as David's priest, eventually made an unwise political decision and was ordered to return to his fields in Anathoth: 'and Solomon expelled Abiathar from being a *kohen* for YHWH' (1 Kgs 2.26–27). Despite the dismissal and the fact that he ceased functioning in a sacerdotal capacity, his descendants were known as 'the *kohanim* who are in Anathoth in the land of Benjamin' (Jer. 1.1). For them in the sixth century BCE, the title appears to have been an honorific.

Early evidence for the use of *kohen* as an honorific may occur in 1 Kgs 4.5, part of a list of Solomon's officials. An individual, Zabud son of Nathan, *kohen*, is provided an official title describing an office, 'king's companion', perhaps meaning personal advisor (cf. Mettinger 1971: 63–9; Fox 2000: 121–28). A different individual, Azariahu son of Zadoq, bears the title of *kohen*. Accordingly, since Zabud did not fulfill any priestly function, the sobriquet may indicate that at one time he had done so. His former title may have been treated as an honorific and 'stuck', as do political, military, and some academic titles such as 'Senator', 'Governor', 'Admiral', 'Professor', and the like in American society. Nothing in this suggestion is affected by assuming that the title should be affixed not to Zabud himself but to his father Nathan, even though the trope markings in the MT militate against such an interpretation.

An interesting datum relevant to this discussion emerges from the story of the contest on Mt Carmel between Elijah and *nebīyēy habbaʿal*, prophets of Baal (1 Kgs 18.19, 20, 22, 25). Both Elijah and the prophets construct altars, slaughter and dress sacrifices, and pray. The ritual involving sacrifice appears to have been sacerdotal, yet none of the protagonists is identified as a priest. In view of the data presented above bearing on the Israelite conception of priesthood, it is apparent that this sacrifice was not a ritual necessitating priests. The place was not a regular shrine bounded by a temenos; the altars were field altars and the participants acted in accord with the general rules of Exod. 20.24–26. Whatever sacrifice was involved, perhaps an ʿōlāh, a holocaust offering, but certainly not a *ḥaṭṭāʾt*, it did not involve blood manipulation. Finally, those in the contest were not regularly involved in performing and supervising such rituals. Absence of the term *kohen* from this context indicates that simply conducting sacrifices was not what defined a person as a *kohen*.

An observation about Josiah's reforms concludes this brief survey. Even as Josiah is depicted as ridding the temple of a host of devices and images considered idolatrous and in violation of YHWH's covenantal requirements, devices that if not installed were maintained by his grandfather Manasseh and his father Amon, he left the Jerusalem priesthood alone. Those entrusted to maintain and minister to the various cults that Josiah purged from the temple and that the Deuteronomistic historians considered a blight on Israel were actually drafted into the reform program. Josiah could do this because the job of a *kohen* was to administer policy, not to set it. This narrative, both with regard to the attitude of the narrator and the description of the protagonists is congruent with what is presented in the story of Micaihu's Levite in Judg. 17.

Strictly speaking, most of the data presented above from the Deuteronomistic history and from P reflect attitudes and perceptions from the seventh through the sixth centuries BCE. The bulk of material from prophetic texts discussed below, but not all, is congruent with this dating.

One additional feature in the job description of priests should also be relevant. After the establishment of the central shrine, Deuteronomy prescribes a court system in which the *kohanim* and an individual described as *haššōpēṭ*, the judge (who may or may not have been a priest), at the central shrine function as an advisory board for difficult cases or those without precedent (Deut. 14.8–10). The conception of such a judicial system may be reflected also in the description of events during Jehoshapat's third year, c. 870 BCE, narrated in 2 Chron. 17.7–9: Jehoshaphat sent Levites and priests to instruct residents of the cities of Judah in the contents of the scroll of the instructions of YHWH, *sēfer tōwrat YHWH*. Minimally, if historical, Chronicles notes publication of a common law which could then be enforced by courts operating with the same system and under a centralized administration. It would attest to the involvement of priests in this system, but not to their control of it.[14]

Prophets versus Priests: The Crucial Passages

Occurrences of the vocable *kohen* in the collected oracles of the Latter Prophets are relatively few: 78, in all, out of a total of 752 occurrences in the Tanakh. These are found in the following books: Isaiah (3); Jeremiah (34); Ezekiel (22); Hosea (3); Joel (3); Amos (1); Zephaniah (1); Haggai (5); Zechariah (5); Malachi (1). The word does not appear in Obadiah, (Jonah), Micah, Nahum, and Habakkuk. Most occurrences throw no light on what the prophet may have thought of the priest. Accordingly, the following discussion considers only relevant passages.

Hosea 4.4–10 may comprise an oracle delivered against a particular shrine, but like so much in Hosea, much is unclear, uncertain, and unknown.

In Hos 4.4–6, whose meaning is uncertain, *kohen* parallels *nabi'*:

14. When the archaeological reality is examined along with the legal and historiographic texts considered above, the picture becomes more nuanced and complex, but not significantly different. Cf. Zevit (2001: 254–60, 457, 479).

1. Let a man not dispute; let a man not reprove, and your people are
    like disputants, (O) *kohen*.[15]
2. You will stumble today; and the *nabi'* will stumble with you tonight;
    and I will destroy your people.[16]
3. My people are destroyed from lack of the knowledge. Because you
    have despised the knowledge, I despise you from serving as *kohen*
    for me.

It may be that the priests are accused of instructing Israel with regard to
rituals that they know to be unacceptable to people like Hosea, but no
specifics are provided. The ultimate result of such waywardness is
proclaimed in Hos. 4.9: 'And it shall be like the people like the *kohen*, I
will punish him for his ways and requite him for his deeds.' But the big
misdeed, as indicated in v. 6, is simply providing the type of instruction
with which the prophet disagrees.

In Hos. 5.1, *kohen* parallels 'house of Israel', and 'house of the king' in a
standard opening: 'Hear this, *kohanim*, pay attention, house of Israel, and
house of the king, give ear because the judgment is for you.' The cultic
specialists, however, are not charged with anything specific in the very
general indictment that follows: 'You made a pit at Mizpeh and spread a
net on Tabor... I will chastise them all' (Hos. 5.2). Hosea's parting shot in
Hos. 6.9 is significant perhaps, but it too is difficult and unclear: 'Like
bands of men who lie in wait, groups of priests murder on the road to
Shechem for they act shamefully'. This may address priests involved in
some specific cult practiced 'on the road to Shechem'. The vague references
to blood and murder in vv. 8–9 disallow understanding exactly what was
objectionable. Elsewhere, in Hos. 2.15–19; 4.12–14; 8.4–6; 10.1–8; 13.1–2
where different specific practices are condemned, they are not mentioned at
all.[17]

Joel 1.14 indicates that *kohanim* were invested with the authority to
declare fasts and public days of work-cessation. The general agricultural
desolation which forms the background of this book is not, however,
attributed to anything that they may have done. Described as those 'who
serve YHWH' (Joel 1.9), they are instructed to mourn because cereal and
drink offerings are not offered on the altar of the temple (cf. also, v. 13). It

15. This translation emends MT *mryby* to *mrybym*. Possibly, the phrases *kimerībey kōhēn*
should be translated, 'like the contentions of priests'. F. I. Andersen and D. N. Freedman
interpret the phrase, 'My contention is with you, priest' after their proposed redivision of the
consonantal text (1980: 344–5). Other emendations may be proposed on the basis of the
versions, cf. BHS and W. R. Harper (1905: 252–53).
16. Connecting the word *'immekā* with *'ummāh*. It can hardly mean 'your mother'.
17. See the discussions in Zevit (2001: 568–74) and the bibliography cited there. Non-
Israelite gods did have cults served by *kohanim* specialists in the care and feeding of the deity.
Jeremiah refers to *kohanim* of Kemosh and of Milkom (Jer. 48.7, 49.3).

is possible to view Joel the prophet as determining the policy that he expects priests to execute.

Zephaniah, whose book is a run-on outpouring of wrath and an announcement of world judgement, warns of a catastrophe that will visit Judah and the inhabitants of Jerusalem. Among those who will be cut off, Hebrew *k-r-t*, are the 'idol-priests, *kemārīm*, with the *kohanim*; and those who bow on the roofs to the host of the heaven, and those who bow, who swear to YHWH and who swear by their king' (Zeph. 1.4–5).[18] Zephaniah accuses priests of idolatry, but lumps them with others who participate in both the YHWH cult along with that of some other deity. They are not accused of leading others or instructing others in this worship. When these verses are compared to Zeph. 1.8–9, it is clear that the social elements condemned for affecting all manner of foreign customs and dress belong to the upper crust and the royal court. Zephaniah, accordingly, contributes nothing to the analysis of prophet-priest antagonism.

Jeremiah, a descendent of priests (cf. Jer. 1.1), mentions *kohanim* as a distinct social group, one wielding influence and authority, along with high- and low-placed people and with *nebi'im* (Jer. 6.13; 8.1). In Jer. 2.8, he castigates them because they – people responsible for holding fast to instruction, *tōrāh* – did not challenge cultic miscreants, including prophets who prophesied through Baal. He accuses them of not doing what they ought to have done, according to his standards and his understanding of their knowledge. Elsewhere, Jeremiah indicts priests for following the teachings of prophets who teach falsehoods: 'Prophets prophesy in lies, and priests rule by their authority, and my people love it so; but what will you do at the end?' (Jer. 5.31). This is most interesting because even as it acknowledges that priests exercise authority over the people, Jeremiah states that ultimately lying prophets are to blame. At worst, the priests that Jeremiah had in mind were misguided in that they accepted from prophets as authoritative what he considered false teachings.

Since nothing suggests that Jeremiah himself ever functioned in a sacerdotal capacity, his sense of what the priests ought to have been teaching may have been derived from family and tribal lore. But whatever its source, it is clear that different priests had different ideas of what constituted proper behavior and of who possessed the proper authority to guide them in their activities. In Jer. 14.18; 23.11, 33–34, priests are faulted for teaching untruths about the past, but not for cultic or other improprieties. From Jeremiah's perspective, priests were not overly tied to a frozen, book-bound tradition.

---

18. The word *mlkm* in Zeph. 1.5 may be a reference to the Ammonite deity Milkom, or to 'their Molech'. Cf. the discussion in Zevit (2001: 581).

Despite the fact that priests were among those accusing him of seditious speech in the temple, Jeremiah did not single priests out for any particular condemnation (Jer. 26.7, 11, 16). The issue in Jer. 26 was not the right of recognized prophets to speak negatively about the temple, but to do so freely on the temple grounds (cf. Spiegel 1976: 41–47). Jeremiah's temporary incarceration could be justified because priests were responsible for and had the authority to restrain the unwanted behavior of *kol 'īyš meššugga'*, 'every madman and prophetic *poseur*' (Jer. 29.27). Ultimately, Jeremiah's right was upheld on the basis of legal precedent, cf. Jer. 26.11–19.

Ezekiel, identified as a *kohen* (cf. Ezek. 1.3), critiqued priestly practices and prescribed for their proper performance. Remarkably, however, he adds little to what we know about the relationship between prophet and priest.[19] In Ezek. 42.14, Ezekiel's divine guide points out to him that *kohanim* fail to change garments between serving within the inner part of the temple designated 'holy' and before going into the outer court where the people are. This is a procedural, technical matter remediable by instruction.

In Ezek. 43, ordinances for the new temple are found. Although the idolatry of the old temple is condemned, vv. 6–9, no special mention is made of priests.[20] The reason for this is clarified by Ezek. 8.3–17 where all manner of cultic activities taking place in the temple are described and condemned. All are led by laity; none involve sacrifice and blood manipulation; none required priests (cf. Zevit 2001: 555–61). Israelites as a whole are condemned. Ezekiel's heavenly guide informs him that in the new temple, he, Ezekiel will inaugurate the sacrificial system by having the Zadokite priests prepare the purification offering whose blood he, Ezekiel, will manipulate on the horns, corners, and ledges of the altar according to instructions (Ezek. 43.19–27).

---

19. A. Mein, is puzzled that Ezekiel is identified as a priest in exile since nobody there needed a specialist in ritual and there was no shrine at which he could officiate. Mein concludes that as priest he was also an instructor in ritual law and justice (Ezek. 44.23–24), and that even in exile, where it had no cultic implications, there was concern with ritual purity (Ezek. 4.13–14), (Mein 2001: 199–201).

The behaviors that Mein identifies as priestly need not have been so in exile. Ezekiel's particular punctiliousness with purity may have been an element of his finicky and strange personality. Cf. also B. W. Anderson's description of Ezekiel as a 'priestly prophet' (1999: 128).

20. Levites are indicted for idolatrous practices in Ezek. 44.10, and the indictment is followed by the words 'they shall bear their punishment'. Ezekiel, however, continues immediately: 'They shall serve in my sanctuary, having oversight at the gates of the temple and serving in the temple.' The notion here is that their ritual error does not affect their status while the punishment, whatever it will be, once completed, will have redressed the wrong and restored to them the right/obligation to serve.

The picture remains unchanged in the post-exilic period. Haggai the prophet sends messages to Zerubbabel, the governor, and Joshua, the high priest, concerning the construction of the temple, which, according to what is presented in the book, are obeyed (Hag. 1.1–15). In Hag. 2.11–19, Haggai directs a *halakhic* query to the priests and turns their response into an oracular parable. In this small book, there is only prophet-priest cooperation.

So too, in Zech. 3 where the prophet announces the role of Joshua, the high priest, in establishing the glorious future of Judah on condition that he walk in YHWH's ways (Zech. 3.7). Zechariah 6.9–15 contains a prophecy directed to Joshua, son of Jehozadak the high priest. The contents of this prophecy regarding a future scion of David, who will rebuild the temple, indicates that the temple and priesthood will be restored and that there will be cooperation between the future king and future high priest. In Zech. 7.4, a prophecy is directed toward 'the people of the land and the priests' whose import is that they should learn from the past that pious activities do not guarantee divine support in the absence of appropriate, socially ethical behavior. But here too, priests are addressed as the religious leaders of the people as a whole. Zechariah is of special interest because like Jeremiah and Ezekiel, he may have been of priestly descent. The son of a man named Iddo, his father's name appears in a list of priests who returned with the exiles (Neh. 12.4, 16). Even he does not show any particular interest in priests beyond what seems appropriate to his particular interest in the rebuilding of the temple (Ezra 5.1–2).

Malachi sounds a slightly different note. In Mal. 1.6–14, the prophet charges *kohanim* with shortchanging YHWH in offerings due him by allowing the presentation of what he, Malachi, considers inferior animals. They are not accused of profiting by this, only of violating what appear to him to be transparently obvious standards of acceptablility. In the continuation of this tirade, Malachi contrasts their behavior with that of their ancestor Levi, who provided Israel with true instruction: 'because the lips of a *kohen* guard knowledge, and they seek instruction from his mouth, because he is a messenger of YHWH of hosts' (Mal. 2.7). Although Malachi himself claims no special knowledge, he assumes his right to challenge what is done in violation of recognized standards. Malachi's remedy is to predict that a messenger will come from YHWH, purifying the officiating sons of Levi – the word *kohen* does not appear in this part of his speech – so that they will do what is right, and only then offerings will again be pleasing to YHWH (Mal. 3.2b-4).

Malachi's debate with the priests apparently boils down to a difference of opinion as to what in the language of P constitutes an acceptable animal, *tāmīym*, one without *mūwm*, a blemish. Here it is possible to imagine that priests allowed minimally acceptable animals, according to their interpretation of P-like legislation, cf. Lev. 22.17–24, in a time of poverty so that the semblance of a dignified cult could continue. Malachi does not treat priests as innovators, but as people expected to follow policy, maintain standards determined by others, and to perform their duties in a conventional, conservative way. From Amos to Hosea, there is no antagonism to the cult as performed properly and no animosity directed to *kohanim* functioning in their priestly capacity. When singled out as subjects of an indictment, it is because as directors of the cult, they occupy a socially prominent position. No prophet, however, except Malachi, accused them of malfeasance in office. Prophets had many extreme and uncomplimentary observations to make about observances and cultic practices of their people, but did not single out priests as targets.

***

This survey indicates that when some prophets did not like the cult, or a particular cult at a particular place, or the attitude of those participating, or certain unsophisticated beliefs about the efficacy of sacrifice (cf. Isa. 1.11–17; Hos. 8.13; Amos 4.4–5, 5.5, 5.21–25), *they did not attack its officiants who were essentially technicians, mechanics.* Had they been opposed to the cult on principle, a position argued by many until the 1960s, they would have had to address those who promoted and administered the system.[21] But they expressed no principled objections to the cult and no principled antagonism against those charged with overseeing and maintaining it.[22] An argument could be made that for many of the prophets the temple cult was conceived as a graceful gift from YHWH to Israel and that conception clarifies their statements. Isaiah and Micah contains a vision of the temple to which nations stream (Isa. 2.2–3; Mic. 4.1–2). Jeremiah declared in the temple: 'Improve your ways and I will cause you to dwell in this place' (Jer. 7.3). The post-exilic prophets certainly seem concerned that the cult not only functioned, but functioned well (Hag. 1.7–8; Mal. 1.6–2.9).

Nothing in Chronicles, a book whose historiosophy – understanding of historical processes – is very much concerned with temple and cultic *Realia*

---

21. See the survey of C. F. Whitley (1963: 63–68) where the major views and pithy citations are presented. R. P. Gordon surveys the same material but more succinctly. Gordon, however, traces how and why the scholarly conception that there was a fundamental opposition between prophecy and cult is no longer accepted (1995: 9–12).

22. It is possible to suppose that prophetic books generally pass over what may have been considered legitimate private sacrifice in silence, focusing only on what was deemed illegitimate, e.g., Hos. 4.12–14, 8.4–6, 10.1–8; Amos 5.26, etc. Cf. Zevit (2001: 514–82) for a catalogue and analysis of relevant pericopes.

on the one hand, and with prophetic explanations of why events developed as they did, on the other, affects this picture.[23]

The Primary Origin of the Antagonism Hypothesis

These conclusions concerning what is actually attested in prophetic literature about priests have significant implications for discovering the origin of the antagonism hypothesis. Since the Hebrew Bible does not provide data supporting it, the question of its origin remains open. At the beginning of this article I cited scholars who suggest that the notion arose at the end of the nineteenth century, during the Enlightenment of the sixteenth to eighteenth centuries, during the Reformation of the sixteenth to seventeenth centuries, and even during the period of the Second Temple, c. first century CE. I suggest that the first two periods proposed actually represent particular moments when the hypothesis may have *regained* popularity and found expression in a guise suitable to the *Zeitgeist*. Since nothing in the Hebrew Bible itself actually supported such a reading, the idea most likely came into existence earlier due to circumstance other than those commonly suggested.

The Enlightenment of the seventeenth to eighteenth centuries combined Renaissance humanism with evolving notions of scientific inquiry and, in the wake of Francis Bacon, René Descartes, and Immanuel Kant, esteemed reason and logic in combination as prime arbiters of truth. Applied to religion, the topic at hand, prophetic speech could be analyzed inductively in terms of logic and reason, compared to acknowledged, manifest civilized moral standards – a particularly ethnocentric concept that was unrecognized as such 350 years ago – and suggest the rationality of revelation. Priestly concerns focused on ritual behavior could not be analysed this way in those times and consequently would have appeared inferior. The moral concerns of the prophets, congruent with the morality of enlightened individuals, justified postulating a God very much like the one which enlightened individuals expected; not so the dogmatic ritualism of priests.

This view also influenced the first wave in psychology of religion because psychology itself was an outgrowth of secular elements in the Enlightenment concerned with the nature of human nature. Among psychologists, however, although there was an objective understanding of the ritual aspects of priests, there was a preference for the natural spontaneity of progressive prophets. Biblical interpreters, however, no matter the enlightenment influences, could not have generated the general antagonism

---

23. See the useful survey in Petersen (1977: 55–104). Petersen analyzes how Chronicles presents levitical singers as prophets (1977: 64–68, 85).

hypothesis on the basis of the texts examined above or even on the basis of all statements directed against the cult.

Possibly, the idea may have arisen in circumstances where exegetes reacted defensively yet aggressively to texts in which priests addressed themselves negatively to prophets. Although the case of the temple priests versus Jeremiah does not fit this scenario, that of Amaziah versus Amos does. Not only was Amos sent away, but Amos's mean-spirited prophecy against Amaziah and his family (Amos 7.17) may have been a trigger forcing exegetes to justify Amos. But this is a singular case, not overly important in the scheme of things, and Amos' predictions that Jeroboam II 'will die by the sword' (Amos 7.11) and that Amaziah 'will die on impure land' (Amos 7.17) never came about. More significant, however, Amos' vindictiveness was personal, not principled.

Another, more important, narrative must be sought.

I propose that the main case which led scholars of an earlier generation to emphasize the antagonism between priests and prophets was that of Caiaphas versus Jesus (Mt. 26.57–68; Mk 14.53–65; Lk. 22.54–65; Jn 18.19–24). In each of the virtually identical synoptic accounts, Caiaphas, the high priest, interrogates Jesus, sits in judgment on him as he is found guilty. Then, priests spit in Jesus' face, someone slaps him and says 'Prophesy to us...' (Mt. 26.58; Mk 14.65; Lk. 22.64). In Acts, Caiphas, the high priest, confronted Peter, while the organized priesthood continually persecuted those who first preached and taught in the name of Jesus (Acts 4.5–12, 40–42), and later those who accepted such teachings (Acts 9.1–3). These images, priests versus Jesus, priests versus the divinely inspired early believers (cf. Acts 2.5–13), and priests versus the early church, may have been retrojected to the first temple period.

Such backreading required little eisegesis in the light of Jer. 20.2: 'Then Pashur struck Jeremiah the prophet and placed him in the cell in the Upper Benjamin Gate of the house of YHWH.' By the time of the gospel writers, experiences with persecution may have lead some in the early church to see themselves as Jeremiah-like in their experiences with priestly authorities. This, in turn, evolved into a topos which influenced elements of the passion narratives written after the events described in Acts.

Read in canonical context, the Matthew version harks back to Mt. 23.34–35, one of Jesus' sermons: '... I send you prophets and wise men and scribes, some of whom you will kill and crucify, and some you will scourge in your synagogues and persecute from town to town, that upon you may come the righteous blood shed upon the earth, from the blood of righteous Abel to the blood of Zecharias son of Berachias whom you slew between the temple and the altar.'

As scholars have long recognized, this alludes to the stoning of a priest, Zechariah son of Yehoiada, who prophesied in the temple (2 Chron. 24.20–21). His name was confused with that of the prophet Zechariah son of Berachiah (Zech. 1.1). What is significant in Matthew is that it alludes to a story in which people commanded by the king stoned Zechariah in the 'courtyard of the house of YHWH' (2 Chron. 24.21). According to Mt. 23.5, he was killed 'between the temple and the altar', a part of the temple off-limits to everybody except priests. Again, priests killed a prophet!

As realized in the passion narrative, it was the priests who persecuted the prophets, but it was the prophets who ultimately triumphed in the triumph of Jesus and the rise of Christianity. The origin of the antagonism hypothesis (most likely) lies in the late antique and medieval reversal of the priest versus prophet antagonism of the gospels and Acts and its being backread into the Hebrew Bible. In the absence of specific interpretations of biblical texts in medieval and Reformation exegesis that recognizably advance the antagonism hypothesis, I cannot demonstrate that it was a constituent element in pre-Enlightenment Christianity, but I do hypothesize its existence. Additionally I propose that the New Testament accounts provided a background against which the antagonism hypothesis appeared so reasonable that it was unnecessary to argue for its acceptance after the Enlightenment.

It gained modern support from Julius Wellhausen and others who accepted his ordering of the Pentateuchal documents: JEDP. In his justly famous *Prolegomena to the History of Ancient Israel* (1878), Wellhausen expressed his personal discomfort with the legal sections of the Pentateuch, Exodus, Leviticus, and Numbers which he associated largely with Israelite priests. He describes his dilemma as being an apparent lack of connection between them and those parts of the Hebrew Bible that he considered of greater importance: '...it was in vain that I looked for the light which was to be shed from this source on the historical and prophetic books. On the contrary, my enjoyment of the latter was marred by the Law; it did not bring them any nearer to me, but intruded itself uneasily, like a ghost...' (Wellhausen 1957 [1878]: 3).

Wellhausen discovered that his search was unnecessary after learning of K. H. Graf's idea that the priestly source was the last to be added to the Pentateuch. Consequently, it could be seen as a blind path down which Judaism eventually filed. Christianity, however, maintained a more healthy religious attitude and continued the prophetic tradition (cf. Zevit 2001: 32–33, 45 and footnotes).

In an intriguing lecture delivered originally in 1984, Jon D. Levenson observed that Wellhausen's autobiographical depictions of his feelings about the law echoed Paul in Rom. 7: 'You have died to the law through the body of Christ...' (v. 4); 'Apart from the law, sin lies dead' (v. 8). 'I was once alive apart from the law, but when the commandment came, sin revived and I died' (v. 9) (cf. Levenson 1993: 11–13). If priests were to be associated with the punctilious performance of the prescriptions of the law, then priests and their law could be viewed as being in permanent opposition to Jesus, the church and the prophets. In this context, it is worthwhile noting the telling 'death' language employed by the psychologists Coe and Clark in their descriptions of priests and priestly institutions cited above.

One major prophet, however, marred Wellhausen's dichotomy between prophets and priests with their law. In the final chapter of the *Prolegomena*, Wellhausen writes about Ezekiel (1957 [1878]: 421):

> Ezekiel first pointed out the way which was suited for the time. He is the connecting link between the prophets and the law. He claims to be a prophet, and starts out from prophetic ideas: but they are not his own ideas, they are those of his predecessors which he turns into dogmas. He is by nature a priest, and his particular merit is that he enclosed the soul of prophecy in the body of a community which was not political, but founded on the temple and the cultus. The chapters xl-xlviii are the most important in his book, and have been called...the key of the Old Testament.
>
> Thus arose that artificial product, the sacred constitution of Judaism. In the Priestly Code we have the picture of it in detail.

For Wellhausen, Ezekiel, both priest and prophet, was a fraud. That which is 'prophetic' in Ezekiel was not original, while that which was original was 'priestly', that is chs. 40–48, chapters which led to the formation of an artificial priestly religion, Judaism.

Wellhausen's statement indicting Ezekiel who advanced the priestly agenda and Kuenen's observation about the prophet–priest antagonism cited earlier are explicable also as a necessary corollary of their dating the Priestly source to the post-exilic period: the original, dynamic religion of YHWH and the gradual rise of a priest-dominated, temple-oriented Judaism found expression in prophetic antagonism towards priests and cult until the latter succeeded and the prophetic voice was silenced, almost.[24] These theological, historical, and critical ideas were developed further by the prominent, critical, Cambridge biblicist R. H. Kennett in an early-twentieth-century study, 'Ezekiel'. Kennett concluded his essay with two paragraphs pitting Ezekiel against the prophets (1928: 58):

> ... When we read his hope that his people shall be cleansed from all uncleanness, and shall be given a new heart, we are inclined to imagine that we are being led to think of a state of spiritual blessedness such as

---

24. S. I. Curtiss (1877: 121–23) attempted to stay the tide represented in the work of Wellhausen, Curtiss' selection of passages from prophetic literature ostensibly showing prophet–priest antagonism differs from mine because he was interested in undermining critical claims that P was post-exilic. I discovered his book after completing this paper and was delighted to discover that the conclusions of my analysis complement his, 125 years after Curtiss' work was published, Cf. pp. 124–44.

our Saviour describes. To Ezekiel, however, the result of the cleansing of men's hearts is not a vision of God, but an increase in material prosperity....

Ezekiel... was the father of Judaism, but of a Judaism in which the Gospel could not germinate. In Jeremiah on thè other hand we see 'as in a mirror darkly' the truth which Jesus Christ made manifest in all its glory. Of Ezekiel's teaching the almost inevitable outcome was Caiphas; while Jeremiah marked out the way which led to Jesus Christ.[25]

***

A history of the prophet versus priest antagonism hypothesis, described at the outset of this paper, then, may be outlined as follows:

1. It appears first in Acts and the synoptic Passion narratives.
2. In late antiquity and the medieval period, it emerged in theologically driven eisegesis that backread New Testament images into the Hebrew Bible.
3. During the Reformation, it maintained itself as a subtle form of anti-Catholicism and, perhaps, of anti-Judaism.
4. By the end of the nineteenth century, it found new justifications in late Enlightenment theology, the socio-political needs of the social gospel movement, and in the developing discipline of psychology of religion.
5. During the last quarter of the nineteenth century it found support in the historical conclusions of Wellhausen's source critical analysis of the Pentateuch.
6. Nowadays, it is maintained as an eisegetical/exegetical trope in institutions of higher learning, parochial and secular. This is (or, may be) due to a general lack of awareness that the hypothesis has been undermined slowly since the 1940s by slowly growing numbers of both inner-biblical studies and comparative studies of religion in the ancient Near East.

Stages 2 and 3 are posited as a matter of logical necessity to bridge between the overt NT passages and the nineteenth-century authors. Evidence from the writings of the Church Fathers and Reformation leaders is necessary in order to establish their factual basis. If, however, such are not to be found, it will be necessary to posit that early in the nineteenth century, some New Testament texts came to be understood in the way that found expression in the writings of late-nineteenth-century Protestant thinkers.

---

25. I am indebted to an audience member at the SBL Annual Meeting in Toronto, November 2002, for providing me with the reference to Kennett's essay.

BIBLIOGRAPHY

Albertz, R.
    1984   *A History of Israelite Religion in the Old Testament Period*
                (Louisville, KY: Westminster/John Knox Press).
Anderson, B. W.
    1975   *Understanding the Old Testament* Prentice-Hall: Englewood, NJ.
                (Englewood, NJ: Prentice Hall, 3rd edn).

    1999   *Contours of Old Testament Theology* (Minneapolis: Fortress Press).
Andersen, F. I., and D. N. Freedman
    1980   *Hosea* (AB, 24; Garden City, NY: Doubleday).
Beebe, H. K.
    1970   *The Old Testament An Introduction to Its Literary, Historical, and
                Religious Traditions* (Belmont, CA: Dickenson Publishing).
Beit-Hallahmi, B.
    1985   'Religiously Based Differences in Approach to the Psychology of
                Religion: Freud, Fromm, Allport, and Zilboorg' in L. B. Brown
                (ed.), *Advances in the Psychology of Religion* (Oxford: Pergamon
                Press): 18–33.
    1989   *Prolegomena to the Psychological Study of Religion* (Lewisburg:
                Buckwell University Press).
    1991   'Goring the Sacred Ox: Towards a Psychology of Religion', in H.
                N. Malony (ed.), *Psychology of Religion. Personalities, Problems,
                Possibilities* (Grand Rapids: Baker Books): 189–96.
Bewer, J. A.
    1922   *The Literature of the Old Testament* (New York: Columbia
                University Press).
Blenkinsopp, J.
    1995   *Sage Priest, Prophet: Religious and Intellectual Leadership in
                Ancient Israel* (Louisville: Westminster/John Knox Press).
Boisen, A. T.
    1962   *The Exploration of the Inner World: A Study of Mental Disorder and
    [1922]   Religious Experience* (Chicago, NY: Willett Clark & Co.).
    [1933]
Brown, L. B.
    1987   *The Psychology of Religious Belief* (London: Academic Press).
Capps, D.
    1997   *Men Religion, and Melancholia: James, Otto, Jung, and Erikson*
                (New Haven and London: Yale University Press).
Carmody, J., L. Carmody and R. L. Cohen
    1988   *Exploring the Hebrew Bible*, (Englewood Cliffs, NJ: Prentice Hall).
Clark, W. H.
    1958   *The Psychology of Religion: An Introduction to Religious Experience
                and Behavior* (New York: Macmillan).
Coe, G. A.
    1917   *The Psychology of Religion* (Chicago: University of Chicago Press).

Curtiss, S. I.
    1877   *The Levitical Priests: A Contribution to the Criticism of the Pentateuch* (Edinburgh: T. & T. Clark).

Dennis, J.
    2002   'The Function of the *ḥaṭṭā't* Sacrifice in the Priestly Literature: An Evaluation of the View of Jacob Milgrom', *Ephemerides Theologicae Lovanienses* 78: 108–29.

Fenton, T. L.
    2001   'Israelite Prophecy: Characteristics of the First Protest Movement', in J. C. De Moor (ed.), *The Elusive Prophet* (Leiden: Brill).

Fox, N.
    2000   *In the Service of the King: Officialdom in Ancient Israel and Judah* (Cincinnati: Hebrew Union College Press).

Ginsberg, H. L.
    1979   *The Supernatural in the Prophets* (Cincinnati: Hebrew Union College Press).

Gordon, R. P.
    1995   'A Story of Two Paradigm Shifts', in *idem* (ed.), *The Place Is Too Small for Us: The Israelite Prophets in Recent Scholarship* (Winona Lake: Eisenbrauns): 3–26.

Gottwald, N. K.
    1959   *A Light to the Nations: An Introduction to the Old Testament* (New York: Harper).

Grabbe, L. L.
    1995   *Priests, Prophets, Diviners, Sages: A Socio-Historical Study of Religious Specialists in Ancient Israel* (Valley Forge, PA: Trinity Press).

Halperin, D. J.
    1993   *Seeking Ezekiel: Text and Psychology* (University Park, PA: Pennsylvania State University Press).

Harper, W. R.
    1905   *Amos and Hosea* (ICC; Edinburgh: T. & T. Clark).

Hayes, J. H.
    1971   *Introduction to the Bible* (Philadelphia: Westminster Press).

Hutton, R. R.
    1994   *Charisma and Authority in Ancient Israelite Society* (Minneapolis: Fortress Press).

Johnson, A. R.
    1944   *The Cultic Prophet in Ancient Israel* (Cardiff: University of Wales Press).

Kennett, R. H.
    1928   *Old Testament Essays* (Cambridge: Cambridge University Press).

Kuenen, A.
    1874   *The Religion of Israel* (London: Williams & Northgate).

Larue, G. A.
    1968   *Old Testament Life and Literature* (Boston: Allyn & Bacon).

Levenson, J. D.
    1993   *The Hebrew Bible: The Old Testament, and Historical Criticism*
                (Louisville, KY: Westminster/John Knox Press).
Lindblom, J.
    1962   *Prophecy in Ancient Israel* (Philadelphia: Fortress Press).
Malamat, A.
    1995   'Prophecy at Mari', in R. P. Gordon (ed.) *The Place Is Too Small
                for Us: The Israelite Prophets in Recent Scholarship* (Winona Lake:
                Eisenbrauns): 50–73.
Mein, A.
    2001   'Ezekiel as a Priest in Exile', in J. C. De Moor, *The Elusive Prophet*
                (Leiden: Brill): 199–213.
Mettinger, T. N. D.
    1971   *Solomonic State Officials: A Study of Civil Government Officials in
                the Israelite Monarchy* (Lund: Gleerup).
Millar, W. R.
    2001   *Priesthood in Ancient Israel* (St Louis: Chalice Press).
Muffs, Y.
    1992   *Love & Joy: Law, Language, and Religion in Ancient Israel* (USA:
                Jewish Theological Seminary).
    2002   'Agents of the Lord, Warrior for the People', *BR* 18.6: 21–27, 56.
Petersen, D. L.
    1977   *Late Israelite Prophecy: Studies in Deutero-Prophetic Literature and
                in Chronicles* (Missoula, MT: Scholars Press).
Plein, J. D.
    2001   *The Social Visions of the Hebrew Bible: A Theological Introduction*,
                (Louisville: Westminster/John Knox Press).
Riley, B. T.
    1988   *The Psychology of Religious Experience in its Personal and
                Institutional Dimensions* (New York and Bern: Peter Land).
Spiegel, S.
    1976   'Amos versus Amaziah', in J. Goldin, *The Jewish Expression* (New
                Haven and London: Yale University Press): 38–65.
Sweeney, M. A.
    2001   'The End of Eschatology in Daniel? Theological and Socio-Political
                Ramification of the Changing Contexts of Interpretation', *Biblical
                Interpretation* 9: 123–40.
Weinfeld, M.
    1995   'Ancient Near Eastern Patterns in Prophetic Literature,' in R. P.
                Gordon (ed.), *The Place Is Too Small for Us: The Israelite Prophets
                in Recent Scholarship* (Winona Lake: Eisenbrauns): 32–49.
Wellhausen, J.
    1957   *Prolegomena to the History of Ancient Israel* (New York: Meridan
    [1878]   Books).
Whitley, C. F.
    1963   *The Prophetic Achievement* (Leiden: Brill).

Wilson, R. R.
    1980   *Prophecy and Society in Ancient Israel* (Philadelphia: Fortress
                Press).
Zevit, Z.
    2001   *The Religions of Ancient Israel: A Synthesis of Parallactic
                Approaches* (London and New York: Continuum).

INDEXES

INDEX OF REFERENCES

INDEX OF AUTHORS

Smith, M.S.   145, 150, 157
Snyman, G.   123
Spalinger, A.   73
Spiegel, S.   206
Spycket, A.   47
Stacey, W.D.   120
Starbuck, E.D.   195
Steiner, R.   73
Steinkeller, P.   55
Stuart, D.   99–101
Stulman, L.   149–52, 154, 157, 160,
    164, 165
Sweeney, M.A.   1, 82, 151, 194
Syrén, R.   28

Theil, W.   150
Toorn, K.   van der 118, 158
Törnkvist, R.   123
Torrey, C.C.   134
Tropper, J.   63

Uffenheimer, B.   116
Utzschneider, H.   177

Van der Toorn, K.   45, 50, 51, 53
Vogels, W.   122

Vriezen, T.   2, 3, 32, 40–42

Wacker, M.-T.   123
Weber, M.   167
Weinfeld, M.   166, 198
Weis, R.D.   135
Wellhausen, J.   65, 178, 180, 183, 184,
    193, 211–13
Whitley, C.F.   208
Wilcoxen, J.A.   159
Willis, J.T.   149
Wilson, R.R.   116, 118, 153, 159,
    193
Wolff, H.W.   80, 98–101, 103, 104
Wong, K.L.   141
Woude, A.S.   van der 81
Wyatt, N.   44

Younger, Jr, K.L.   135
Yoyotte, J.   74

Zevit, Z.   8, 10, 11, 16, 160, 193,
    203–205, 208
Ziegler, N.   47, 58
Zimmerli, W.   66, 71, 134, 138,
    139